The Criminology of
Edwin Sutherland

The Criminology of Edwin Sutherland

Mark S. Gaylord

and

John F. Galliher

Transaction Books
New Brunswick (USA) and Oxford (UK)

Second Printing 1990
Copyright (c) 1988 by Transaction Publishers
New Brunswick, New Jersey 08903

Library of Congress Catalog Number: 87-20156
ISBN 0-88738-181-2
Printed in the United States of America

Library of Congress Cataloging in Publication Data

Gaylord, Mark S.
    The Criminology of Edwin Sutherland/Mark S. Gaylord and John
F. Galliher.
    p. cm.
    Bibliography: p.
    Includes index.
    ISBN 0-88738-181-2
    1. Sutherland, Edwin Hardin, 1883-1950. 2. Criminologists–United
States–Biography.   3. Differential association theory.   4. Criminal
behavior. I. Galliher, John F. II. Title.
HV6023.S87G39 1987
364.2–dc 19
                                                        87-20156
                                                        CIP

To Diann and Jeanne

Contents

Acknowledgments

This study owes much to the generous assistance of colleagues and friends, some of whom shall go unnamed, none of whom shall go unthanked. Donald Cressey and Karl Schuessler deserve special thanks. Had it not been for their offer to share their Sutherland files and knowledge of invaluable data sources with us, our work might never have moved beyond contemplation. We owe a great debt also to Alfred Lindesmith for contributing the foreword. We especially thank our friends William Chambliss, Richard Quinney and James McCartney who read early drafts of our research and gave insights on how to improve the manuscript. Sam Gaylord lent seasoned editing skills in a careful reading of the document. Our thanks, too, to Lynn Brown who, with alacrity and grace, typed numerous versions. And finally we gratefully acknowledge the University of Missouri-Columbia for its support in awarding us a portion of the publication costs.

Foreword

Alfred R. Lindesmith

I first became somewhat acquainted with Professor Edwin Sutherland when I enrolled in the University of Chicago in 1932 for graduate work in the department of sociology. I was born on a farm in southern Minnesota near the rather small town of Owatonna. When I finished high school I entered Carleton College in the even smaller town of Northfield, twenty to twenty-five miles north toward the Twin Cities. I received my B.A. there in 1927 at the age of twenty-two. My brother Emery, who was older than I by four years, graduated in the year prior to my enrollment. My mother was an ardent advocate of and believer in the virtues of education and insisted strongly that my brother and I go to college.

During the five years between my graduation from Carleton and my enrollment at Chicago, I taught one year each in Sleepy Eye, Minnesota, Council Bluffs, Iowa, and at the Stevens Point Teachers' College in Wisconsin. I also took time out from teaching to go to Columbia University to get an M.A. in education. I was married about a year before moving to Chicago for a graduate education in sociology. I was then twenty-seven years old and had made no study of criminology, nor had I experienced any significant encounter with delinquents or criminals or witnessed the commission of a serious criminal act. Living in Chicago soon changed this.

One of the first courses I took at Chicago was Sutherland's criminology. It was based on the 1924 edition of the text that he compiled and published at the University of Illinois at the suggestion of Professor E. C. Hayes. I was very favorably impressed by his knowledge, his reasonable and friendly manner, and his lack of the arrogance that some Chicago graduate students have attributed to their professors.

Some time after taking this first criminology course, I took another from Sutherland in which I had a very important and interesting experience. I was sitting in the classroom waiting for things to get started when Sutherland arose and said that a guest lecturer would take over the class and then introduced a professional thief named Broadway Jones. I was at first shocked by this until Broadway arose and remarked that "there are people who, when they have stealing to do, are damn fools enough to do it themselves. There are others who get hold of someone who knows how to do it. That's where I come in."

This was the first professional thief I had ever met. Also, he was the first opiate addict I had met and became an important, if not a crucial, figure in determining what my dissertation topic and research would be. My initial choice had been homosexuality, and I interviewed a number of subjects concerning it. However, I became disenchanted by the subject matter and also by the negative reactions of the professors I talked to about it. I then briefly changed my mind in favor of a library study of German sociology, since I had learned considerable German from my mother and her relatives. I spoke to Professor Louis Wirth about my idea but nothing came of it. What happened was that I chose instead to do a study of opiate addiction and matters connected with the narcotics traffic.

As I pondered what my dissertation should be, I resorted to some tactics to give myself more time to study the sociological literature that my professors seemed to stress most and presumably viewed as important. In order to speed this study process I went so far as to stop taking courses for a quarter in order to prepare for a scheduled comprehensive preliminary exam. I spoke to Professor Ellsworth Faris about my plan to take the exam. He looked at some of my records and asked if I had taken his course in "Social Attitudes." My answer was negative, and he responded that if I were his son he would want me to take that course before taking the exam, implying that I would perhaps run into trouble if I didn't.

I was disappointed because I now felt I had to delay my exam even though I believed that I was very well prepared for it. I thought about what I ought to do and decided to try for a job in the flophouses for homeless men. I applied to the state of Illinois and was awarded a job. Before taking it, however, I managed to take Faris's course on "Social Attitudes." When I went down to the flophouses for my first day of work, I was surprised to find that Broadway Jones—ex-thief, ex-drug addict—had acquired a job in the same office on the same day. Other persons who worked there did not know of Broadway's background and I recall two of them disagreeing. One said he (Broadway) was an ex-lawyer, the other said an ex-journalist. I never enlightened them.

During the months that Broadway and I worked in the flophouses for homeless men we became better and better acquainted, and he offered to introduce to me acquaintances of his who he might meet when they came to Chicago. He also assured me that he would assure them that they would be in no danger of betrayal to the police if they talked freely to me. The help he offered and the advice he gave made it much easier for me to locate addict subjects for interviews and had the effect of fully confirming my choice of addiction as the topic of my dissertation. I began to organize and write my dissertation after interviews with about fifty addicts. I had not finished it when, in the early fall of 1936, I received a phone call from Indiana University inviting me to join the department of sociology there. I accepted the invitation and finished my thesis there early in 1937. I mailed my dissertation to Ellsworth Faris to prepare for the oral examination on it, and it was lost for a time on the shelves in the entry to Faris's office. I was told that his secretary had found it. The oral examination on the thesis took place during the summer of 1937.

It should be noted with respect to Sutherland's criminological career that it seems not to have really begun when he obtained his Ph.D. from the University of Chicago. His 1913 dissertation, for example, was entitled "Unemployment and Public Employment Agencies." It reflected his interest in political economy and political science. He also took courses in the history department and in the Chicago divinity school. In 1912 he took six political economy courses, two sociology courses, and one history course. He appears to have become absorbed in criminological theory only during his 1919 to 1926 stay at the University of Illinois, when E. C. Hayes suggested to him that he compile a textbook in that field. This text was published in 1924. Subsequent editions, designed by Sutherland to improve and correct the multiple factor theory represented by the 1924 edition, appeared in 1934, 1939, and 1947. Additional editions have been published since Sutherland's death in 1950 by Donald Cressey. The last two editions that Sutherland produced were designed to substitute the "differential association" theory for that of multiple factors and to include corrections and other ideas. During this same period Sutherland's reputation soared, and his criminological textbook has dominated the field for more than half a century.

During my stay in Chicago from 1932 until 1936 I had relatively few close contacts with Sutherland and his family. For example, I did not meet his wife or his young daughter. One day he did talk to me on the way to his class about the possibility of using autobiographically detailed items to discover the real causes of a person becoming a criminal. I expressed skepticism of this method and he agreed with me. There was a tendency in Chicago at that time to prepare and publish case histories, such as Shaw's The Jack-Roller. I met a few evenings with Sutherland and Herbert Blumer for general conversation and amusement. Once, two professional thieves and ex-addicts were included, and I recall only that I laughed more that night than I ever had before or since. Broadway Jones was there, and I think both Blumer and Sutherland were quite well acquainted with him and that they probably talked about and approved of my choice of opiate addiction as my dissertation topic. Blumer exercised more influence and control over my course work and research than any other professor, and if Sutherland exerted some influence it was through him. In my 1947 book *Opiate Addiction*, which was derived from my dissertation, Blumer wrote a generous introduction. In brief Acknowledgments I also noted that the "materials and methods of the study were discussed at length" with Professor Sutherland. This would have been after my move from Chicago to Indiana University.

In Sutherland's position as chair of the small and informal department of sociology at Indiana, communication between professors and graduate students was stimulating, relaxed, and frank. Sutherland continued to engage in examination of the theories stated in the 1924, 1934, and 1939 editions of his criminology text. In the process, biologically oriented theories such as that of Lombroso, instinct theories, and Sutherland's initial statement of multiple factor theory were progressively changed, eliminated or replaced by new sociological theories embodied in the expression "differential association." This expression and its implications were spelled out in seven propositions in the 1939 edition and in nine in the edition of 1947, the last one prepared by Sutherland before his death.

During his 1935 to 1950 tenure at Indiana, Sutherland's prestige and reputation increased greatly as he worked on his white-collar crime project and continued to improve and refine his differential association theory. When Sutherland's monograph on white-collar crime was completed in 1949, he presented it to Dryden Press, but the publisher objected to including all of the names of the corporations covered by the study and charged with legal offenses. The book was published and for about the next thirty years the identities of the white-collar criminals were not revealed. A recent edition from Yale University Press has remedied this flaw. Sutherland, as the president of the American Sociological Society and in other similar situations, made speeches commenting on his study and work of it spread rapidly in the United States and abroad. A German emigré criminologist teaching in London called the study a "milestone" and said that "it should become the starting point of a new line of research." A survey of 1940-1950 publications selected Sutherland's study as the most important one of the decade.

The authors of this book have interviewed a number of persons who were graduate students or young members of the Indiana sociology faculty. Their reports on Sutherland's personality were invariably favorable, and they were impressed by his willingness to engage in self-criticism and to take others' comments seriously when warranted. The authors note that when Frank Sweetser and I went along with Sutherland to meetings in Indianapolis by automobile, Sweetser on the way home once asked if the processes that produced juvenile delinquency might not have something to do with murder in the South and Sutherland agreed. On my part, since I spent considerable time during my first year at Indiana finishing the writing and organization of my dissertation, I felt pleased and flattered when Sutherland and students in my classes accepted my view of the exceptional instance as the growing point of science. I recalled that when I took statistics courses at Chicago, my professors almost always warned that a statistical correlation has nothing to do with causation in a scientific sense.

Perhaps a final note that I may add here is that Broadway Jones made repeated visits to Bloomington, in which he talked to a number of classes during the day, scheduled a talk in the early evening, and after his talk went to a party in Sutherland's or my home. Broadway had begun to work in a Chicago liquor store and sometimes brought us presents from it. After a considerable number of years Sutherland told me that he had received a letter from Broadway which indicated to him that he had resumed the use of opiates. Sutherland told me that he replied that if Broadway had relapsed, the thing for him to do was to report to the Lexington, Kentucky Public Health Service Hospital for treatment. The next letter from Broadway confirmed Sutherland's idea and Jones once again broke his habit. My memory, which might well be wrong, tells me that Broadway continued to correspond with us after Sutherland died. Now and then he would tell us that a medical problem had caused him to go to a Chicago hospital for treatment. Ultimately we received a notification from the hospital that Broadway had died. A day or two later we received a long distance telephone call from a Chicago woman who was totally unknown to us. She scolded us bitterly and at length for not having called her to tell her about Broadway. The latter had never mentioned her to my wife or me.

Besides the visits that Broadway made here, there was a short-change artist who was a friend of David Maurer of the University of Louisville from whom Maurer obtained the argot of addicts and criminals. We arranged to have this man visit Indiana University and explain to a class how the short-change racket is handled. One graduate student in my class learned the technique so well that when she went home to a northern Indiana city she tried it with three cashiers in shops owned by her father and succeeded in all three of them. At the evening party for the short-change artist, he said he needed someone to drive his car for him during the coming summer and asked me if I wished to. I answered that I couldn't because I feared that university officials would disapprove.

One more item of interest is that the author of the screenplay for *The Sting* used Sutherland's book *The Professional Thief* to learn the details of the "con game," and did a good job of it. A number of Bloomington acquaintances commented that the movie was very much like a lecture that Broadway Jones gave!

Bloomington, Indiana
November 1986

Introduction

This is a study of the origin and development of Edwin H. Sutherland's differential association theory. Among sociological students of criminal behavior, there is considerable agreement that this is the single most important innovation during the past fifty years. As Chambliss has observed, "Edwin Sutherland . . . developed the most influential of all sociological perspectives on criminal behavior: the differential association theory."[1] Correspondingly, Cressey has claimed that "the most significant criminological works of the past half-century are those which have, in one way or another, tried to *extend* Sutherland's principle [of differential association], to say something he did not say, rather than trying to improve the form of his statements."[2] The precise dimensions of the legacy of differential association theory are reflected in the many publications that have attempted to defend, criticize, or empirically verify this theory.[3]

Here we will examine the origins of differential association theory and show how it evolved with Sutherland's development as a criminologist. Sutherland thought that, compared to American sociology, criminology in the 1920s and early 1930s was in dire need of new ideas and direction. He rejected biological determinism and the extreme individualism of psychiatry, as well as economic explanations of crime. His search for an alternative understanding of crime led to the development of differential association theory—a theory which both increased the prominence of American criminology and made the sociological influence on it profound. For the past fifty years American criminology, and criminology courses, have been found largely in sociology departments. Without the legacy of differential association theory it is not at all clear that this would have been the case. The influence of Sutherland's theory is made all the more important by virtue of the recent reemergence of classical criminology, stressing insufficient punishment as the cause of crime, and by the even more recent resurfacing of claims emphasizing genetic origins of criminal behavior, thus implying biological initiatives in crime control. In contrast to both classical and biological theories, differential association theory poses no obvious threats to the humane treatment of those identified as criminals.

Our research has drawn on both published and unpublished materials

1

for details about the life and background of this eminent scholar, including, but not limited to, introductions to books written by Schuessler[4] and Geis and Goff,[5] and unpublished dissertations by Goff[6] and Snodgrass.[7] We also made heavy use of a collection of letters written by Sutherland mainly between 1912 and 1927, as well as interviews with former students and colleagues.

Notes

1. William J. Chambliss, "White Collar Crime and Criminology," *Contemporary Sociology*, 13 (March 1984), p. 161.
2. Donald R. Cressey, "Fifty Years of Criminology: From Sociological Theory to Political Control," *Pacific Sociological Review*, 22 (October 1979), p. 462.
3. Using the *Social Science Citation Index*, the *Sociological Abstracts*, and the *Criminal Justice Abstracts*, forty-two published articles were located.
4. Karl Schuessler, "Introduction," in *Edwin H. Sutherland: On Analyzing Crime*, Karl Schuessler, ed. (Chicago: University of Chicago Press, 1973), pp. ix-xxxvi.
5. Gilbert Geis and Colin Goff, "Introduction," in Edwin H. Sutherland, *White Collar Crime: The Uncut Version* (New Haven: Yale University Press, 1983), pp. ix-xxxii.
6. Colin Goff, "Edwin H. Sutherland and White-Collar Crime" (unpublished Ph.D. dissertation, University of California, Irvine, 1982).
7. Jon Snodgrass, "The American Criminological Tradition: Portraits of Men and Ideology in a Discipline" (unpublished Ph.D. dissertation, University of Pennsylvania, 1972).

1

Edwin H. Sutherland's Legacy

One April evening in 1942, Edwin H. Sutherland stood before the members and guests of the Ohio Valley Sociological Society. As retiring president it was his privilege to give an address following the Society's annual dinner meeting. His listeners saw Sutherland as the dean of American criminology. That evening he spoke to them on the "Development of the Theory." The theory to which the title of his address referred was differential association.

Sutherland was then fifty-eight years old and at the peak of his profession. In 1939 he had been elected president of the American Sociological Society in recognition of his scholarship and his service to the profession. In 1940 he had been elected president of the Sociological Research Association. He was currently chair of the department of sociology at Indiana University, which in 1935 he had established as an independent department. Sutherland was in constant demand to lecture, to consult with crime commissions and other study groups, and to teach at other universities.

Three years earlier, Sutherland had presented the first explicit statement of the theory of differential association in the third edition of his criminology textbook, *Principles of Criminology* (1939). Now, before this audience, he chose to reveal something of the theory's origin and development over the course of two decades. He began his address by announcing:

> I shall present a personal account of the hypothesis that criminal behavior is caused by differential association. This is to be a biography of the hypothesis and a report on its present status or its rise and decline. It is a story of confusion, inconsistencies, delayed recognition of implicit meanings, and of much borrowing from and stimulation by colleagues and students.[1]

The theory about which he spoke that evening—differential association—represented a major landmark within the discipline. Nearly forty years after Sutherland's death, his theory continues to guide research, stim-

3

ulate debate, and organize empirical findings. Students of criminology are still taught the theory of differential association as an essential part of their education. Although most criminologists cite Sutherland's textbook, his theory of differential association, and his ground-breaking work on white-collar crime as his most important intellectual achievements, this study will focus attention on the theory of differential association.

This theory postulates that criminal behavior is learned behavior. It is learned through interaction with other persons, usually within intimate personal groups. In such a context one learns the techniques of committing crime and acquires the motivation to do so. All of us are exposed to statements favorable and unfavorable to the violation of law. However, when a person's association with definitions favorable to the violation of law is in excess of his or her association with definitions unfavorable to the violation of the law the person will become criminal. "Differential association" emphasizes the variable character of each person's exposure to both kinds of definitions. The theory is sociological in the sense that it places emphasis on the social origins of criminal behavior.

In the decades immediately preceding the development of the theory of differential association, theoretical criminology was of little value in attempts to understand the causes of crime or for purposes of social control. In fact, in the first decades of the twentieth century there was no indigenous American criminology. Instead, American social scientists looked across the Atlantic for theories to explain New World criminality. Compared to American sociology, which by the 1920s had created a profound new social psychology and developed an empirical methodology, American criminology was intellectually backward and unscientific. From the start of the century, American criminology struggled for twenty years to free itself from the Lombrosian legacy of biological determinism, with its notions of "born criminals," criminal types, and eugenics. Until the 1930s, American criminology was characterized by multiple factor theory, a misnomer that represented an intellectually flaccid and atheoretical stance toward understanding crime causation. Out of this unpromising background, Sutherland's efforts to develop a theoretical understanding of crime causation will be documented.

It is the thesis of this study that Sutherland's dissatisfaction with contemporary American criminology, together with a personality marked by perfectionism, professional ambition, diligence, and the desire to win acceptance from his colleagues, led him to search for a scientific sociological criminology. His seeking resulted in the development of the theory of differential association, which gave new direction and intellectual respectability to American criminology.

From the very beginning, Sutherland's theory was widely accepted by his fellow sociologists, an acceptance that arose from two sources. First, as a system of ideas, the theory of differential association was generously accommodative to the concepts and perspectives shared by his colleagues. It not only explained most of the criminological findings of its day, but did so from a determinedly sociological perspective. His colleagues responded favorably to his efforts to develop a consistently sociological account of criminal behavior. Second, Sutherland was sociology's able and staunch supporter against attacks from such disciplinary rivals as psychiatry and psychology. In his articles, book reviews, and speeches, he effectively solidified his stance against opponents from other disciplines. He used his ideas to further the interests of sociology as a profession as well as a discipline. By the 1930s Sutherland was deeply embedded within the professional organization of American sociology. He worked long and conscientiously on behalf of the American Sociological Society and other professional institutions and was highly respected and trusted by colleagues. While it cannot be proven, it is likely that his work won easy acceptance and loyal support in no small part because of his position as an effective and loyal member of the sociological profession.

But what sets Sutherland's theory of differential association apart from most others is that it has continued to influence American sociological criminology for nearly half a century. Even after all the years since Sutherland's death, current criminologists are just as familiar with his theory as were his contemporaries. Clearly the continuing influence of the theory of differential association must be attributed to the significance of its ideas rather than to the esteem in which Sutherland was held by his colleagues, friends, and students.

The theory of differential association was conceived, developed, and accepted because of three factors. First, Sutherland's early career was marked by disillusionment with sociology and the absence of a clear professional identity. His first academic position following graduate study at the University of Chicago left him discontented and fearful that he might never achieve the professional recognition he sought. Later, when offered a position at the University of Illinois, he used the opportunity to establish himself as a criminologist. His textbook, *Criminology* (1924), incorporated the concepts and perspectives of general sociology and won instant acceptance as *the* sociological criminology textbook of its day. Although Sutherland failed to recognize it at the time, the seeds of a sociological theory of crime causation were present in that first edition of his criminology textbook.

Second, Sutherland was an active member of a group of Chicago-trained sociologists, including W. I. Thomas, Robert Park, Clifford Shaw, and Henry McKay, who drew from (and added to) the concepts and perspectives of the wider sociological community as well as from each other's work to develop a general theory of human behavior. Sutherland considered his own endeavors to be merely a part of this collective effort. While he is remembered as a criminologist, he thought of himself as a sociologist first and as a criminologist second. That is, he saw himself as a sociologist whose data were the criminal law, criminals, and the agencies for the administration of justice. Sutherland's genius as a criminologist was to adapt the concepts and perspectives of sociology to his particular field and in so doing create the theoretical underpinnings for sociological criminology. In addition to the University of Chicago-trained sociologists already mentioned, Sutherland's theory building was also aided by his assocation with Thorsten Sellin, Frank L. Sweetser, Charles H. Cooley, and Alfred R. Lindesmith.

Third, the Great Depression created, in part, an intellectual climate in which a sociological theory of crime causation was readily accepted. The idea that deviant behavior had its roots in the fabric of society made sense in the context of those millions who experienced personal upheaval and the social dislocation of unemployment and material want that the Depression left in its wake.

What follows will be an intellectual biography of Sutherland and his theory, focusing on the ideas, institutional settings, and persons that most influenced Sutherland's work. His growth as a sociologist will be traced over the course of more than forty years and the origin and development of his thinking on crime causation will be documented, mainly through an examination of his published and unpublished work, his letters to friends and colleagues, and the work of his professional reference group. While it is true that Sutherland provided some insight into the origins of his theory, it is believed that more detached observers should be able to provide a more balanced and complete statement.

Edwin H. Sutherland: The Early Years

In order to understand Sutherland's life and career it is necessary to have some appreciation of the family in which his personality and character were formed. Most of what is known about his early years is found in Snodgrass (1972), Goff (1982), and Geis and Goff (1983). Jon Snodgrass's Ph.D. dissertation ("The American Criminological Tradition: Portraits of Men and Ideology in a Discipline") contains a chapter on Sutherland entitled "The Gentle and Devout Iconoclast." What Snodgrass knew in 1972 about Sutherland's early years apparently was all that had been discovered at that time. And precious little it was. Snodgrass writes:

> Any attempt to recapture and retrace Sutherland's past associations to account for his own personality, life-history, and intellectual career, fails miserably. The fact is very little is known about him, particularly about his childhood, youth, and pre-university days. It is somewhat ironic that Sutherland, a most famous and widely known criminologist, with innumerable students, colleagues and friends, is the least well known.[2]

That we now know more about his family background than we did a decade ago is largely due to the efforts of Colin Goff, whose 1982 Ph.D. dissertation ("Edwin H. Sutherland and White-Collar Crime") contains considerable biographical material on Sutherland.

Edwin Sutherland was born on August 13, 1883 in Gibbon, Nebraska. He was the third of seven children born to George and Lizzie T. (Pickett) Sutherland. He grew up and was educated in Ottawa, Kansas, and Grand Island, Nebraska. In 1904 he received the bachelor of arts degree from Grand Island College, where his clergyman father, George Sutherland, was president.

That Edwin's father made a lasting impression on his son is generally recognized by those who have written on the subject. George Sutherland had been raised in a deeply religious and sober family. As an adult he was opposed to vice in all forms, especially alcohol. He was a member of the Anti-Saloon League, the Nebraska State Temperance Union, and the Nebraska Prohibition Party. In his "Reminiscences" he refers to alcohol as the "great corrupter of mankind."[3] He endeavored to pass on such values as these to his children. Schuessler writes that Edwin's parents "presided over a Protestant parsonage in a rural community, and in that setting they succeeded in giving their son a sense of the moral importance of carrying out one's duties."[4]

Snodgrass has described George Sutherland as a religious fundamentalist who "followed all the austere and strict practices of the Baptist faith."[5] Card playing, dancing, and other "sinful" activities were not permitted in the Sutherland home. Snodgrass quotes one relative who remembers George Sutherland as

> a man of stern discipline. Even in those days there was a generation "gap" and he could not adjust to it. He punished his children severely for what seemed to them small lapses. Especially the older ones became bitter over the treatment of their little brothers and sisters. Arthur [the oldest brother] retained this bitterness through life, but Edwin, in the middle of the family, and by naturally wishing to please, seemed to me to have escaped most of the punishment and resentment.[6]

Thus, from what is known of George Sutherland, it must have been somewhat oppressive to live under his stern and unbending rule. His presence was forceful. He wrote in his "Reminiscences": "I was asked to withdraw from the teaching force of [Grand Island] college for the reason that my personality was so striking and impressive that no president could stand up against me."[7] It seems likely that early in his life Edwin developed respect for authority and learned to please powerful others as a way to gain acceptance.

Snodgrass's Sutherland family informant alluded to a falling out between Edwin and his father and a break with the Baptist church, yet few details on these events are known. As an adult Edwin enjoyed golf, bridge, cigarettes, movies, magazines, and jigsaw puzzles. Today, in most circles, these activities would scarcely brand him libertine, but George Sutherland would have disapproved had he known about them. One writes "had he known about them" because it was said of Edwin that "he still went behind the barn to smoke his cigarettes as an adult when he went home to visit his parents in the summer."[8] In point of fact, however, as an adult Edwin returned to Grand Island only occasionally to visit his parents. According to Snodgrass, "[f]riends did not know Sutherland came from a large family and recalled that there was no mention of, nor visits by, its members. One cannot help but gain the impression that relations must have been strained."[9]

Geis and Goff see the relationship between father and son as a "familiar" one:

> A strict father with children who rebel to the extent of casting aside some of the more superficial aspects of the parent's behavior and values. . . . But the father's fundamental attitudes and commitments permeated the ethos of the son . . . the impress of his father's strong personality was bred into him; so were the sense of righteousness and toughness.[10]

This suggests that Edwin was no rebel, for he retained his father's fundamental ethical values throughout his life. Moreover, both father and son have been characterized as "intellectually demanding, sharply critical of the work of colleagues which failed to meet their rigorous standards, as well as unstintingly self-critical."[11]

Snodgrass has described Edwin Sutherland as a "man of compulsive virtue and integrity. While he may have given up the orthodoxy of his Baptist upbringing, he never lost its scruples."[12] His personality seems to have been a blend of the Christian humanist and cool scientist "unsparing in his exposure of the false syllogism, sloppy logic, the unsupported inference, and the generalization rooted in fancy rather than fact."[13] He was passionately committed to ethical human and business relationships, personal integrity, social reform, and disciplined hard work.

The son inherited many of the father's intellectual characteristics as well. Edwin was an outstanding student and acquired a classical education in languages, history, literature, natural science, and religion. He also participated in many extracurricular activities, among them oratory and debate, baseball, basketball, and football. Goff has described a picture of Sutherland that appeared in the 1904 college yearbook. There stood a "tall broad-shouldered young man, attired in full football uniform—leggings, padded pants, and roll neck sweater. On the football team, Sutherland played offensive fullback."[14]

Edwin embodied the ideals of the Rhodes Scholar. And, in fact, his athletic prowess and academic record almost won him that scholarship. He passed the Rhodes scholarship examination and hoped to be among the first contingent of young Americans to study at Oxford University. However he tied with another student for the honor. Unfortunately for Sutherland, the other student was offered the scholarship and accepted it.

After graduation from college in 1904, Sutherland taught Latin, Greek, history, and shorthand for two years at Sioux Falls College in South Dakota, where his sister Nellie May was teaching English. It was here in 1905 that he enrolled in a correspondence course in sociology offered by the home study department of the University of Chicago. The course was titled "Introduction to Sociology," and was supervised by Dr. Annie Marion MacLean, an assistant professor, who had received her Ph.D. from the University of Chicago in 1900. This course was Edwin's first formal exposure to sociology.[15] At that point in his life he was planning to undertake graduate work in history at the University of Chicago, and a course in sociology was then required for acceptance. He had no way of knowing then that a university requirement would set him on a new life's course.

Chicago

In 1906 Sutherland left Sioux Falls College and entered graduate school at the University of Chicago. It would be difficult to appreciate the kind of education he received there between 1906 and 1913 without first understanding something of the city of Chicago and of the nation at large during the preceding half century.

From its beginnings as a swampy village called Fort Dearborn, the city grew by leaps and bounds throughout the nineteenth century. From approximately 10,000 inhabitants in 1837, when it was first incorporated, Chicago grew to be a major city of over 1,000,000 people and the host of the Columbian Exposition by 1893. No large American city grew faster in the 1890s than did Chicago. By 1910 its population had doubled and stood at 2,185,283. By 1920 another half million had been added and Chicago's population numbered 2,701,705. Between 1880 and 1920 the population increased four-fold.[16]

Well before the turn of the century, Chicago had captured the attention of the rest of the country and of Europe. Capital and people flowed into the city at a mind-boggling rate. By 1900 Chicago was established as a commercial and industrial powerhouse whose people and machines transformed the agricultural and natural resources of the West into foodstuffs and finished products for an ever-expanding domestic market.

Chicago, itself neither West nor East, was strategically situated at the crossroads of this vast country, linking both ends. The railroad was both an essential ingredient in making Chicago what it had become and, at the same time, a symbol of the city and its significance to the country.[17]

> Chicago presented a readily observable raw dynamic of industrial urban growth. It was unencumbered physically, socially, politically, and culturally with the layers of the past. The elites of Chicago were speculative (brash and/ or bold) entrepreneurs, and the Swifts, McCormicks, Pullmans, and Yerkes could trace their new wealth to nearby stockyards, factories, and transportation terminals.[18]

Of course Chicago had its underside as well as its elites. The lives of the poor, the immigrants, and the working class were as raw and as observable as those of the "speculative entrepreneurs." These less-favored groups provided the strong backs and nimble fingers that kept the great industrial machine turning. Today it is difficult to accurately assess whether these groups were better or worse off in their new urban lives. The sheer fact that Chicago and other similar cities continued to attract wave upon wave of newcomers is a bold testament to their imagined opportunities. Between 1900 and 1910 approximately one-third of Chicago's population was foreign born, and another one-third the children of the foreign born.[19] Against these irrefutable statistics stands the equally undeniable fact that currents of discontent were simultaneously at work. In the 1890s, Chicago was the site of gathering "armies of reform,"

> the labor unionists, the free silverites, the civil service reformers, the female suffragists, the settlement workers, [and] the Populists. These armies may have been fighting different campaigns against different enemies, but each group was driven by feelings of anger or disappointment or disillusionment at the discrepancy between an American ideal they cherished and an American reality they were enduring.[20]

However, it would not only be misleading but simply wrong to give the impression that the overriding temper of the times was discontent and despair. The mood at the end of the nineteenth century was essentially optimistic. Progress, science, and growth were the appropriate watchwords. But the truth of any period is generally more complex than we are ready to admit. The United States was changing from one kind of society into another, and that has never occurred without personal and social pain and dislocation. This period gave rise to various forms of public protest and social reform that tried, each in individual fashion, to alter the direction and pace of social change, or at least to understand its dynamic.

> The Grangers (or the Patrons of Husbandry), the Knights of Labor, and the later American Federation of Labor became specialized organizations for the occupational interests of the farmer and worker; the Greenback, Single-Tax, Populist, and Progressive political movements developed; from the Protestant Churches came the Social Gospel Movement as a vehicle for reform; and through the medium of the emerging popular literature of the period the muckraker exposed economic, political, and social injustices. Among those who hoped to employ science in the amelioration of social evils were the sociologists.[21]

In the *Hull House Maps and Papers* (1895), articles described the "grinding poverty, ending only in death or escape to some more hopeful occupation. Within the [sweatshop trades] there has been and can be no improvement in wages while tenement-house manufacture is tolerated."[22] While the city may have represented an improvement to the people who came there to begin a new life, it was still the case that those on the bottom were unable to earn enough money to support their families. For example, Diner reports that in 1915 the average wage of men working in the stockyards was $503 a year, while the minimum amount needed to support a family of five was said to be $800.[23] Goff writes:

> The results were evident if you walked through Chicago's poorest neighborhoods. Six and seven people commonly lived in one or two rooms; the disease rate was high; criminals operated freely; prostitutes were numerous; animal waste choked the stockyards; and pollution from the steel mills oftentimes made life in South Chicago almost unbearable. Political power was decentralized, and city politicians often were corrupt. In the poorest districts, ward bosses financed their organizations through kickbacks from corrupt politicians, money given them from gambling operators, and bribes accepted from a variety of sources, including companies wanting to receive city contracts.[24]

From the little that Sutherland has written about his graduate school days at the University of Chicago we can conclude that he was not insensitive to his surroundings. Writing in 1927, he described his initial motivation for studying sociology as an interest in the methods of improving social conditions. This was a missionary interest. . . . When I became an officer of the Juvenile Protective Association, I saw for the first time in my life the conditions of life in the immigrant sections of a large city. These impressed me very much, as had some of the earlier literature I had read (Jacob Riis, etc.), and I developed a somewhat radical attitude. I was impressed with the slightness of modification that could be made by reform organization, and I wanted something like socialism . . . that would make a great and somewhat sudden change.[25]

For most sociologists—indeed, for most intellectuals—material progress was viewed with ambivalence. The tremendous industrial and commercial growth of the last half of the nineteenth century created vast new fortunes, but it also spawned teeming neighborhoods of unacculturated immigrants, official corruption, crime, and disillusionment. These changes were felt especially in the urban midwest, which only decades earlier had been hardly more developed than the frontier. The contrast between the society that existed before the Civil War and the one that followed was so stark that its effects could not help but draw the attention of the midwestern sociologists. These social conditions constituted, in part, the backdrop for young Sutherland as he embarked upon his graduate studies at the University of Chicago.[26]

Organization of Chapters

Chapters Two and Three trace Sutherland's intellectual development from the time he entered the University of Chicago to study history until the crystallization of his professional identity around sociological criminology. Between 1906 and 1926 he passed through three academic settings—the University of Chicago (1906-1913), William Jewell College (1913-1919), and the University of Illinois (1919-1926). Each left its mark on Sutherland, although not, of course, in equal measure or in the same way. It will be seen that his initial development was characterized by false starts and much indecision. But once he set about to make his mark as a criminologist, Sutherland hewed to it with a single-mindedness that is rare within sociology. Throughout this early period in his intellectual and professional development there was nothing to suggest that Sutherland would develop a criminological theory that would reorient the discipline.

Chapter Four follows Sutherland's career to the University of Minnesota, at the fourth-ranked department of sociology in the country. There, his colleagues were as ambitious as he was, and the pressures within the department to publish were palpable. Between 1926 and 1929 Sutherland strove to solidify his reputation as one of the country's leading criminologists. During these years he wrote articles that promoted the idea that sociology was a scientific enterprise whose goal was the understanding and control of social problems, including crime. A few hundred miles to the southeast, the University of Chicago and the Institute for Juvenile Research were giving birth to sociological criminology. Men such as Robert E. Park, Ernest W. Burgess, Clifford R. Shaw, and Henry D. McKay constituted Sutherland's reference group and he followed their theoretical and research activities closely. Through his activities within the profession, his correspondence with McKay and Burgess, and his occasional visits to the University of Chicago, he participated in these developments. During this period Sutherland was a follower of what was called multiple factor theory. While he was critical of this contemporary criminological theory, he was unable to formulate an alternative theory of his own.

Chapter Five describes six crucial years in Sutherland's career. For one year (1929-1930) he worked as a researcher for the Bureau of Social Hygiene in New York City. Then, for five years, he was a research professor in the department of sociology at the University of Chicago. His was definitely an upwardly mobile career path. But these years are important not so much for what they meant to Sutherland's career as for what they contributed to his ideas on crime causation. The early 1930s witnessed Sutherland's first efforts to state a theory of crime causation. Drawing on the concepts and perspective of his reference group, he began to move toward what later would be called the theory of differential association. This chapter will examine the people and ideas that contributed to Sutherland's theoretical breakthrough.

Chapter Six traces the temporary setback in Sutherland's career when his contract at the University of Chicago was not renewed after the 1934-1935 academic year. The next year he assumed the position of chair in the newly established department of sociology at Indiana University. Within four years he had published three books, including the third edition of *Principles of Criminology* (1939). This edition contained the first explicit statement of the theory of differential association. That same year he was elected president of the American Sociological Society. The persons and events that contributed to Sutherland's evolving ideas on crime causation in the late 1930s will be described. Throughout the next decade Sutherland was widely recognized as the dean of American criminology and he continued to sharpen and refine his theory. The transitional stages that the theory assumed between 1939 and 1947 will be discussed, along with Sutherland's reasons for their consideration and ultimate rejection. Finally, the 1947 version of the theory will be analyzed to reveal Sutherland's final published ideas on crime causation.

Notes

1. Edwin H. Sutherland, "Development of the Theory," in *Edwin H. Sutherland: On Analyzing Crime*, Karl Schuessler, ed. (Chicago: University of Chicago Press, 1973), p. 13.
2. Jon Snodgrass, "The American Criminological Tradition: Portraits of Men and Ideology in a Discipline" (unpublished Ph.D. dissertation, University of Pennsylvania, 1972), p. 218.
3. George Sutherland, "Reminiscences," Manuscript (Rochester, N.Y.: American Baptist Historical Society, 1935), p. 155, quoted in Gilbert Geis and Colin Goff, "Introduction," in Edwin H. Sutherland, *White Collar Crime: The Uncut Version* (New Haven: Yale University Press,, 1983), p. xxi.
4. Karl Schuessler, "Introduction," in *Edwin H. Sutherland: On Analyzing Crime*, Karl Schuessler, ed. (Chicago: University of Chicago Press, 1973), p. x.
5. Snodgrass, p. 221.
6. Ibid.
7. George Sutherland, p. 177.
8. Snodgrass, pp. 221-222.
9. Ibid., p. 219.
10. Gilbert Geis and Colin Goff, "Introduction," in Edwin H. Sutherland, *White Collar Crime: The Uncut Version* (New Haven: Yale University Press, 1983). p. xx.
11. Ibid., p. xviii.
12. Snodgrass, p. 227.
13. Geis and Goff, p. xxi.
14. Colin Goff, "Edwin H. Sutherland and White-Collar Crime" (unpublished Ph.D. dissertation, University of Calfornia, Irvine, 1982), pp. 60-61.
15. Ibid., p. 63.
16. James T. Carey, *Sociology and Public Affairs: The Chicago School* (Beverly Hills, California: Sage Publications, 1975), p. 114; Albert Hunter, "Why Chicago? The Rise of the Chicago School of Urban Social Science," *American Behavioral Scientist*, 24 (1980), pp. 216-217; Goff, p. 73.
17. Albert Hunter, "Why Chicago? The Rise of the Chicago School of Urban Social Science," p. 216.
18. Hunter, pp. 216-217.
19. Goff, pp. 73-74.
20. Robert McCaul, "Dewey's Chicago," *School Review*, 67 (Summer 1959), p. 268.
21. Roscoe C. Hinkle and Gisela J. Hinkle, *The Development of Modern Sociology: Its Nature and Growth in the United States* (New York: Random House, 1954), p. 2.
22. Goff, p. 74.
23. Steven J. Diner, *A City and Its Universities: Public Policy in Chicago, 1892-1919* (Chapel Hill: University of North Carolina Press, 1980), p. 53.
24. Goff, pp. 74-75.
25. Edwin H. Sutherland, Letter to Luther Bernard, 13 July 1927. Luther L. Bernard Papers, Pennsylvania Historical Collections, Pattee Library, Pennsylvania State University, University Park, Pennsylvania.
26. Hinkle and Hinkle, pp. 1-4.

2

The University of Chicago, 1906-1913

This chapter divides Sutherland's graduate studies at the University of Chicago into two phases. The first phase, 1906 to 1908, will reveal a young man undecided about the direction his studies should take. It will explain why he changed his major from history to sociology and will show how he fell under the influence of Charles R. Henderson and then, later, W. I. Thomas. The second phase, 1908 to 1913, will describe Sutherland's growing disillusionment with sociology. It will show how he turned toward Robert F. Hoxie and political economy in search of a value-free and objective social science by which human behavior and society could be understood and controlled. This chapter will show how, in 1913, he emerged from the University of Chicago with an ambiguous professional identity and a collection of research interests more suited to an economist than to a sociologist, albeit with a doctorate in both sociology and political economy.

Early Graduate Student Years, 1906-1908

In order to understand the sources of major influence over Sutherland's graduate work at the University of Chicago, and the modes in which this influence was exerted, it is necessary to apply the techniques of the historian as well as of the sociologist. Through an examination of the men and ideas to which Edwin Sutherland was exposed at Chicago, one may begin to understand the sources of his later development and output.

So little is known about his experiences at Chicago that radically different opinions as to the instructors who bore the most influence on him are held by Karl Schuessler (who in 1973 edited and wrote an introduction to a collection of Sutherland's major articles on criminology), on the one hand, and Gilbert Geis and Colon Goff (authors of a recent introduction to the "uncut version" of *White Collar Crime*) on the other. Schuessler believes

[h]is training there was largely in the hands of Charles Henderson, Albion Small, and W. I. Thomas, whose collective influence is quite evident in Sutherland's earlier writing, with its emphasis on social process. It is also evident in his theory of criminal behavior, which may be regarded as an adaptation of interactional sociology as expounded by W. I. Thomas; it is further evident in his empirical research, which is based on those techniques of careful investigation that came to be known as the hallmark of the Chicago school of sociology.[1]

Geis and Goff, to the contrary, argue that Sutherland became "disenchanted" with Chicago's department of sociology and chose to concentrate his energies in the department of political economy.[2]

It will be argued here that both accounts, as cited, are correct. While it is true that Sutherland did become disenchanted with his instructors in the department of sociology, Henderson and Small had a collective influence on him, if only in a negative way. W. I. Thomas's influence, however, was significant, lasting, and positive.

One source of information about Sutherland's graduate school years and his possible intellectual filiation is contained in an interview Colin Goff conducted with Stuart A. Queen in November 1980. At the time of this interview Queen, then ninety years old, was the "last surviving graduate student from Chicago during this era."[3] Queen's close relationship with Sutherland makes it possible to secure insights into a facet of Sutherland's graduate school experiences not likely now to be secured in any other way.

From 1911 to 1913 Queen was a master's degree candidate at the University of Chicago. Sutherland was seven years older than Queen and a Ph.D. candidate, yet these differences did not stand in the way of their forming a close and lasting friendship. Queen, recalling those years long ago in Chicago, stated that he and Sutherland "treated each other almost as brothers."[4] In Goff's interview with Queen, the latter recalled how Sutherland would join in informal discussions about sociology along the Midway at the university with such graduate students as Emory S. Bogardus, Ernest W. Burgess, Ellsworth Faris, and others. While definitely not the pushy sort, Sutherland could more than hold up his end of a good debate: "[Sutherland] was thoughtful, he thought for himself, he could definitely but pleasantly disagree with anybody. He was admired by the faculty and the students. He was a person I think everybody liked."[5]

Another source of information on Sutherland's graduate work at Chicago may be found at the Pennsylvania Historical Collections and Labor Archives, Pennsylvania State University, where a collection of Sutherland's correspondence with Luther L. Bernard (1881-1951) is located. Sutherland and Bernard became good friends during their graduate school years at Chicago, and through the years, as each man moved about the country in pursuit of his career, they maintained a faithful correspondence. The letters were written mainly between 1912 and 1927. A good number of them contain Sutherland's thoughts on his instructors at the University of Chicago. The general impression these letters leave with a modern-day student of the history of sociology is how little has changed in the daily reality of graduate students. The Luther L. Bernard Collection contains hundreds of letters sent to him by W. I. Thomas and Robert E. Park, as well as by Edwin H. Sutherland. Bernard was particularly interested in the history of social thought, and this may have prompted him to retain his correspondence with these eminent men within the discipline.

When Sutherland entered the University of Chicago he intended to take graduate work in history. That being the case, it is curious that the first courses he enrolled in were offered by the University of Chicago divinity school: "Introduction to the Books of the New Testament," "Outlines of Church History," and "Psychology of Conduct." There are a number of possible explanations for Sutherland's enrollment in these courses, the most likely being that they were taken at the suggestion of his father, George Sutherland, a Baptist minister and educator. Perhaps the son enrolled in these courses because he, too, thought his future lay in the ministry, but it is more likely that he took them in order to please a domineering father.

Sutherland also enrolled in a sociology course that first summer at Chicago. When he had been teaching at Sioux Falls College in South Dakota he had received a letter from his correspondence course instructor, Dr. Annie Marion MacLean. In that letter she praised him for his work in "Introduction to Sociology." She also invited him to call on her when he began his graduate work at the University of Chicago. When he arrived in the summer of 1906 he did so. She persuaded Sutherland to enroll in Charles R. Henderson's course "Social Treatment of Crime." The suggestion was probably not difficult to follow since, at that time, Sutherland was apparently still eager to please authority figures. This event marked the first major turning point in his academic career.

Sutherland was familiar with Professor Henderson's work because Dr. MacLean had used one of Henderson's texts in her sociology correspondence course. In a letter written to his friend Luther L. Bernard in 1927, Sutherland recalled that Dr. MacLean

> spoke to Dr. Henderson about me, so that when I entered Dr. Henderson's course, I received personal attention. He spoke to me, knew me, was interested in me. Consequently I was interested in pursuing sociology, and interested in the type of sociology that Professor Henderson presented.[6]

Lacking an apparent professional direction in 1906, it is likely

Sutherland turned toward sociology for no more compelling reason than that Henderson took a personal interest in him. A number of sources suggest that these two men should have found themselves compatible. Geis and Goff have argued that Professor Henderson and George Sutherland, Edwin's father, were made in the same image.[7] Each was a Baptist minister, each had graduated from the Baptist Union Theological Seminary at Chicago, and each had a confident, self-assured, and outgoing personality. Yet it is possible that whatever strain Sutherland felt in his relationship with his father may have been reflected in his relationship with Henderson. As was true for most of Sutherland's instructors, his relationship with Henderson was ambivalent. Nevertheless, he once wrote that Henderson was the greatest influence on him during his first year of graduate work.[8]

As time passed, however, Henderson's influence waned, even though he served as Sutherland's advisor in the department of sociology from 1906 to 1913. Eventually Sutherland came to believe that Henderson was much too concerned with social reform and not concerned enough with developing sociology as a science. This was because Henderson conceived of his civic work, his teaching and research, and indeed his entire professional activity as a sociologist as the secular side of an essentially pastoral approach to mankind and the problems of society.[9]

In an article titled "The Ministry of Today—Its New Equipment," Henderson wrote: "To assist us in the difficult task of adjustment to new situations God has providentially wrought out for us the social sciences and placed them at our disposal."[10] Social science, and especially sociology, was seen by Henderson as the "new equipment" that would promote the ends of the progressive "social gospel" movement. Henderson was no theorist, but rather a man of practical action. His involvement with civic organizations furnished data that found their way into his publications. While it is true that he was one of the original members of the department of sociology at the University of Chicago, his contribution to the development of sociology was slight. In fact, he was the only member of the early department not elected president of the American Sociological Society.

Geis and Goff have stated that throughout his life Edwin Sutherland harbored a strong sense of "indignation" and "vituperation" toward the selfishness and greed of white-collar crimes and white-collar criminals.[11] Perhaps this is one of the lessons he learned from Henderson, for it is not difficult to find similar expressions of indignation and contempt in his writings.[12] For example, in his 1901 textbook, *Introduction to the Study of the Dependent, Defective, and Delinquent Classes*, Henderson wrote:

> Social position affects conduct. Crime is more frequent among the lower classes than among the upper classes. Criminals are recruited from their own

kind. But it should be added that rich criminals are more likely to escape detection, arrest, and punishment, and that we must in justice discriminate carefully between the "lower classes" and the great majority of the worthy and honest working people of small incomes. These latter often belong to the true "upper classes." The real distinction is one of character, not of income. The crimes of merchants are those of cunning and intrigue rather than of force. The immoral and cruel acts of employers which drive men to strike are usually within the technical forms of law, and are not outwardly sensational and tangible, while the beating of a non-union workman is covered by statute.[13]

Within this same textbook, which one assumes Sutherland studied carefully in Henderson's courses, one may find other examples of the cool detachment of the social scientist giving way to the heat of the indignant moralist appalled by the behavior of the "upper classes":

The corruption of partisan politics, the entire spoils system, favors the increase of crime. The successful politician is the demigod of the immature youth of a city ward, and his example is more powerful than that of Washington or Lincoln, because these respectable gentlemen are not so well known, and have no places to fill. Bribery in all its forms stimulates cupidity and dulls conscience. The saloon-keeper is an authority and guide in the evil ways of politics. Under a vicious system of appointments to office the police, who should suppress vice, sometimes derive private revenue from gambling-dens and brothels as the price of immunity from interruption of their wicked trades. When the unscrupulous agents of city railways, railroads, and other great corporations purchase the nominations and control the elections of aldermen in their own interest and against the public, crime is fostered through the very institutions of justice and law, and by those whose intelligence and strength makes them most responsible and guilty.[14]

In the final analysis, then, how may Henderson's influence on Sutherland be judged? First, Henderson was responsible for Sutherland's changing his major from history to the "type of sociology that Dr. Henderson presented." Second, his initial conception of how sociological research should be conducted was learned from Henderson. Henderson was never comfortable with abstract theory. Instead, he placed emphasis on direct observation and generalizations based on their findings. He encouraged his students to pursue concrete descriptions and analyses of urban life, especially the lives of the poor, the immigrants, the orphaned and deserted, and the criminals.[15] When Sutherland later conducted research for his dissertation Henderson's was the model he followed. But as Sutherland matured to become an independent scholar he changed his mind about the value of abstract theory. In the 1930s and 1940s he sought to develop a general theory of criminal behavior. This, of course, resulted in the theory of differential association.

When the fall quarter of 1906 began at the University of Chicago, Sutherland had finished his three courses in the divinity school and Professor Henderson's course, "The Social Treatment of Crime." During his first full year in graduate school he took six courses in the department of sociology. Three of the courses were taught by Albion Small: "Outlines of General Sociology," "Ethics of Sociology," and "The Class Struggle in Society." In addition to Small's courses, Sutherland enrolled in "Social Origins," which was taught by W. I. Thomas, "Contemporary Charities," under Charles Henderson, and "Public Opinion," one of George E. Vincent's courses.

Among those regarded as having had an influence on Sutherland's education at the University of Chicago, Albion Small (1854-1926), chair of the department of sociology, is often mentioned. Small was founder and chair of one of the world's first departments of sociology. He was dean of the graduate college, and coauthor of *Introduction to the Study of Sociology*, the first sociology textbook in America. With this background and as editor of the *American Journal of Sociology*, Small was in a strategic position to influence Sutherland's progress as he worked toward his Ph.D. in sociology. Whether (and if so, to what degree) that potential for influence was realized is difficult to assess today.

Sutherland's theory of differential association suggests, however, that propinquity is not sufficient to assure influence. Sutherland's receptivity to Small's teaching and ideas is crucial, and it is precisely here that the test of "significant influence" is weakest. It is difficult, if not impossible, to find in Sutherland's published work the hand of Small. For example, in all four editions of Sutherland's criminology textbook not a single reference is made to Small. Actually, in much of Sutherland's correspondence with fellow graduate student Luther L. Bernard he writes negatively of Small. In a letter written to Bernard on November 24, 1912, Sutherland complained:

> As a matter of fact, Small now speaks more frequently about objective standards and objective points of view, and other objectives than he used to speak about Sabbath Day's journeys; I have not heard him mention storage tanks for the last year, and he says the only value of "General Sociology" is in working out some concepts—a sort of sociological dictionary—that is, of course, aside from the interpretation of Ratzenhofer, Spencer, Schaeffle, and the others.[16]

In another letter to Bernard, Sutherland described the Sociology Club's efforts to develop an introductory sociology course, "i.e. to determine its general content and nature. . . ." He explained the strategy they hoped to employ to convince the sociology faculty that a drastic change was needed:

> We have asked Tufts, Mead and are going to try to get Marshall, Hoxie and

one or two others outside the department to tell us how to teach the introductory course in sociology, and shall ask Small to give his opinion afterward, as a sop to his position.[17]

By most accounts, Small was an uninspiring teacher. Stuart Queen, among fellow graduate students, remembered him as "reading his manuscripts to the students, leaving little time for discussion."[18] Everett C. Hughes, who was a graduate student at Chicago between 1923 and 1928 and a good friend of Sutherland's, recalled a funny incident in one of Small's courses:

> I was in a class of his and he fell asleep in the class once, reading the correspondence that he'd had with Lester Ward. And a student named Eyler Simpson . . . stepped into the breach and took over and started lecturing and after a while Professor Small woke up brightly and acted as if he hadn't been asleep at all and as if Eyler Simpson had been appointed to run the class.[19]

In conclusion, it is difficult to believe, as Schuessler does, that Small's influence, to whatever extent it may have existed during Sutherland's university days, had any lasting effect on his mature thought as an independent scholar.

W. I. Thomas is the third sociology professor named by Schuessler as having had strong bearing on Sutherland's sociological education at Chicago. The hand of Thomas (1863-1947) is so evident in the work of Sutherland that, despite the latter's statement, written in 1927, in which he disclaims much "constructive influence" by the members of the department of sociology on his thinking, it is encumbent upon any of his biographers to trace the major lines of that influence.

It is known that Sutherland was deeply impressed by Thomas, for in an autobiographical statement prepared for his friend Luther L. Bernard he wrote:

> During my first year in graduate work at the University of Chicago I became impressed with the great complexity of social problems and the great difficulty of solving them. I developed a moderate skepticism regarding social reform. My brother had taken a course under Dr. Thomas and had been greatly impressed by it and by Dr. Thomas. I decided that if I placed more emphasis on ethnology, specializing in that, I could deal with a situation that was specific and concrete, and thus get rid of the troublesome and practically impossible problems of social reform.

> I had started in my graduate work in sociology with economics as a minor, related somewhat to the interest in social reform. I suspect that the courses in economics added more to my skepticism in regard to social reform than did the courses in sociology. At any rate, as I became interested in ethnological

material, I also developed an interest in psychology, and I changed from economics to psychology as a minor.[20]

When Thomas arrived at the University of Chicago in 1893 to begin the graduate work that ended with his receiving a doctorate in 1896, sociology was in its infancy and Thomas was just beginning to find his way within its existing forms. From the very beginning, he felt himself to be working at the margin of the dominant concerns of the discipline. If one recalls that most sociologists of that day, including Small, Henderson, and Vincent, were steeped in history, philosophy, theology, and to a lesser degree political science and economics, Thomas's "marginality" then stands out in high relief. Thomas claimed: "I read largely and in marginal subjects—biology, psychology, ethnology—" And "I never became influenced by philosophy as offering an explanation of reality."[21] Here was a man deeply interested in "anthropology, biology, Egyptology, Assyriology, literature, history, and biography"[22] who was sorting out for himself what sociology was and might possibly become. On this same point, Faris wrote:

> None of the original faculty of the Chicago department was trained in sociology because there had been no department to train them. Thus there was still a large amount of uncertainty about what the task was to be—what sort of sociology was to be created. It was to be nearly thirty years before their successors could feel confident that they were at last on the true road.[23]

It is very difficult to locate the social and intellectual origins of Thomas's sociological thought. This is not just a biographer's complaint, for Thomas has said as much himself.

> It is certainly a misapprehension of the truth, however, to trace influence predominantly to personalities or "masters." This represented the truth more completely at the time when primary group norms prevailed in society, when outstanding personalities assembled disciples and followers and created cults and schools. But at present the influences are as diverse as the "great society" is diverse in its models and attitudes. We tend to be more influenced by trends of thought and method than by particular persons, and we tend to be influenced by dissent from, as much as acquiescence in, the systems of other persons. We may be influenced by a person and at the same time reject his conclusions.[24]

In a letter written January 10, 1928, to Luther L. Bernard, Thomas expressed his sense of independence from his teachers and colleagues and the degree to which he felt himself to be an original thinker whose work bore the stamp of no one quite so much as Thomas himself.

> You will notice that I have added the names of Mead and Cooley to those

who influenced me. [This letter mentioned Spencer, Loeb, Jennings, Watson, and Park as "influences."] I have preferred to say nothing about Dewey. When he came to the University I was already offering a course in "Social Origins." I gave him materials used in his address as President of the Philosophical Society about that time and it would be more correct to say that he came under my influence than that I came under his. It is true that I was interested in his thought and certainly attempted to use some of it in my classes, but Dewey has always seemed to me to be essentially a mystic and a metaphysician and I found—or rather thought I found—that I was repudiating almost everything he said, or ignoring it. It may be, nevertheless, that he had more influence on me than I remember. The same of Mead. I am saying this to you by way of explanation and as a private matter.[25]

It is a fact, however, that Thomas studied under both Dewey and Mead. Dewey had come to Chicago from the University of Michigan in 1894. Thomas's book *Source Book for Social Origins* (1909) made use of some of the basic concepts of functional psychology that Dewey and Mead were developing.

Control is the end to be secured and attention is the means of securing it. They are the objective and subjective sides of the same process. Attention is the mental attitude which takes note of the outside world and manipulates it; it is the organ of accommodation. But attention does not operate alone; it is associated with habit on the one hand and with crisis on the other. When the habits are running smoothly the attention is relaxed; it is not at work. But when something happens to disturb the run of habit the attention is called into play and devises a new mode of behavior which will meet the crisis. That is, the attention establishes new and adequate habits, or it is its function to do so.[26]

This passage makes plain that Thomas's view is based on the role of problems in thought and action as conceived by Dewey and Mead. The "subjective side of the process" results from the interpretation of an ongoing activity (or habit), while the "objective side of the process" is the effort to restore the activity.

While Thomas's interests would later lead him to develop such sociological concepts as definition of the situation, wishes, attitudes, and values, his approach remained that of functional psychology. Ernest W. Burgess, first a student and later a colleague of Thomas, writes:

In his general orientation he was profoundly affected by the pragmatic philosophy of John Dewey, whose influence still pervaded the university although he had departed for Columbia five years earlier [1904], by the social thinking of George H. Mead, also a colleague, and by the anthropological studies of Franz Boas.[27]

When Sutherland entered the graduate program in sociology at Chicago in 1906, Thomas was a forty-three-year-old associate professor, whose genius was recognized by his colleagues. The courses that he taught were designated "purely anthropological"[28] and fell within that part of the department's program variously called "Folk Psychology," "Social Psychology," and "Social and Racial Psychology." The courses that were included often changed in title and content. However, Thomas often advised his students not to take more than two or three courses from him, "explaining that although the titles were different, the material was the same."[29] This was not to be taken literally, however, for Thomas's method of conducting his courses was to bring into the classroom materials on which he was currently working. Burgess described Thomas's method:

> His custom was to read quotations from the literature upon a given topic, supplementing these by his own immitable [*sic*] comments. Students in his courses were alternately shocked and thrilled by an extract on behavior widely different from our own or by a penetrating interpretation which showed among the great diversity of human behavior a manifestation of human nature akin if not identical with our own.[30]

As Thomas's interests shifted, so did the titles and contents of his courses. They dealt with such topics as primitive art, women, occupations, primitive races, folk psychology, sex, and racial development. As a teacher, Bernard remembered Thomas as "very open, leisurely, almost confiding, enthusiastic, and a bit open to flattery."[31]

In 1909 Thomas's first influential book, *Source Book for Social Origins*, was published. This book, "which was required reading for most graduate students at Chicago during the next quarter century,"[32] was undoubtedly read by Sutherland, since he "specialized" in ethnology. It was a book interesting not only in its content, but also in its organization. It contained ethnological source materials and Thomas's "careful introductions to and his comments on each selection and his bibliographic annotations."[33]

Sutherland's graduate school years straddle the middle of Thomas's twenty-five-year association with the University of Chicago as student and teacher. Between 1906 and 1913 Thomas was moving from the first to the second phase of his career. It was a transition from traditional ethnographer to empirical social psychologist, a notable shift in interests. Burgess has clearly documented this phase in Thomas's teaching career:

> By 1900 the viewpoint and organization of his teaching had become stabilized around five main courses: namely, Sociological Function of Art and Play, Origin of Social Institutions, Race Development of Mind, Sex in Social Organization, and Primitive Social Control. The names of some of these

courses are changed; for example, Origin of Social Institutions becomes Social Origins and is the only course in the above group which Thomas continued to teach during his tenure at Chicago. Race Development of Mind was changed to Mental Development in the Races and was offered for the last time in 1916.

New courses appear in the Annual Register and indicate Thomas' continuing shift of interest in subject matter more than in his point of view. These are listed with the approximate years in which they were offered: Origin and Psychology of the Occupations (1902, 1906, 1909); The Negro in Africa and America (1906-1907); The Mind of the Oriental (1908); Savage Childhood (1909); the Mind of the Negro (1913); The Immigrant (1910-1912); The European Peasant (1913); Social Attitudes (1913-1917); Psychology of Divergent Types (1914-1916); Prostitution (1914-1916); The European Peasant (1914-1916); The Jew (1914-1915); Divergent Types (1916); Races and Nationalities (1917); and Theory of Social Disorganization (1917).

An examination of the above courses discloses definite trends in Thomas' interests and theoretical orientations. He became much less concerned with ethnological subject matter and much more attracted by studies of the Negro, the immigrant, the European peasant, and the Jew.[34]

One might also add that he became interested in studies of children and delinquents, but these came in later years.

Goff has speculated that one reason Thomas displaced Henderson as the "major influence" on Sutherland during the 1907-1908 academic year was that

> Sutherland became critical of Henderson's style of reform. . . . [H]is reforms were oftentimes defeated, and therefore failed to bring about effective social changes. Sutherland also became critical of Henderson because business control of the law-making process defeated many attempts at reform. Henderson, in Sutherland's opinion, failed to realize this because he was always "careful to keep the approval of the substantial businessmen." As a result, tenement reforms were revised to include only unenforceable building codes and other similar minor changes. . . . From divinity student to Henderson's protégé, and then on to a follower of Thomas' style of ethnographic research, Sutherland began to become more involved with theoretical and methodological questions than moral ones.[35]

Scholars have only quite recently "discovered" the extent of Thomas's interest and involvement in social reform.[36] That interest was the direct result of his ideas on the human relationship to society. The problem of social change and its impact on the individual was central to his approach to sociology. He found himself deeply involved in the great transformation of his own society and the impact of this on the individual: massive immigration, rapid urbanization, increasing international tensions and their attendant threat of "world war," and the conflict between capital and labor.

These problems were not "social problems" in the sense of being merely troublesome features of an otherwise wholesome society. Instead, they were part and parcel of the transformation wrought by the wrenching change from one mode of social organization to another. Thomas believed societal transformation was inevitably conflictual: full of the clash and accommodation of groups vying for the favored positions within society.

For Thomas, social change was a series of transformations in which social organization gave way to disorganization, to be followed by reorganization as shifting and competing groups achieved an integration at a different level. While the transformation itself might be anything but tranquil, Thomas's attitude toward such events was essentially hopeful, for "it is always possible that groups would become more democratic in spirit, more rational in direction, and more functional in organization."[37] In this sense, Thomas's general theory of social change admitted the possibility of social progress.

What role did his theory of social change permit the sociologist to play, either as a social scientist or as a concerned citizen, in furtherance of this process? Thomas placed emphasis on the role of education, broadly defined, in enhancing a group's success in the evolutionary struggle. A group could do much to further its own ends, yet a role could also be played by those individuals who chose to act benevolently toward others less favored at the moment than themselves. Such individuals recognized that greater security for all could be achieved if contending groups voluntarily cooperated with each other. Thomas favored promoting "mutually advantageous forms of interaction;" one specific way this was being done in Chicago, which received his endorsement, was in the settlement houses. W. I. Thomas and Jane Addams were close friends and mutual supporters. Addams's Hull House, which she founded in 1889 with Ellen Gates Starr, became a focal point for the reform activities of Thomas. This institution represented the twin ideas of education and the "mutually advantageous" mixing of representatives of different social classes. Settlement houses were islands of middle-class values situated in deteriorated lower class neighborhoods. Within these settlement houses, patterns of middle class "adjustment" could be taught to those immigrants struggling to master a new language, new mores, and, in the case of immigrants from rural Europe, new modes of economic survival.

The question remains whether Thomas's model of sociological practice represented a real alternative to Henderson's. Goff suggests that it did. One suspects that the feature of Thomas's model that attracted Sutherland had more to do with the attempt to establish what Sutherland called "standards." In a letter to Luther L. Bernard dated November 1, 1915, Sutherland wrote:

The epithet "scholastic" which you shied [*threw*] at me in your last communication grows out of your failure to understand the evolutionary doctrine. It seems to me that a person must be either a "scholastic" or a demagogue, and I prefer the former. [Scott] Nearing is a good case of the latter. I don't mean to justify his dismissal, but to refer to his loose, inaccurate and superficial pronouncements on questions of social reform. His method seems to constitute a real danger, and I would prefer the settlement of questions by the strength of popular parties and classes than by such a quasi-rational method as he used. Dr. Henderson used the same method but was more conservative and more careful to keep the approval of the substantial businessmen. Neither one made any attempt, worth mentioning, to determine standards; they simply assumed them. . . . Any attempt to determine standards takes a person into social psychology. . . .[38]

During Sutherland's years of graduate study at Chicago, Thomas was laying the foundation for a theory of social organization and change. His attempt to establish a scientific basis for "standards," that is, his attempt to derive a statement of what constituted the "social good," was highly attractive to Sutherland. From Thomas, Sutherland learned a definition of sociology that emphasized its potential to become a science based on direct empirical observation. In the decade between Thomas's appointment as assistant professor (1896) and Sutherland's entry into the graduate program at Chicago, sociology was beginning to move from a "primitive and diffuse idea and mainly a bookish and speculative subject" to an empirical science based on direct observation and primary source material.[39] This transition paralleled Sutherland's own later slow development from social amelioration to social science.

In addition to his sociology courses, Sutherland enrolled in four political economy courses during his first year at Chicago: "Trusts," taught by Chester W. Wright; "Public Finance," under Herbert J. Davenport; "Scope and Method of Political Economy," a course given by Robert Hoxie; and "History of Political Economy," under Thorstein Veblen.

As Edwin Sutherland progressed in his graduate studies his interests underwent a number of interesting and somewhat puzzling shifts. He had begun his studies with divinity school courses, although his intention had been to pursue an advanced degree in history. He then transferred into the sociology program to learn methods of improving social conditions. At first he was attracted to Charles Henderson's type of sociology, but by the beginning of the 1907-1908 academic year he had fallen under the influence of W. I. Thomas. Sutherland chose political economy as his minor field of interest when he entered the university, but when he finished his studies he had earned a Ph.D. in both sociology *and* political economy, with a minor in psychology. These changes raise a number of "interesting questions about the true nature of Sutherland's educational goals and his social consciousness upon his arrival at Chicago."[40]

> It remains an enigma why Sutherland chose political economy as his minor field of study when he was entering the Divinity School. While his moralism had yet to be tempered by sociology, Sutherland was selecting courses such as "Public Finance" and "Trusts" rather than the more conservative offerings of the department of political economy. Perhaps he had brought with him from the midwest a knowledgeable and politicized attitude about certain political and economic issues, a result of the agrarian unrest of the Populists and, later, the Progressive point of view. His unsureness about sociology as compared to Divinity School courses remains in marked contrast to his immediate selection of political economy courses.[41]

In spite of our uncertainty concerning Sutherland's motivations and political/economic sophistication, it is clear that he was not so much committed to a particular discipline as eager to understand the social forces at work as America rushed into the twentieth century. Sutherland sought to acquire a scientific method by which he could determine objective standards. In his first two years at Chicago he failed to find such a method within sociology, although in W. I. Thomas he had at least found a man who thought such ought to be sociology's goal. He enrolled in political economy courses to learn whether he could locate in that discipline the scientific method he found lacking in sociology.

In one of those instances of "what if," he registered in a course titled "History of Political Economy" given by Thorstein Veblen (1857-1929) in the fall quarter of 1906. As Sutherland's choice of sociology seems to have been the result of Charles Henderson showing a personal interest in him, one wonders if Sutherland's academic career might not have been very different if he had studied with Veblen. Perhaps unfortunately for Sutherland (but perhaps fortunately for sociological criminology), Veblen left the University of Chicago to accept a position at Stanford University before the fall quarter began.

Later Graduate Student Years, 1910-1913

After the winter quarter of 1908, Edwin Sutherland returned to his alma mater at Grand Island, Nebraska, where he taught sociology, economics, and psychology. He remained in Grand Island for two and a half years. Except for the summer quarter of 1910, he did not return to his graduate studies until the summer quarter of 1911.

One imagines that his return to small-town life in Nebraska, after the intellectual stimulation of Chicago, must have encouraged Sutherland to evaluate his graduate program up to that point and to begin making plans for his studies upon his return to the university. At some point during this period he decided to take a major in sociology and political economy and a minor in psychology. The addition of political economy and psychology to his program was explained by Sutherland in these words:

> Life in a small town and teaching in a small college took me back somewhat to the reform type of sociology, but with a considerable increase of interest in the psychological processes involved. When I returned to graduate work in Chicago after an absence . . . of three years, I had as my dominant interest the material conditions—geographical and economic—by which life seemed to be controlled.[42]

When Edwin returned to the University of Chicago in the summer of 1910 he was twenty-seven years old. He seemed to have a surer sense of purpose. In any event, his academic course was now set and he pursued it without the sudden shifts that characterized his first two years at the University. In the summer of 1910 he enrolled in three psychology courses: "Educational Psychology," taught by Charles Hubbard Judd and Frank Nugent Freeman; "Experimental Psychology," taught by Harvey Carr; and "Social Psychology," taught by George Herbert Mead. Of the three "psychology" courses, only "Experimental Psychology" was offered through the department of psychology. Mead's course was taught in the department of philosophy and Judd and Freeman's course was taught in the department of education. In addition, he also registered in two other courses offered by the department of education—"Experimental Education 1" and "Experimental Education 2," both under Walter Fenno Dearborn. Finally, Sutherland enrolled in "Health of Working Men," taught by his advisor, Charles Henderson. While it is impossible to know with any degree of certainty how much work these courses demanded of Sutherland, it seems safe to assume that he was indeed a fully occupied graduate student that summer quarter.

Sutherland's decision to enroll in a course with George Herbert Mead (1863-1931) was in keeping with his decision to make psychology his minor field of study. It is important to understand what ideas Sutherland likely encountered in this course. Mead was one of the founders of what is today called symbolic interactionism. And that theory is fundamental to the theory of differential association.

In 1910 Mead was engaged in an "elaborate analysis . . . still in the making," which would later represent much of the core of what we today call symbolic interactionism. But even then "certain great features in it [stood] out with sufficient clearness to warrant comment."[43] Mead developed his theory of the emergence of the self and the nature of the mind within functional psychology. Exactly what "functional psychology" meant to Mead may be understood by examining what he recognized its subject matter to be:

> That phase of experience within which we are immediately conscious of conflicting impulses which rob the object of its character as object-stimulus, leaving us in so far in an attitude of subjectivity."[44]

Mead's name is missing among the list of Chicago functionalists. This is not because Mead viewed the development of functional psychology as a scant improvement. Mead was clearly a functionalist,[45] yet he stands apart from his Chicago colleagues in one very important respect. He thought their emphasis on individual psychology fundamentally distorted the true nature of psychological processes. In Mead's view the concentration on the individual, abstractly viewed apart from his social environment, ran counter to the insights and concepts from which functionalism originally developed. Something of Mead's disapproval of his colleagues' tendency to emphasize the individual over his environment may be seen in the following passage:

> Psychology . . . has not been interested in these epistemological and metaphysical riddles, it has been simply irritated by them. It has shifted its interest to the processes, where phenomenalism is most harmless, appearing as physiological psychology, as functional psychology, as dynamic psychology, and has ignored the problems for which it had no care. The effect of this has been to give the central nervous system a logical pre-eminence in the procedure and textbooks of psychology which is utterly unwarranted in the analysis of the experience of the individual. The central nervous system has been unwittingly assimilated to the logical position of consciousness. It occupies only an important stage in the act, but we find ourselves locating the whole environment of the individual in its convolutions. It is small wonder, then, that behaviorism has been welcomed with unmistakable relief, for it has studied the conduct of animals in necessary ignoration of consciousness.[46]

This quotation reveals Mead's point of view on a number of issues. First, he appeared to deplore the tendency of psychologists of his day to dismiss consciousness as merely "metaphysical," and therefore abstruse philosophical nonsense. Mead believed the study of consciousness is critical. By indirection, Mead criticized behaviorism as the study of the "conduct of animals in necessary ignoration of consciousness." Second, Mead also criticized functional psychology in this passage. "Psychology . . . has not been interested in these epistemological and metaphysical riddles. . . . It has shifted its interest to the processes, where phenomenalism is most harmless, appearing as . . . functional psychology . . . and has ignored the problems for which it had no care." Mead's displeasure toward functionalism appears to be based on his judgment that functionalism had a tendency to focus intently upon individuals as conceived apart from their social environment. Mead's psychology was a decidedly *social* psychology, and as such represented a deviation from the Chicago school of functional psychology.

It is clear that Mead intended to carve out a distinctive role for social psychology. It included both observable behavior and "those phenomena which are accessible to the individual alone."[47] Therefore, both overt and covert aspects of human behavior were the province of Mead's social psychology.

> Social psychology is behavioristic in the sense of starting off with an observable activity—the dynamic on-going social process, and the social acts which are its component elements—to be studied and analyzed scientifically. But it is not behavioristic in the sense of ignoring the inner experience of the individual—the inner phase of that process or activity. . . . It simply works from the outside to the inside, in its endeavor to determine how such experience does arise within the process. The act, then, . . . is the fundamental datum in both social and individual psychology when behavioristically conceived, and it has both an inner and an outer phase, an internal and an external aspect.[48]

The Meadian framework for understanding human behavior differed from psychologist John Watson's behaviorism in that it insisted on the importance of "those phenomena which are accessible to the individual alone," which may be called consciousness, the central activity, or the covert aspects of behavior. On the other hand, the Meadian framework set itself apart from the functional psychology of, for example, Robert Angell, which, in Mead's opinion, had "got too far from the social context within which that individual was possible."[49]

It is interesting to note that in 1927 Sutherland listed Mead as one of his "teachers of sociology" rather than psychology or philosophy. Yet with the exception of Mead's article on "The Psychology of Punitive Justice" (1918), which is cited in all four editions of Sutherland's criminology textbook, no other citation appears to signify Sutherland's intellectual debt to Mead. It is curious that Sutherland has said so little about George Herbert Mead's influence on the theory of differential association. It would be incorrect to assume that since Sutherland had studied under him, Mead's influence would have been lasting. But Mead was no ordinary instructor, even by the standards then established at the University of Chicago. Also, Mead's teaching has been seen by some of Sutherland's biographers as highly relevant to his later theoretical work. Why then was Sutherland so silent about the role Mead had played in shaping his conception of social psychology?

Apart from the direct influence of his instructors at the University of Chicago, Sutherland credits Charles H. Cooley ("more than any other writer") and Edward A. Ross ("especially his Social Psychology and his Social Control") as having exerted a "principal influence" on him.[50] Even though there was no personal contact with either, each strongly influenced Sutherland's thinking during the latter part of his graduate work.

Any inference that may be drawn from such clues of intellectual influence as citations and intellectual autobiographies such as the one Sutherland composed for Luther L. Bernard in 1927 is at best only suggestive. It is quite apparent that Sutherland's theory of differential association drew on the social psychology of Mead, Cooley, Thomas, and Dewey. If today we attribute the principal role in the genesis of symbolic interactionism to Mead rather than to Dewey, Thomas, or Cooley, this does not mean Sutherland may not have felt otherwise about the matter.

In the final analysis, then, the conclusion that seems most faithful to the evidence is that Mead's contribution to Sutherland's understanding of social psychology was strong, although indirect. Mead's conception of social psychology was passed on to Sutherland through the teaching of W. I. Thomas, with whom Sutherland worked closely at Chicago. Although Thomas denied that he was greatly influenced by Mead, his conception of social psychology clearly shows that influence.

During the summer quarter of 1911 Sutherland enrolled in "Comparative Psychology," which was taught by John Broadus Watson (1878-1958). The contrast between Watson's and Mead's courses must have been quite clear to a student as bright as Sutherland. It is no exaggeration to say that Watson and Mead represented opposite ends of a continuum of thought on human learning and behavior.

Mead thought behavior had both overt and covert aspects, and saw the latter not merely as by-products of the former but as the very stuff that determines human action. This position was in direct opposition to Watson's assertion, perhaps most clearly enunciated in his paper entitled "Psychology as a Behaviorist Views It" (1913), that "mentalistic concepts,"—the study of consciousness, images, and language—were chimerical distractions whose continued ability to interest psychologists could only prevent the development of a truly scientific psychology. Watson's ideas had little impact on Sutherland, who accepted Mead's and Thomas's interactionist perspective.

In addition to Watson's "Comparative Psychology," Sutherland also enrolled in three other courses during the summer of 1911: Harvey Carr's "Experimental Psychology"; "Rural Communities," taught by Charles Henderson; and "Problems of American Agriculture," given by William Hill in the department of political economy.

After the summer quarter of 1911, Sutherland began a full and productive year at the university. He enrolled in a year-long seminar entitled "Social Amelioration," taught by Charles Henderson and offered through the divinity school's department of ecclesiastical sociology. In addition to Henderson's seminar, Sutherland enrolled in two courses offered by the department of sociology: "Problems in General Sociology," a seminar taught by Albion Small, and "The Immigrant," taught by W. I. Thomas. To round out his studies that fall quarter he enrolled in Harvey Carr's "Experimental Psychology 1." This last course completed Sutherland's minor in psychology.

Sutherland had always been a bright and willing student (as witnessed by his Rhodes scholarship candidacy), and now that he approached that phase in his graduate work when he would be expected to develop his own line of inquiry, his qualities of critical intelligence, rigorous analysis, and disdain for empty speculation turned him into a devastating critic of his own discipline. He increasingly came to believe that sociology, as represented by Henderson and Small in particular, was too short on empirical knowledge and too long on unsupported social nostrums. What Sutherland was searching for was a "scientific" sociology based on research that put the investigator close to his subject matter. He believed the topics that the sociologist ought to study should be those identified by the community and not those of academic interest alone.

As a result of these growing misgivings about sociology, Sutherland began to turn his attention toward other disciplines in the hope of learning methods that would provide an objective understanding of the social world in which he lived. By 1911 he had formed the opinion that psychology was not the direction in which to turn. At least this seems to be a reasonable view when it is noted that after he fulfilled his minor-field requirements he never again enrolled in a psychology course. Why would Sutherland react in this fashion? One of his biographers believes Sutherland came to perceive psychology as a discipline that "dealt with social problems only in the experience of the individual, and ignored crucial social structural elements that also had to be analyzed."[51] If this analysis is correct, then one must conclude that Mead's point of view had indeed made an impression on Sutherland and that Watson and the other psychology instructors had failed to demonstrate to Sutherland's satisfaction the utility of individual psychology as a method for developing an understanding of collective phenomena.

The extent of his displeasure with sociology's tendency to lapse into empty moralizing may be seen in his correspondence with Luther L. Bernard, as this excerpt from a letter written August 13, 1915, shows:

> In one of your letters you tried to prove that you were not an absolutist, or

that if you were, it is not a bad thing to be an absolutist, and you offered the eight-hour law for women as an illustration. Now I am quite willing to favor an eight-hour law for women, but recognize that I do so from sentiment and not on the basis of scientific standards. A woman presumably produces less wealth in eight hours than in ten hours, but it is more trying on her, uses up her vitality and reduces the length of her life, and has various other subordinate effects. Which is more conducive to general social welfare—the extra production or the increase of the woman's health? How can they be compared? One group of people says one thing about it, another group says another thing. Which is right? How can either be right on any scientific grounds? As I understand it, you use your criterion, assumed to be scientific, of social conservation: more wealth or less health? The answer to that depends not on a general criterion, such as social conservation, or social welfare, but on the sentiments, impulses and general experience of the person making the answer. Just as those impulses and sentiments and experiences vary, the answer will vary. The right answer is, therefore, the one which is in harmony with the previous experiences of the particular group in question, and any so-called scientific answer seems to me to be merely a method of persuading the uninitiated and unsophisticated. My own sentiments and experiences are of such a nature that I should prefer the increment of health for women, but I cannot prove that that is preferable if I try to take an entirely impartial attitude toward the question. Now I declare that you are an absolutist in that you are trying to do that very thing.[52]

In order to avoid becoming a prisoner of his own closed system of thought, Sutherland turned increasingly toward political economy, history, and political science. At this point in his development he was quite fed up with what had come to pass for sociology. He yearned for a method that would allow him to stand apart from the subjective standards to which everyone must to some extent be prisoner.

Park is a "pure scientist" or tries to be. He studies people just as the chemist studies his materials. There are some things about him that I can not write, but they furnish, if true, good illustrations of this point. . . . Both Mead and Cooley carry their analysis over into ethics in a way which is not justified, but both of them help me in understanding social movements as they actually go on. Park's attitude seems to me the one that a good many of us must take for a long time yet. I don't see how we can pronounce upon right and wrong at the present time, for our standards are all representative of our particular experiences, which experiences are limited in their range. . . . As long as standards are group standards or class standards—as they are now even for sociologists—the only ethical application I see is to try to induce some sort of group tolerance, even welcome group differences and let the groups fight it out.[53]

Between 1911 and 1913, Sutherland turned from sociology (and the sociology faculty at Chicago) in the hope of finding a scientific method by which he could study social problems. During the winter quarter of

1911-1912 he enrolled in one political science course, "Legislation Methods," and two political economy courses, "Theory of Value" and "Vital Statistics." "Legislation Methods" was taught by three of the university's most distinguished professors, Charles Edward Merriam, Ernest Freund, and Harry Pratt Judson. The title of their course does not suggest the interest it held for Sutherland. "Legislation Methods" explored "the role and application of the social survey in the making of social legislation."[54]

At the beginning of the twentieth century, the social survey was thought by social scientists to hold the promise of generating impartial data which could then be used to formulate "scientific" social policy.

> Problems of policy . . . are political and legislative. Most social investigations in recent years have been made in the interest of some legislative program or for the purpose of creating a more intelligent public opinion in regard to certain local problems.[55]

Today, the social survey is so widely used (over-used, some would say) that we tend to forget that its introduction into modern social science was greeted with great hope and enthusiasm. Its proponents had eagerly sought a means to establish a scientific status for their research.

The remaining two courses in which Sutherland enrolled during the 1911-1912 academic year were "Theory of Value," under Albert C. Whitaker, and "Vital Statistics," taught by James Alfred Field. Both of these courses were offered by the department of political economy. Field was an important figure in Sutherland's education, particularly since Sutherland "could not find [a] theory that amounted to anything"[56] and felt the social reforms proposed by the sociologists lacked scientific standing. Field, as a statistician, represented a type of social science that held great appeal for Sutherland. Field's importance to Sutherland's education is also indicated by the fact that he was one of the five men (also including Thomas, Henderson, Small, and Hoxie) who were present at Sutherland's oral doctoral examination on June 2, 1913.

The following entry appeared in the sociology section of the University of Chicago handbook in 1911:

> Special attention of students in "social technology" [this was Edwin Sutherland's area of concentration within the graduate sociology program] is called to the courses of Mr. James A. Field in statistics; statistics of population . . . introduction to statistics . . . and vital statistics. The courses in the Family, Urban Communities, Rural Communities, . . .Dependents, Defectives and Delinquents, and [on] social legislation, rest in great part on a statistical basis and can be pursued with profit by those who have had careful drill in the precise methods of statistics.[57]

Statistics was not nearly the sophisticated discipline in 1911-1913 that it is today. As a consequence, even though Sutherland's training was advanced for his time, his level of knowledge would strike a contemporary social science graduate student as rudimentary. Sutherland never considered himself to be "expert" in his understanding and use of statistics, yet, as one of his colleagues once remarked, he was never deceived by the careless or disingenuous use of statistics—especially by those whose points of view were contrary to his. For this, Field can be given credit.

Sutherland enrolled in three courses during the summer quarter of 1912: "The Family," with Charles Henderson (his last course with him), Marcus Jernegan's history course, "American Society and Industrial History, 1750-1820"; and Leon C. Marshall's political economy course, "Railway Transportation."

The fall of 1912 found Sutherland entering into his final year as a graduate student. By all indications it was a full year: he enrolled in six political economy courses, two sociology courses, and one history course. In addition to course work he was writing his dissertation and correcting papers for Professor Hoxie's trade unionism course. And as if all this were not enough to occupy his time, he involved himself actively in departmental politics.

With each passing month Sutherland found himself increasingly dissatisfied with the quality of instruction graduate sociology students were receiving. These students were particularly unhappy with Small's teaching. Twenty-five years prior to Small's retirement, Mead had written in a letter to his wife, "the grad students in Sociology are up in arms about the thin and valueless pabulum which Small gives them. Unfortunately the man has no philosophy and no psychology and his work is practically an application of both."[58] Small was described as "formal," "urbane," "reserved," and "not wholly frank in his attitudes." He was considered "monotonous" besides. But it would be misleading to suggest that Small was held in contempt by Sutherland and the other sociology graduate students of his time; this was not the case. Rather, there appeared to be a "generation gap" between Small, the erstwhile "systematizer" trained in history, theology, economics, and political science, and the newer generation, which hoped for a sociology based on scientific methods leading to the solution to pressing social problems. What they received instead, especially in Small's courses, were abstract speculation and philosophical discourse.

By the fall of 1912, Sutherland decided he would take no more sociology courses "unless I am absolutely held to it."[59] He tried to make the best of his last course with Small ("Problems in General Sociology"), and he suffered through Scott Bedford's version of "The History of Sociology."

I want to tell you about our latest move. Bedford's History of Sociology is the point of attack. The course . . . is worse than I thought it would be. Bedford had a written quiz last week, in which one of the questions was to state the purpose of the course. Queen, Ware, and I took the occasion to jump on the course. . . . Because Ware and Queen stated more clearly what their objections to the course were he gave Ware "E" and Queen "C — " and because he did not understand mine he gave me "A + ." But as a matter of fact Queen and Ware and I were all trying to say the same thing. . . . Well, Queen went to Small this morning and raised a kick about the nature of the course, and said he was not alone in it; Small asked him to have those who had objections to send them in writing to him . . . and if the objections were serious enough the course would be thrown out and a new one organized for next year, intimating that some one else would teach it. We have written out our objections to such a course, and will send them in tomorrow. There will be seven objectors. . . . I do not suppose this kick will be of any direct value, but it may add one more to the accumulation.[60]

This "kick" aparently had no effect. Scott Bedford remained at Chicago until his resignation in 1925.

The six political economy courses taken by Sutherland that last year were Field's "Statistical Theory and Method," the two-quarter course "Principles of Political Economy" (instructors unknown), and Robert Hoxie's "The Labor Movement," "Trade Unionism," and "Research in Labor Problems." Finally, Sutherland enrolled in "History of the South," taught by William E. Dodd.

Sutherland's first two years at the University of Chicago were a time for clarifying values. As a first-year graduate student he worked as a field investigator for the Juvenile Protective Association, giving him the opportunity to witness firsthand the ills of the city's poor, about which, to this point, he had only done some reading. He alternated between the belief that social problems were virtually intractable due to their great complexity and a wish for a "somewhat radical" change. When he was in the former frame of mind he felt a "moderate skepticism regarding social reform." His doubts, confusion, and frustration led him to search for a problem worthy of his best efforts, yet something "that was specific and concrete, and thus . . . rid of the troublesome and practically impossible problems of social welfare."[61] He turned to the study of ethnology, believing it to be a subject sufficiently specific and concrete, and to which he could diligently apply himself. He eventually lost interest even in this, however, and began to drift toward political economy.

Sutherland increasingly took refuge in courses outside the department of sociology. By 1912 he had concluded that meaningful sociological theory was nonexistent. Therefore, in his view, the only possible justification for sociology was its usefulness in solving social problems. And by this criterion it was a total failure. He had seen how sociologically informed legislative action failed to affect in any meaningful way the lives of those most in need of help. Too often, the social reforms that held the promise of significant change for the poor and powerless were blocked by powerful interests that benefited from the status quo.

Fortunately for Sutherland, he did not become an embittered cynic. He turned to political economy as a discipline and method by which he hoped to make headway against "troublesome and practically impossible problems of social reform." In his 1927 autobiographical statement he expressed the view that Robert F. Hoxie of the department of political economy "exerted more constructive influence in determining my thinking than did any of the sociologists." Sutherland greatly admired Hoxie's "desire to understand" and his ability to "discover the truth and exhibit it so that it could not help but be recognized."[62]

What was the basis of Sutherland's high regard for Hoxie? Both men have been described as "toughminded," given to the habit of "merciless self-criticism" in relation to their work.[63] Apart from personal qualities that may have formed the basis of their close friendship, Sutherland came to appreciate Hoxie for his goals and methods. In a letter to Luther L. Bernard written shortly after Hoxie's death, Sutherland wrote of him:

> My dear Bernard ... [d]id you see Johnson's statement regarding Hoxie in the last number of The New Republic? That desire to understand seems to me was characteristic of Hoxie. Doubtless you would say that is a mere esthetic interest and of no importance. Hoxie was more interested in reforms at the times when he was off guard than any person I know, but his whole sociological interest was in the work of understanding. He agreed, of course, that understanding was not the end in itself, but who does not? We sociologists are in a sort of combine to fool or bluff the public, as Small admits in his recent history ["Fifty Years of Sociology in the United States," *American Journal of Sociology*, May 1916] and as Blackmar admitted to me a couple of years ago. ... Hoxie, on the contrary, wanted to understand, instead of bluff. Now which is the better way?[64]

Sutherland's regard for Hoxie grew during his last two years at the University of Chicago. He helped Hoxie grade student papers and he registered for three of Hoxie's courses during the 1912-1913 academic year. In addition to this interaction, Hoxie worked closely with Sutherland as he wrote his dissertation. Charles Henderson, Sutherland's advisor, was on sabbatical leave in India for much of this school year. Sutherland's correspondence with Luther L. Bernard suggests, however, that Henderson's absence was far from being a sore point. At one place in a letter written January 31, 1913, Sutherland complained mildly of "some suggestions for improvement of [employment] exchanges—made a la Henderson—in view of [his] German experience."

Two months earlier Sutherland had sent Bernard a report on the "progress" of his dissertation. Tongue firmly in cheek, he had written in mock-complaint:

> My thesis is moving with a rather delayed time. I have picked out a dedicatee, written the title, author, preface, and introduction, comprising eleven pages in all; but that does not begin to describe it—I have turned in that introduction five times to Hoxie and read it before his seminar three times, each time after re-writing it; the criticism has been very good, and it has been improving all the time, and with a little increase in speed, I think I shall be able to get through it by spring.[65]

The following April, Sutherland wrote to Bernard to apprise him of his further progress toward the completion of his dissertation.

> Henderson is back from the Orient, and is making a series of speeches, containing the same things he would have said if he had taken a year off in Woodland, or in Berlin with his friend Dr. Zacher. I have not seen him yet, but shall go soon and pay my respects, with a copy of my thesis in its unfinished state—which, by the way, I have worked almost entirely under Hoxie. Hoxie has done a lot for me this year.[66]

The degree to which Sutherland came to emulate Hoxie is revealed by the event of Hoxie taking leave from Chicago in 1914-1915 to work as special investigator for the United States Commission on Industrial Relations. Sutherland was invited, in Hoxie's stead, to teach two of his courses, "Trade Unionism" and "Socialism." Sutherland was a natural choice for the task since he had become Hoxie's closest academic disciple. He was more qualified than anyone to continue Hoxie's distinctive approach and style in dealing with these areas of scholarship.

Hoxie committed suicide on June 22, 1916. Poor health and the feeling that his work was unappreciated were most often mentioned by those who knew him best as the cause of his action; it is also true that he had been under a physician's care for a number of years for treatment of depression. Newspaper accounts during his last months suggested that his work was biased owing to his "labor affiliations and socialist leanings. He denied this, and seemed overanxious to maintain a position of scientific neutrality in his studies."[67]

In two letters to Bernard in July 1916, Sutherland expressed his sorrow and bitterness that Hoxie had so tragically ended his own life:

> You have undoubtedly learned by this time as much about Dr. Hoxie's death as I have. At any rate the enclosed clipping will tell all I have heard. . . . [Y]ou may consider that at your disposal . . . I have no further use for it. I believe

however that ill health and what Hoxie thought to be lack of recognition and appreciation are responsible for this. A man like [Scott] Nearing would have no excuse for suicide, any more than Henderson would. Such people get lots of recognition. But there is little return for attempting to do scientific work in sociology.[68]

   The years Sutherland spent at the University of Chicago saw him subject to the salutary influence of a number of teachers in numerous disciplines. After some initial indecision over what discipline to study, he settled on sociology, principally because of the personal interest shown in him by Charles Henderson. Sutherland's first year of graduate study was directed towards the kind of sociology Henderson represented: practical, reformist, and atheoretical. His second year at Chicago saw him develop a skepticism toward meaningful social reform. He became disenchanted with Henderson's approach and turned toward W. I. Thomas. At first Sutherland believed he had found in Thomas's ethnological studies a worthy and concrete subject that could be studied with profit. However, in those years Thomas's work did not represent a significant alternative to Henderson's. Sutherland eventually came to value Thomas mostly for his ideas on the directions sociology should take (objective, empirical, and theoretical) rather than for his ethnological studies. For the rest of Sutherland's life, he also espoused Thomas's interactionist social psychology and his antipathy toward psychiatry.
   The last two years at Chicago saw Sutherland becoming more and more frustrated at the insubstantiality of sociology. He desperately wanted to find a method by which to rise above personal, occupational, or class values in order to establish scientific standards. His search led him to James Field in statistics; to Charles Merriam, Ernest Freund, and Harry Judson in political science; and, especially, to Robert F. Hoxie in political economy. The extent of Sutherland's dissatisfaction with sociology is revealed in his eventual decision to take his Ph.D. in sociology *and* political economy. By 1913, Hoxie had become, unquestionably, Sutherland's closest mentor. Sutherland then saw himself as a political economist as well as a sociologist. His professional identity was thus ambivalent. While his breadth of training no doubt strengthened Sutherland's capacity to see problems from different points of view, it was the kind of overreaching that made it difficult for him to envision a clear career path upon graduation from the University of Chicago in 1913.

Notes

1. Karl Schuessler, "Introduction," in *Edwin H. Sutherland: On Analyzing Crime*, Karl Schuessler, ed. (Chicago: University of Chicago Press, 1973), pp.x-xi.

2. Gilbert Geis and Colin Goff, "Introduction," in Edwin H. Sutherland, *White Collar Crime: The Uncut Version* (New Haven: Yale University Press, 1983), pp. xxiv-xxv.

3. Colin Goff, "Edwin H. Sutherland and White-Collar Crime" (unpublished Ph.D. dissertation, University of California, Irvine, 1982), p. 103.

4. Ibid., pp. 103-104.

5. Ibid., p. 104.

6. Edwin H. Sutherland, Letter to Luther Bernard, 13 July 1927. Luther L. Bernard Papers, Pennsylvania Historical Collection, Pattee Library, Pennsylvania State University, University Park. Pennsylvania.

7. Geis and Goff, p. xxiv.

8. Edwin H. Sutherland, Letter to Luther Bernard, 13 July 1927.

9. Steven J. Diner, "Department and Discipline: The Department of Sociology at the University of Chicago, 1892-1920," *Minerva*, 13 (1975), pp. 524-525.

10. Charles R. Henderson, "The Ministry of Today—Its New Equipment," *University of Chicago Record*, 3 (1899), p. 281, quoted in Diner, p. 524.

11. Geis and Goff, pp. xiv-xv.

12. Ibid., p. xxiv.

13. Charles R. Henderson, *Introduction to the Study of the Dependent, Defective, and Delinquent Classes*, 2nd ed. (Boston: D.C. Heath, 1901), p. 240.

14. Ibid., p. 244.

15. Edward Shils, "Tradition, Ecology, and Institution in the History of Sociology," *Daedalus*, 99 (Fall 1970), p. 771.

16. Edwin H. Sutherland, Letter to Luther Bernard, 24 November, 1912.

17. Edwin H. Sutherland, Letter to Luther Bernard, 31 January 1913.

18. Stuart A. Queen, interview with Colin Goff, 8 November 1980, quoted in Goff, p. 102.

19. Lyn H. Lofland, ed., "Reminiscences of Classic Chicago: The Blumer-Hughes Talk," *Urban Life*, 9 (October 1980), p. 255.

20. Edwin H. Sutherland, Letter to Luther Bernard, 13 July 1927.

21. Paul J. Baker, "The Life Histories of W. I. Thomas and Robert E. Park," *American Journal of Sociology*, 79 (September 1974), p. 248.

22. Ibid.

23. Robert E.L. Faris, *Chicago Sociology, 1920-1932* (Chicago: University of Chicago Press, 1967), p. 9.

24. Baker, pp. 249-250.

25. Ibid., p. 245.

26. W. I. Thomas, *Source Book for Social Origins* (Chicago: University of Chicago Press, 1909), pp. 16-17.

27. Ernest W. Burgess, "W. I. Thomas as a Teacher," *Sociology and Social Research*, 32 (March-April 1948), p. 760.

28. Morris Janowitz, "Introduction to W. I. Thomas," in *On Social Organization and Social Personality*, Morris Janowitz ed. (Chicago: University of Chicago Press, 1966), p. xiii.

29. Burgess, p. 761.

30. Ibid.

31. Diner, p. 539.

32. Faris, p. 15.

33. Janowitz, p. xxi.

34. Burgess, p. 763.

35. Goff, pp.88-89.
36. Mary Jo Deegan and John S. Burger, "W. I. Thomas and Social Reform: His Work and Writings," *Journal of the History of the Behavioral Sciences*, 17 (January 1981), pp. 114-125; Berenice Fisher and Anselm Strauss, "The Chicago Tradition and Social Change: Thomas, Park and Their Successors," *Symbolic Interaction*, 1 (Spring 1978), pp. 5-23.
37. Fisher and Strauss, p. 7.
38. Edwin H. Sutherland, Letter to Luther Bernard. 1 November 1915.
39. Janowitz, p. xix.
40. Goff, p. 81.
41. Ibid.
42. Edwin H. Sutherland, Letter to Luther Bernard, 13 July 1927.
43. George Herbert Mead, "The Psychology of Punitive Justice," *American Journal of Sociology*, 23 (March 1918), p. 578.
44. George Herbert Mead, "The Definition of the Psychical," in *Investigations Representing the Departments; The Decennial Publications of the University of Chicago*. First Series, 3, Part 2 (1903), p. 109, quoted in Darnell Rucker, *The Chicago Pragmatists* (Minneapolis: University of Minnesota Press, 1969), p. 64.
45. Functionalism, the school of psychology founded by William James, emphasizes the uses or functions of the mind in the adaptive process. Behaviorism, on the other hand, is the study of observable behavior only. It investigates relationships between stimuli and responses.
46. George Herbert Mead, "The Genesis of the Self and Social Control," *International Journal of Ethics*, 35 (April 1925), pp. 253-254, quoted in Rucker, p. 77.
47. Rucker, p. 79.
48. George Herbert Mead, *Mind, Self, and Society* (Chicago: University of Chicago Press, 1934), pp. 7-8, quoted in Rucker, p. 79.
49. Rucker, p. 81.
50. Edwin H. Sutherland, Letter to Luther Bernard, 13 July 1927.
51. Goff, p. 102.
52. Edwin H. Sutherland, Letter to Luther Bernard, 13 August 1915.
53. Edwin H. Sutherland, Letter to Luther Bernard, 26 April 1915.
54. Goff, p. 109.
55. Robert E. Park and Ernest W. Burgess, *Introduction to the Science of Sociology* (Chicago: University of Chicago Press, 1921), p. 46.
56. Edwin H. Sutherland, Letter to Luther Bernard, 13 July 1927.
57. *Official Publications of the University of Chicago*, Circular of the Departments of Political Economy, Political Science, History, Sociology and Anthropology, 1911, quoted in Martin Bulmer, "Quantification and Chicago Social Science in the 1920s," *Journal of the History of the Behavioral Sciences*, 17 (July 1981), pp. 317-318.
58. George Herbert Mead, Letter to Helen Mead, 26 May 1901. George Herbert Mead Papers, Department of Special Collections, University of Chicago Libraries, quoted in Diner, p. 539.
59. Edwin H. Sutherland, Letter to Luther Bernard, 24 November 1912.
60. Edwin H. Sutherland, Letter to Luther Bernard, 23 October 1912.
61. Edwin H. Sutherland, Letter to Luther Bernard, 13 July 1927.
62. Edwin H. Sutherland, Letter to Luther Bernard, 11 July 1916.
63. Goff, p. 123.

64. Edwin H. Sutherland, Letter to Luther Bernard, 11 July 1916.
65. Edwin H. Sutherland, Letter to Luther Bernard, 24 November 1912.
66. Edwin H. Sutherland, Letter to Luther Bernard, 17 April 1913.
67. "Prof. R. F. Hoxie Takes His Life," *Chicago Daily Tribune*, 23 June 1916, Section 2, p. 15, col. 2, quoted in Goff, p. 123.
68. Edwin H. Sutherland, Letters to Luther Bernard, 6 July 1916 and 11 July 1916.

3

Sutherland's Early Career, 1913-1926

This chapter will trace Sutherland's early career after his graduation from the University of Chicago in 1913. It begins with his first teaching position at William Jewell College, where he was discontented and longed for professional recognition and upward mobility. It then traces his path to the University of Illinois. Here a request by the department of sociology chair, Edward C. Hayes, that Sutherland write a criminology textbook would become a major turning point in Sutherland's career, serving to center his professional identity on sociological criminology.

Several early twentieth-century textbooks will be reviewed in order to understand what American criminology was like prior to the mid-1920s. Sutherland's *Criminology*, unlike competing texts, will be shown to be sociological in approach, and it was widely accepted for that reason and brought Sutherland the recognition which he coveted.

William Jewell College, 1913-1919

During his final year at the University of Chicago Sutherland was offered a teaching position at William Jewell College in Liberty, Missouri. In a letter to Luther L. Bernard written November 24, 1912, he stated:

> I just learned this week that the man who was teaching economics and sociology and history in William Jewell . . . was fired for theological reasons, and I am going there to do work which the founder of the chair wants to make socialistic, which the President wants to make practical evangelism, and which I wish to use as a source of income and promotion. My father is a praying man, and may lead me through the difficulties.[1]

Sutherland's words make it clear enough that he wished to save neither souls nor society. What he wanted was an opportunity to establish himself as an academic and to rise within the ranks. Still, after all the time and effort he ultimately invested to earn his Ph.D. degree from the University of Chicago, one wonders why he would accept a position at a small college, deprived of colleagues and with so little time and a minimum of facilities to permit research. That he did so, despite all, suggests how desperate he was to establish himself as an academic—at no matter what cost. The following spring he wrote Bernard again, to voice a complaint:

> First the men who are going out this year [from the University of Chicago graduate sociology program] are pretty well fixed for positions; Clark gets the job in Colgate, at $1800; Knapp is going to a settlement job in Brooklyn at $1500, Queen is going to Cumberland Gap, Ware is on the track of a job in Canada, which will be very good, while I go to William Jewell, about the poorest job immediately in the bunch.[2]

Unlike his predecessor, the Reverend Charles W. Moore, Sutherland's contract called for him to teach sociology only, yet as the school year approached he found himself about to carry as varied a load as the Reverend Moore had:

> The courses I shall give are as follows: Introductory Sociology, Family, Rural Sociology, Modern Industrial Organization (which means a study of trade unions and employer's associations—they objected to a course on trade unions, so I changed the name), Socialism, and Charities and Corrections. That means two courses each term; in addition I shall have to take' the following courses for a year or two: Psychology, Ethics and Logic, one each term. This means 12 or 13 hours a week each term.[3]

The quotation cited here indicates that Sutherland was definitely his own man and had firm ideas about the kind of sociology he wanted to teach. And, perhaps putting it more accurately—about the kind of political economy he wanted to teach. For this was a time when he was disillusioned with sociology and quite the disciple of Robert Hoxie's scholarship.

"Charities and Corrections" was the equivalent of criminology in those years, illustrating that in the first third of the twentieth century "social pathology" was a broad field of study within sociology. It included the investigation of poverty and dependency, personal maladjustments and disorganization of the personality, and the study of crime and delinquency.[4] Sutherland's course was typical of its day in that it cut across these categories to integrate, in a single course, poverty and dependency (charities) and crime and delinquency (corrections).

To understand the kind of pressure Sutherland faced at William Jewell it is mandatory to examine the manner in which sociology was introduced permanently into the curriculum at this Baptist college. A St. Louis, Missouri, banker and member of the college's Board of Trustees, John E.

Franklin, made a substantial gift to William Jewell College to create the position of "J. E. Franklin Professor of Sociology." This chair was to be occupied by a socialist.[5] The president of William Jewell College at that time was Dr. John Priest Greene, former pastor of the Third Baptist Church of St. Louis. Greene most definitely did not want a socialist on his faculty, yet Franklin's gift was too generous to refuse. How could President Greene reconcile his own wishes with those of Mr. Franklin? Perhaps he thought he had found a solution in the person of Edwin H. Sutherland, son of a Baptist minister and educator, and product of a Baptist home and education. It might have been Greene's agenda that the young Sutherland could be persuaded to use his courses (whatever they might be titled) to promote an ecclesiastical style of sociology. If this is what Greene had hoped to accomplish, he soon was disappointed. The brand of sociology that Sutherland wished to teach would disappoint both Franklin and Greene. It was an approach designed as much as possible to avoid political and religious dogma, one that sought as its goal an objective knowledge of society.[6]

With the aplomb of an experienced academic infighter, Sutherland played off the demands of the Christian socialist Franklin against those of the "practical evangelist" Greene.[7] The following passage from one of Sutherland's letters to Bernard reveals both the pressure he faced and the skill he used to turn it to his own advantage:

> I had quite a little controversy with the president and one member of the faculty; they wanted me to give a course on Biblical Sociology; I replied fervently that since the department was being established by a Christian Socialist, I felt compelled to give especial attention to Christian Socialism in the course on Socialism, and in that connection would teach all the Biblical Sociology I could lay my hands on. I guess that settled the matter, for they have not referred to it since that statement.[8]

The six years (1913-1919) spent at William Jewell were not very satisfying to Sutherland. This may be inferred from the clash between his stated academic ambitions and the reality of teaching in a relatively isolated, small, underfinanced, church-related college with its whole program directed to the "thorough literary and scientific training of young men [it merged with a women's college in 1914] for Christian service."[9]

Sutherland's letters reveal that he began his new position in good spirits, willing to give the college the benefit of doubts that assailed him. For example, on September 13, 1913, during his first term, he wrote: "There are two or three very influential men on the faculty here who are trying to hold the standards up, to make this different from the ordinary denominational schools and are succeeding pretty well. It appears to be a pretty good bunch

to get in with." But as time passed (and not too long a time) disenchant-
ment began to creep in. Exactly two months later, while still basically
positive about his position, he wrote:

> The class of work done here is not very high grade; the students depend
> entirely on text-books in most of their courses, and no one ever uses the
> library except for studying their texts, reading the magazines, and working up
> debates. . . . Then, the students do not . . . understand [Cooley], most of it
> seems to be over their heads. . . . Then my explanations have been even more
> over their heads: the best students and the most mature are getting it very
> well, but the rank and file are merely learning the words, and not assimilating
> it."[10]

By the second term both Sutherland and Bernard were corresponding
with W. I. Thomas concerning an opening at the University of Pittsburgh.
Thomas wrote Bernard: "I will back either yourself or Dr. Sutherland very
warmly for the position. . . ."[11] Sutherland indicated an interest but was
unwilling to stand in Bernard's way: "I feel I am getting along pretty well
here, but of course if I get a chance at a bigger job, I am open to change. But
I certainly would not want to—or be able to—interfere with your running."[12] This statement shows Sutherland was a professional and a gentleman from the very beginning of his career. Although he was eager to
advance himself, he would never do so at a colleague's expense. He refused
to place personal ambition above ethical human relationships.

On February 4, 1914, two weeks after receiving a reply to a letter he had
written to Pittsburgh, Sutherland wrote to Bernard:

> I am not at all sure that I want the Pittsburgh job. The work that is laid out,
> according to the catalogue, does not appeal to me very much, it is too much
> like Cooley's stuff. My interests are confined almost entirely to investigation
> of such things as farmers' organizations, trade unions, socialism, and similar
> movements of "the people" to improve themselves. Here I have complete
> liberty to work along any line I see fit; I am given complete sway; no one
> dictates to me. I do not have to teach anything I do not want to teach.[13]

These words suggest Sutherland's uncertainty concerning his professional identity; he was more interested in trade unions, socialism, and
farmers' organizations than he was in sociology, or at least the kind of
sociology that Cooley represented. His statement is interesting in view of
how far he changed later in his career. Over the next two decades
Sutherland developed a strong appreciation for Cooley's work and incorporated much of it in his theory of differential association.

If it were not for the lack of good equipment and the constant importun-
ing to teach Sunday school, lead chapel, and go to church, Sutherland

thought he could stay at William Jewell until "there is an opportunity to get in a school with good facilities, and with better salary, and considerable freedom to teach what I want. . . ."[14]

When he wrote those words, Sutherland did have considerable freedom, if allowance is made for the occasional course in psychology, ethics, and logic that he was obliged to teach. He taught the same courses for the first five years, except that the course title "Modern Industrial Organization" was changed to "Trade Unions" in 1914-1915. He also added "Social Politics," a course dealing with "social insurance," to his schedule in 1916-1917. During Sutherland's final year he was appointed professor of sociology, history, and political science. This change was not made on his own initiative; instead, it reflected the hard times that had befallen the college. America's entry into the First World War cut heavily into enrollment, and the college was unable to support both Sutherland and the history and political science instructor. Added now to his regular seven sociology courses was responsibility for three history courses, "The Nineteenth Century," "Political and Constitutional History of England," and "Constitutional History of the United States." In addition he taught three political science courses, "American National and State Governments," "Municipal Government," and "Comparative Governments."[15]

Throughout these years Sutherland kept abreast of sociology openings at other colleges and universities and with the comings and goings of his friends and acquaintances from his years at Chicago. In the spring of 1914 he learned there would be a position available at the University of Illinois. But he was unable to try for this, explaining to Bernard, "they do not allow two persons of the same family on the faculty."[16] The reference was to Arthur, his oldest brother, then (1910-1914) an instructor of psychology at Illinois.

The following year Illinois had another vacancy in the department of sociology, and the younger Sutherland was in a position to try for it, since Arthur had by then accepted a position at Yale (1914-1917). In this he was unsuccessful,[17] so that, apart from teaching "Trade Unionism" and "Socialism" during the spring quarter of 1915 at Chicago and during the summer session at the University of Kansas in 1918, Sutherland carried on at William Jewell as best he could. On a very few occasions he extended "feelers," for example to President George E. Vincent at the University of Minnesota (1915) and to Charles H. Cooley at the University of Michigan (1916). Letters to Bernard during this period reveal Sutherland to be reluctant to put himself in a position where he would be unable to teach courses of his choosing. Like many in his field, he felt his present position was both good and bad: "good" because of the latitude he enjoyed to make sociology at William Jewell what he wanted; "bad" because of the sense of isolation he experienced in western Missouri, and because of the quality of his students and the lack of facilities to further his research. He complained to Bernard: "I am teaching here, but find it awfully hot [July 1916] and the work is not very satisfactory. I am entirely shut off from news here. Let me know if you hear anything important."[18] And earlier that year: ". . . but the big things that hinder the students here are a static point of view, a rationalistic and absolutistic view of life, and a good deal of aristocracy and blue blood."[19]

No doubt William Jewell College seemed increasingly unattractive in 1916 as he pinned hope on receiving word from the University of Chicago that he would be selected to fill the vacancy created by Hoxie's untimely demise. Unfortunately for Sutherland, no such request was forthcoming, which was surely a cause for discouragement.

> No appeal has been made to me to fill Hoxie's place. I would accept it on a moment's notice. But I doubt if they would try me. Hoxie did not really stand well with the department for he was too sociological and too much of a social psychologist especially. Then, I am from the department of sociology and they will want an economist. No, I expect no call in that direction.[20]

His inability to write and publish frustrated Sutherland most of all. In his six years at William Jewell he wrote just one article, "What Rural Health Surveys Have Revealed" (June 1916). It was published in the *Monthly Bulletin: State Board of Charities and Corrections*—hardly the vehicle to advance his reputation or career. Perhaps his failure to publish was a reason he was not hired to fill the sociology position at the University of Illinois in 1915 or Hoxie's position at Chicago in 1916. Here is his comment.

> I wish I could finish some of the investigations I have undertaken since I came. It is extremely difficult for me to finish anything. When a person criticizes others as freely as I have, he is rather ashamed to turn out anything that he himself criticized severely. And yet, there seems to be no other way to get ahead.[21]

Sutherland's lament was not just a rationalization for laziness; he had indeed set high standards for himself and the demands of his teaching schedule and extracurricular responsibilities made it all but impossible to realize his goals.

> It is exceedingly difficult in an institution such as this to keep out of the side-show enterprises. I was made debate coach last year, last night I talked to a county Sunday School convention, along the lines of Ross' idea of modern sin, I am presiding officer in an oratorical contest tonight. That is the way it goes. It is mighty difficult to stick to definite constructive work, and I doubt

whether I shall ever be able to turn out anything worthwhile as long as I remain in colleges such as this. Of course such work has some value and is somewhat entertaining while it is going on.[22]

With all of these encumbrances, one might well ask why Sutherland had accepted the position at William Jewell. And if he failed at the outset to realize the problems that would face him in his efforts to do "constructive work" there, it surely should not have taken six years to drive the point home. What then were his motives at this stage of his life and career? First, as to why he accepted the position, it is not at all facetious to suggest that Sutherland needed a job upon graduating from the University of Chicago and William Jewell College offered him one. An old friend of his, Raymond Huntington Coon (1883-1935), helped Sutherland secure the position. They were the same age and had known each other since their boyhood in Grand Island, Nebraska. They attended Grand Island College together, both graduating in 1904. But whereas Edwin's interests led him to the social sciences, his friend Raymond pursued the humanities, receiving an M.A. in classical studies from Oxford University in 1907 and a Ph.D. in the same field in 1916 from the University of Chicago. Coon, having joined the William Jewell faculty in 1909 as an instructor of Latin, was already there when Sutherland began his search for an academic position. Actually, Coon and Sutherland had served together as young instructors at Grand Island College during the 1908-1909 academic year, when Sutherland had interrupted his graduate studies at Chicago in order to earn money to finance his further work there. At William Jewell College they were again together.[23]

If it is not too difficult to understand Sutherland's reasons for accepting the position at William Jewell, it is somewhat harder to know why he remained there so long. His own words tell us that he would not accept just any other position but the negatives associated with William Jewell seemed to be more than sufficient reason to nudge him to seek elsewhere. The answer may be as simple, and as complex, as love. Already in his early thirties, Sutherland was not interested in becoming a confirmed bachelor. He had simply not met a suitable woman until he arrived in Liberty, Missouri. Writing to Bernard in the fall of 1913, he lamented: "I am thinking of spending the Holidays in Chicago, putting the finishing touches on my thesis . . . Besides, I have got to find some female with whom I can link my destinies sooner or later, and I have no chance here in a male college."[24]

As it turned out Sutherland had no need to look so far as Chicago; he found his bride in Liberty, Missouri, after all. The object of his romance was Myrtle Crews, his landlady's daughter. They were married on May 11, 1918, enjoying a devotion to each other severed only by Edwin's death in

1950. Although there was some concern within Sutherland's family over the discrepancy between the educational backgrounds of the pair, it wasn't long before Myrtle completed her academic work for a bachelor's degree, earning a Phi Beta Kappa key in the process. In another respect they were well suited from the start: they were a bit older than most couples beginning married life in those years.[25]

One may conclude that once Sutherland was married he began to look around in earnest for a more promising position than William Jewell could offer, especially in light of the college's deteriorating financial structure and his greatly increased workload during 1918-1919. In 1919 he was offered a position as assistant professor of sociology at the University of Illinois. Although Sutherland may not have realized it at the time, this opportunity was the second major turning point in his career.

The University of Illinois, 1919-1926

The manner in which Sutherland secured the position at Illinois illustrates the workings of the Chicago "old boy network." The chair of the department at that time was Edward C. Hayes (1868-1928), himself a Chicago Ph.D. (1902). By virtue of attending the December 1905 meeting that established the American Sociological Society, Hayes was a charter member of that organization. He was elected president of the American Sociological Society in 1921 and for many years was an advisory editor of the *American Journal of Sociology*. His textbook, *Introduction to the Study of Sociology*, remained a principal text in sociology in this country for at least a decade after its publication in 1915. He was editor of the Lippincott series in sociology, a role in which he was destined to play a highly significant part in Sutherland's career.

In 1919 the department of sociology at Illinois was small, made up of two full-time professsors. Sutherland must have felt fortunate to get the post, since once before he had tried to win Hayes's favor and failed. This time, however, Sutherland had the inside track on the job because of his good friend from Chicago, Stuart A. Queen. Queen was a member of the Illinois department of sociology during the 1918-1919 academic year, and before he left to accept a position at Goucher College, on the outskirts of Baltimore, Maryland, he put in a good word for his friend Sutherland.

> I recommended Sutherland at Illinois to follow me. I taught criminology there and I told Hayes "you've got a young sociologist out here in a small college in Missouri that can do a better job on criminology than I can. And he's got a well balanced teaching background." Which is what Hayes was looking for, and so he followed me there.[26]

In 1921, Hayes asked Sutherland to write a criminology textbook for the Lippincott series. Sutherland was doubly fortunate: not only had he been lifted from an isolated, overburdened, and professionally dead-end position at William Jewell College, he was now being offered an opportunity to send up his colors within the discipline. His subsequent success in criminology demonstrates that his was a classic example of the right person being at the right place at the right time.

> Hayes ... believed that the younger faculty, for their own good, should be engaged in some major project. Since Hayes was both chairman of the department and editor of the Lippincott Sociological Series, Sutherland had to give some weight to his opinion. In any event, Sutherland did the book for Lippincott.... Although this somewhat cynical version appealed to Sutherland's puckish humor, and he enjoyed repeating it, it is unlikely that Hayes, who was not considered a reckless man, would have offered much encouragement if he had scant confidence in Sutherland's competence and dependability. Whatever its auspices, *Criminology* had the effect of binding Sutherland to the field of criminology, which he cultivated until his death.[27]

Hayes's offer indeed had the "effect of binding Sutherland to the field of criminology." Until this time, Sutherland's professional identity had oscillated between sociology and political economy. The idea of writing a criminology textbook had undoubtedly never occurred to him, but from this point on Sutherland began to devote himself to criminology almost exclusively. Given his personality, one assumes Sutherland tried his utmost to write a book that would please his colleagues and gain for him the professional acceptance and recognition he desired. It is easy to imagine that if Hayes had asked Sutherland to write an urban sociology or a social psychology textbook, Sutherland would have poured his best efforts into that assignment as well, pursuing that direction, rather than criminology, for the rest of his academic career.

As he began instead to focus on the task of writing a criminology text, Sutherland immersed himself in the existing literature. "Preliminary to writing a manuscript, I attempted to review all of the literature on criminology and especially the research studies."[28] His review of the literature on criminology revealed that early American criminology was primitive and virtually without structure. In the three or four decades preceding Sutherland's *Criminology*, an indigenous American criminology simply did not exist. Instead, European theories were imported to explain New World criminality. Even as those theories were losing credibility in their countries of origin, American criminologists were only slowly beginning to free themselvees from the Lombrosian legacy of biological determinism. American criminology, its contemporary practitioners deeming themselves broadminded, by the 1920s was still characterized by multiple factor theory.

Mabel Elliot (1952) has described how in 1909 the Northwestern University School of Law was the venue for the National Conference of Criminal Law and Criminology. To help celebrate the school's fiftieth anniversary, more than one-hundred and fifty distinguished leaders in medicine, psychiatry, penology, the criminal court system, and sociology were invited to discuss the nature of the criminal justice system and the scientific knowledge about crime and criminals that underlay public policy.

Out of this conference a committee was established that took responsibility for publishing, in translation, nine books by noted European criminologists, including Lombroso, Ferri, and Aschaffenburg. These books, together with a very few publications in the United States, constituted the available criminological literature of that era for American students of crime.

In 1893 Charles Henderson published *Introduction to the Study of the Dependent, Defective, and Delinquent Classes*. As the title indicates, only part of the book was devoted to criminology, the rest being a treatment of topics that today are the concern of other disciplines. Henderson's book was published in a second edition in 1901 and used as a textbook at the time Sutherland was studying with Henderson at Chicago. Sutherland's opinion of its value may be inferred from his failure to cite it in any of the four editions of his own criminology textbook.

It is difficult to know quite how to evaluate books that are at least seventy years old. But Henderson's *The Cause and Cure of Crime* (1914) may be examined as representative of this generation of writing in the field in order to get a sense of what ideas were then in the mainstream of criminological theory. *The Cause and Cure of Crime* was published under the editorship of Frank L. McVey, then president of the University of North Dakota. It was one of five volumes in the "National Social Science Series" published by A.C. McClurg and Company of Chicago. Dr. McVey, in the editor's preface, lauds Henderson for his emphasis "upon the fact that crime is not a disease." While this statement is factually correct, it is misleading. Actually, Henderson appears unable to decide whether the criminal is the product of his environment (including the physical as well as the social environment, "as climate, seasons, storms, and electrical changes, are known to affect crime, directly or indirectly") or of his biological makeup.[29] Henderson wrote:

> Crime is not a disease of the body. There is no physical "germ" which causes crime as the tubercle bacillus causes tuberculosis, and other specific microorganisms cause typhoid fever and venereal disease.

Multitudes of persons have precisely the same environment and outward temptations as criminals and yet do not fall. The difference must be something peculiar in the criminal himself. This peculiarity has been called "moral depravity," a selfish disposition, and is often accompanied by a narrow and perverted judgment and a confused vision of the relation of acts and consequences. The criminal is a weak man; generally he is defective in his body, in intellect, and will, at least in some point.

Mr. Z. R. Brockway, who has no superior in the understanding of criminals, declared: "It cannot too often be stated that prisoners are of an inferior class, and that our prison system is intended for treatment of defectives."[30]

Henderson devoted a scant five pages to a discussion of the causes of crime, while fourteen pages were spent on a chapter entitled "The Power of Religion," offered as a "constructive measure" to combat crime. Perusing this book today, one readily understands why Stuart Queen, writing in the 1932 edition of the *Encyclopedia of the Social Sciences*, branded Henderson a "social worker": "Although nominally a sociologist his contributions were to social ethics. . . . He was less an originator than a compiler and promoter but he was a man of wide influence."[31]

Henderson was also open to the charge of sexism, but in this he was not alone. As Gibbons (1974) has written in reference to Maurice F. Parmelee: ". . . the reader can find some comments in the book [Parmelee's *Criminology*, published in 1918] which brand [him] a 'male chauvinist pig,' but one should remember that 'male chauvinist pig' beliefs were among the eternal verities in the early 1900s."[32] Below is the kind of passage that earns Henderson the same label:

One of the crying needs of all our cities is the establishment by the states and by private philanthropy of an adequate number of reformatory schools for weak girls who have been neglected by parents and enticed by boys and men into evil ways. . . . The judges of juvenile courts testify that they are obliged to send back to vicious surroundings a vast number of such girls, who ought to receive training in a school. . . . Many of these girls are diseased and require medical treatment; they are centers of physical and moral contamination. A lady superintendent of such a school declared that one bad girl can do more harm than fifty depraved boys. She attracts about her a swarm of undisciplined and passionate youth and helps to drag them down with her into a common ruin.[33]

If, after reading this passage, one is tempted to dismiss outright *The Cause and Cure of Crime*, one should recognize Henderson's occasional insights, which in different hands later became conventional sociological explanations of crime. For example, does not the following passage suggest something like Sutherland's theory of differential association?

A man is known by the company he chooses. Long before the man selects his associations his surroundings may have made a choice for him. This poor widow with five children never voted to place a saloon or a brothel in a residence district; but, being poor, she must take rooms in a district where rents are low, and there are saloons and brothels. Her children are reared in a neighborhood where modesty is frostbitten, purity mocked, honesty despised as weakness, public opinion favorable to bribery. Here crime is a natural product.[34]

Passages like this give the impression that Henderson was an active researcher, unafraid to follow where his theories and research interests led him. In fact, Henderson had no direct, personal experience with neighborhoods such as he described. He did, however, send his graduate students into various areas of the city. W.I. Thomas proved to be an invaluable aid to Henderson as well, since he would report on his visits to a variety of saloons. According to Thomas, Henderson had never visited a saloon or tasted beer.[35]

Another representative book, published a few years earlier than *The Cause and Cure of Crime*, is Philip A. Parsons's *Responsibility for Crime* (1909)—"An investigation of the Nature and Causes of Crime and a Means of its Prevention." This book was Parsons's Ph.D. dissertation, written under the supervision of Professor Franklin Giddings of Columbia University. In the preface Parsons described his book "as the outcome of a three years' study of the subject of crime in all its phases on the general basis of Professor Giddings' explanation of society as a product of like response to stimuli." And: "Owing to the widespread aversion to the subject in general, a special effort has been made to present it in as popular phraseology as possible, under the impression that reforms can come only as a result of a general understanding of the situation in the minds of the people."

But Parsons's book is very disappointing to the reader looking at it seventy-five years after publication. Although Jerome Hall considered it a book of major importance, claiming that *"Responsibility for Crime* adopted and presented the ideas of the Positivist school in detail," Gibbons's assertion that Parsons "produced a brief and superficial volume . . . that was a textbook of sorts," seems to be a fairer, if less flattering, appraisal.[36]

Chapter two, "The Criminal Classes," contains Parsons's typology of criminals. It is based on the work of Lombroso, Ferri, and Henderson and contains six sub-classes: (1) the insane criminal—"Capable of perpetrating any crime which may be conceived in his idiot brain, he looms above our social life, an ever-present menace to our peace and happiness"; (2) the born criminal—"The born criminal is cruel and remorseless . . . savage or brutal. . . . They do not suffer in prison. They are like a painter in his studio dreaming of his next masterpiece"; (3) the habitual criminal—"Such persons are . . . true moral imbeciles; their moral insensibility is such that in the presence of temptation they have no control over themselves. . . . Men of this type are almost invariably degenerates, moral imbeciles, or insane, and the family trees of such individuals indicate clearly the causal relations which heredity bears to crime. They represent about ¼ to ⅓ of all offenders; and, together with the instinctive criminal element (about 10%) compose perhaps 40% of the total recalcitrant population"; (4) the professional criminal—"frequently of a high order of intelligence, often a college graduate. His profession becomes an art in which he sometimes becomes a master. Bound by no social tie, he is a true parasite"; (5) the occasional criminal—"The occasional criminal is essentially a born criminal, but . . . while the normal function of our born criminal is crime at all times, the occasional criminal yields to his inherent tendencies intermittently, sometimes periodically."[37]

Parsons quotes Lombroso on the fine distinction between occasional criminals and born criminals, apparently agreeing with him:

> Occasional criminals or criminaloids have shown me the weakened but still very visible characteristics of criminals born. Sensibility is less obtuse, reflexes are less irregular, anomalies are less frequent especially in the skull. Some abnormal characteristics, however, appear, as, hair blacker among domestic thieves and left-handedness among common thieves. Great impulsiveness is found among all, and what one least expects, great precocity.[38]

And finally (6), the criminal by passion or accident—"The only grave question raised by this classification is in regard to the criminality of this group. Is the criminal by passion or accident a true criminal? So slight are the physical indications of criminality found in him that one must hesitate to identify him as such upon this ground."[39]

Chapter ten, "Propagation," also reveals Parsons's inclination to take the stump for biological causes of crime. Here he praises the Department of Agriculture for spending large sums of money for the improvement of strains of cattle, hogs, turkeys, and horses, but laments that similar efforts are not made toward the propagation of improved strains of humankind.

> In addition to utter neglect of the matter of race perpetuation there exists our blundering methods of dealing with our delinquent, defective and dependent classes which not only permit such classes to exist and propagate, but often assist and encourage them to do so. . . . Lax laws governing marriage make it possible in almost any state for the most vicious, degenerate and afflicted to marry, and, in many cases, they have been encouraged to do so . . . it is time the wilful production of a child doomed before its birth to insanity, imbecility, or disease would be placed upon the catalog of crimes parallel with

arson and manslaughter. . . . If the same amount of funds were devoted to this subject annually as are given to the improvement of our domestic animals our criminal problem might be practically solved in the lifetime of the present generation.[40]

In chapter five, "Heredity and Environment," Parsons is willing to concede that biology is not the only cause of crime, for "let not society forget it is responsible for the criminal in a large measure and for many of the stimuli which have stimulated him to criminality."[41] But the thrust of this chapter is to suggest that environment is relevant to crime only insofar as it serves to draw out, or make manifest, tendencies to criminality that lie dormant within individuals. This is more the case, Parsons argues, with the insane and born criminals, less so with habitual and professional criminals. But even with the occasional and passionate/accidental criminals, heredity plays a part. Heredity and environment were not seen as contending hypotheses, but rather mutually reinforcing causes, where one or the other plays a relatively larger role, depending upon the criminal subclass.

In 1926 Parsons wrote another criminology text, *Crime and the Criminal*. The seventeen years between the publication of *Responsibility for Crime* and *Crime and the Criminal* brought few changes in Parsons's thinking about the subject. This is curious, given his reason for the second book as explained in its preface:

> Ever since the publication of my *Responsibility for Crime* in 1909 . . . I have entertained a desire to produce a revision of that very fragmentary work. In fact, I was so dissatisfied with it at the time that the Preface was made to carry an announcement of my intention to produce a revision at an early date.[42]

The "revision," unfortunately, was just as unmemorable as the original.

Parsons generously acknowledged his dependence on the work of John L. Gillin *(Criminology and Penology*, 1926) and Edwin H. Sutherland (*Criminology*, 1924) in writing *Crime and the Criminal*.[43]

In fact, *Crime and the Criminal* is more or less a popular interpretation of criminological theory of its day. It devoted nine chapters to the criminal, but only two to the subject of crime. The title of the book should have been *The Criminal and Crime*. Parsons propounded a positivist conception of criminology: first in his concentration on the criminal rather than on crime, second in his insistence on determinism as opposed to free will, and third in his acceptance of a definition of crime that was legalistic rather than sociological. Unfortunately, "positivism" is in that class of terms on whose meaning sociologists seem unable to agree. Parsons, for example, used the term to refer to theories that explained criminal behavior on the basis of anatomy rather than psychology.[44]

Today, Parsons is essentially a forgotten man in the history of American criminology. His role was that of making known to an audience on this side of the Atlantic theories and perspectives that were rapidly losing credibility in Europe. Don Gibbons wrote: "Whatever became of Philip A. Parsons? for although he wrote several early criminology texts, was listed in *Who's Who*, and held academic positions at Syracuse and Oregon, his name certainly failed to become a household word."[45]

John L. Gillin was the author of another early criminology textbook, *Criminology and Penology* (1926). In the 1920s Gillin was a professor of sociology at the University of Wisconsin. In 1926 he was elected president of the American Sociological Society. He published a number of books, among them *A History of Poor Relief Legislation in Iowa, Poverty and Dependency*, and *Outlines of Sociology* (the last co-authored with F. W. Blackmar).

Looking back at *Criminology and Penology* from today's vantage point it seems not too different from many criminology texts now in print. The book contains five parts. Part one introduces the reader to "The Problems of Crime and Criminals," with discussions of the definition of crime and the extent of crime in the United States. What Gillin calls "The Physiognomy of Crime" the modern criminologist might call the "facts of crime" or the epidemiology of crime. This chapter describes crime in relation to such characteristics as geographic distribution, race, age, urban-rural distribution, marital status, and nationality. Part two, "The Making of a Criminal," discusses the various theories of crime causation, revealing an eclectic (or multiple factor) approach that was the fashion of the day. But the movement away from anatomical explanations and toward psychological-sociological explanations is quite clear. Gillin uses many case studies from the work of Dr. William Healy, Nels Anderson, W. I. Thomas, Sophonisba Breckinridge and Edith Abbott.

Part three, "History of Punishment," is just two chapters long. Its treatment of the subject is conventional. Parts four and five, "Modern Penal Institutions" and "The Machinery of Justice," cover all the topics one can find in a contemporary criminology or criminal justice textbook. Again, Gillin's treatment of these topics is conventional. On the whole, *Criminology and Penology* compares quite favorably with Sutherland's *Criminology*, published two years earlier but mentioned not once in Gillin's book.

The last criminology text from this century's first few decades that deserves attention is Maurice F. Parmelee's *Criminology*, written in 1918. Parmelee was one of the one-hundred and fifty participants at the National Conference of Criminal Law and Criminology held at the Northwestern University School of Law in 1909. It must have been apparent to him that the American audience was sorely in need of an American criminology textbook and that translations of European criminologists' works were insufficient to account for the American experience with crime and criminal justice. Nine years later he published his *Criminology*, the first thoroughgoing criminology text published by an American.[46]

Chronologically, Parmelee's *Criminology* (1918) stands between Henderson (1893, 1914) and Parsons (1909), on the one hand, and Sutherland (1924) and Gillin (1926), on the other. The book is divided into six parts, the first of which concerns the nature of crime. Here Parmelee takes a position more like that of his predecessors than his successors. Like Henderson and Parsons, Parmelee portrays crime as abnormal and pathological behavior, best explained by personal inadequacy. However, there appears to have been some indecision on Parmelee's part as to whether all crime was simply bad behavior or, rather, the product of "religious, despotic, and class legislation."[47] For example, he writes:

> But there has probably been more penal legislation in the interests of classes. Whenever a class has succeeded in gaining the ascendancy politically, economically, or otherwise, it has invariably enacted more or less penal legislation in its own interest.[48]

In spite of statements like this his general attitude was that crime is abnormal and pathological behavior, and like all behavior is fundamentally rooted in biology. Thus, we see references to instincts, "aments" (i.e., mental deficients, sometimes the result of infectious fevers), "dements" (i.e., insane persons), and psychopaths in Parmelee's *Criminology*.

In Part two Parmelee describes environmental factors that bear on criminality; but, unlike today's emphasis on the social environment, Parmelee concentrated on the relationship between crime and seasonal and climatic variation. Part two also examines the variation of crime by population density (urban vs. rural) and by economic status. These factors were presumed to affect criminal behavior to the degree that they propelled toward crime those who were already at risk by virtue of inherited tendencies.

Modern criminology textbooks do not discuss climatic and seasonal variations, except insofar as they are correlated with the incidence of various crimes; in no way is it suggested today that climate and season have a causal relationship to crime. Yet, it is noteworthy that Gillin's 1926 text, *Criminology and Penology*, devotes a chapter to the "Factors of the Physical Environment" in the "making of the criminal."[49] And Sutherland's first edition of *Criminology* (1924) discussed the relationship of "stimulants and narcotics" to crime.[50] However, Gillin and Sutherland both reveal a noticeably tentative, if not skeptical, attitude toward these environmental/physical factors in crime causation.

Part three of Parmelee's book examines criminal traits and criminal types. Seven chapters describe such criminal types as occasional criminals, professional criminals, and evolutive criminals (i.e., radicals and revolutionaries whose criminal behavior is aimed at the state). In this respect we find Parmelee following the Italian positivists' tradition of searching for criminal types. This tradition is also found in Henderson (*The Cause and Cure of Crime*, pp. 22-40) and Parsons (*Responsibility for Crime*, pp. 11-45), but not in Sutherand and Gillin.[51] However, the search for criminal traits and criminal types is a time-honored one, and while neither Sutherland nor Gillin ever took up the task, others have, and quite recently, too. Today, however, these criminologists are more likely to be biologists or physician/psychiatrists than sociologists. As a general statement, typologizing has lost the allure it once held, especially in light of the current and widely held opinion that criminals are not nearly so specialized in their crimes as was once thought.

Parts four and five deal with agencies of social control. Their treatment is conventional and, in the words of Gibbons, "undistinguished."[52] Part six discusses the relationship of crime, especially evolutive crime, to social change, and suggests that crime often serves a positive function in society.

Criminology (1924)

Sutherland's review of the existing criminological literature convinced him that a better textbook was needed. He wrote:

> I had taken a course in criminology in 1906 under Charles Richmond Henderson, in which we used as a text his *Dependents, Defectives, and Delinquents*, first edition, 1893, second, 1901. I had taught a course in criminology each year from 1913 to 1921 . . . the only texts, Parmelee and Wines, were inadequate. . . .[53]

What kind of book was Sutherland's *Criminology*, and how did it differ from its cohorts? In many respects his book was only marginally superior to its predecessors and contemporaries; in others it was merely conventional. What set it apart, however, was its avoidance of the pitfalls of biological theories of crime and its attempt to promote a sociological perspective on its subject. It adopted a sociological definition of crime and used sociological concepts then common within the discipline.

> I made some effort from the first to apply sociological concepts to criminal behavior, especially Thomas's attitude-value and four wishes, but also imitation, isolation, culture-conflict (implicitly rather than explicitly), and a little later Park's and Burgess's four processes.[54]

In this statement, Sutherland refers to the first three editions of his criminology text, yet not all of the sociological concepts that he lists are present in the first edition. Imitation, for example, appeared only once (p. 75) as Sutherland described the "debate over theory between Lombroso and his followers and the adherents of the French school, who claimed that crime is primarily the result of imitation. . . ." Park and Burgess's four processes (i.e., the historical, the cultural, the political, and the economic) are not discussed as such in the first edition, although they do make up part of the multiple factor theoretical scheme.

All things considered, Sutherland had produced a solid book, yet it contained some problem areas.

> I organized the results topically—economic factors, political factors, physiological factors, etc., . . .—rather than abstractly or logically. I made no effort to generalize, and consequently I had a congeries of discrete and co-ordinate factors, unrelated to each other, which may be called the multiple-factor theory. I was not aware that the relations among these factors constituted a problem, except as to the relative importance of the several factors. I took pride in my broadmindedness in including all kinds of factors and in not being an extremist like the geographic determinists, economic determinists, the biological determinists, or the mental-tester determinists.[55]

This candid appraisal was written by Sutherland in 1942. At that time *Principles of Criminology* (the title was changed with the second edition) was in its third edition. Sutherland's appraisal is absolutely correct; his presentation was not significantly better than Gillin's *Criminology and Penology*. But its publication was greeted very warmly and it immediately became the dominant criminology text in America, a status it was to maintain for decades.

A year after its publication, Ernest Burgess wrote a laudatory book review for the *American Journal of Sociology*. He was complimentary of his University of Chicago classmate's attempt to write a sociological criminology book. After first pointing out that several books on criminology and penology had appeared within the past few years, Burgess called Sutherland's *Criminology* "the first sociological textbook in the field."[56] In particular, Burgess felt the book's strength lay in the chapters on the causes of crime, chapters that used a "sociological definition of crime" and an "introduction of sociological concepts like human nature, personality, the four wishes, isolation, mobility, and assimilation."[57] *Criminology* was the first step toward a sociological approach to crime and punishment, but it also exhibited a "mature grasp of the bearing of research in psychiatry upon the study of delinquency." Sutherland's first attempt had produced a good book but one that as yet only "point[ed] the way to a work devoted exclusively to the sociology of crime."[58]

It is interesting to compare Sutherland's appraisal of his first edition to that of Gilbert Geis, writing in 1976 as the editor of *Criminology*, the journal of the American Society of Criminology. Unlike Sutherland, Geis approves of the multidisciplinary approach of Sutherland's "pioneering volume."[59] Later editions, according to Geis, "would move increasingly into consideration of more parochial matters of sociological concern, producing a somewhat lopsided emphasis in contemporary American criminology."[60]

This "lopsided emphasis" seems to have resulted from two factors. First, those disciplines that were just as favorably positioned to capture criminology as was sociology did not do so. As Sutherland noted in 1924, "No law school employs a professor who gives full time to the study of criminal law."[61] With few exceptions, law, psychiatry, psychology, and social work showed relatively less interest in criminology than did sociology. In this context, Geis notes, "academic homesteading was readily done [by sociology]."[62] Second, Sutherland and other sociologists moved ahead briskly to develop a singularly sociological approach which, while not denying the relevance of other disciplines, attempted to subsume multiple factors within a unified, sociological theory.

On this second point Sutherland wrote:

> My other principal interest at that time (1924) was opposition to the view of Hayes and others that sociology is a synthetic science, organizing and interpreting the findings of other sciences. In contrast I insisted that sociology is a specialized science with special problems. I did not realize that this conception of general sociology was inconsistent with my synthetic view of criminal behavior; I was not even vaguely aware that the two positions were inconsistent.[63]

Sutherland eventually began to see the inconsistency and moved to rectify his mistakes. With the help of his colleagues and friends he moved steadily toward, in his words, a "point of view and a general hypothesis"[64] by the second (1934) edition of his criminology textbook.

Although Sutherland disagreed with Hayes's conception of sociology as a synthetic science, he did acknowledge Hayes's work on the concept of social process. In 1929 Sutherland wrote: "[According to E. C. Hayes] the sociologist's proper object of attention is the social process. Professor Small who wrote much regarding the social process gives to Professor Hayes the credit of being the first to formulate the concept of the social process."[65] And he recalled in 1927:

> I think that it was about 1918 when I began to have an interest, or a renewed interest, in sociology as a general theory of behavior. [He had been put off by

the kind of social theory he had encountered in Small and Henderson's courses at the University of Chicago and had turned to Robert Hoxie's method and substantive interests.] The change was not abrupt but within the course of two or three years I had changed my interest from the study of social problems, to the study of social processes and social mechanisms, in which the problem merely furnished the data, and limited the field.[66]

In Hayes's hands, the social process was made up of interrelated social activities, and it was to those recurrent and related social activities that the sociologist should direct his attention, rather than to the social organism, the group, or the person. The point is not that Hayes was the "father" of social process, since it is extremely difficult to attribute authorship for concepts that become widely used in a discipline, but that Sutherland and Hayes shared a common background in Chicago-style sociology and maintained a dialogue that perhaps influenced the shape which *Criminology* assumed.

As he wrote *Criminology*, Sutherland was aware of the inadequacy of his theoretical understanding of the causes of crime. In a book of twenty-five chapters and 633 pages, only five chapters and 114 pages are devoted to the causes of crime.

> The consideration of the causes of crime has been like a gesture or ceremony coming prior to a procedure, but not influencing that procedure to a great extent. For this theoretical sociology is undoubtedly in part, at least, responsible. . . . Materials are just beginning to appear that give promise of the development in the near future of such a knowledge of causation as will be of direct assistance in the construction of scientific laws in the field of criminology.[67]

However, the following passage demonstrates just how advanced was Sutherland's thinking in comparison to the previous generation of American criminologists.

> So far as there is any evident [criminal] type it is the young-adult man living in the city; perhaps the negro should be included in this type, but it is by no means certain that the greater criminality is a racial rather than a cultural or economic trait. There seems to be little difference between criminals and non-criminals with reference to mentality or nationality.[68]

Unlike others before him Sutherland was not content to cite the increasingly untenable "criminal types" of the Italian school of criminology. The passage quoted indicates he had a healthy skepticism, a respect for research data, and a tentativeness that yearned for more and better data upon which to build solid generalizations.

Sutherland's first attempt at writing a sociological criminology textbook, then, produced a fundamentally sound book only occasionally marred by remarks that startle the modern reader: "Work as a servant girl seems especially important as a cause of delinquency, and especially of prostitution. . . .Very much the same statement may be made regarding waitresses."[69] But even here the context of these statements suggests that Sutherland meant to say (and came to state in later editions) that these occupations are not themselves the cause of crime, but that they place their incumbents in situations likely to expose them to "definitions favorable to the violation of law."

> This class [i.e., servant girls] is well fed and housed, they supply a universal demand and have no economic anxieties. But they are treated as an inferior class, shown no courtesies, come and go by the back door; their work is monotonous and long, and they rebel against what they call "that hard graft," and seek pleasure, response and recognition in the evening.[70]

Sixty years following its publication, Sutherland's *Criminology* reveals personal characteristics that were his stamp and identity: intelligence, logic, seriousness, honesty, and skepticism. The book is equally remarkable for its lack of intellectual faux pas. When one pauses to consider all of the platitudes and biases, as well as all of the rhetoric and irrationality of his time that might have appeared in his book but did not, Geis's statement takes on even more significance: "if it were used as a text today, the 1924 edition would provide an undergraduate with an excellent understanding of important modes of reasoning about key matters involved in criminal behavior and responses to it."[71]

Economic and Class Theories of Crime

From the very first edition of his criminology textbook Sutherland revealed a skepticism about the opinion that poverty was the causal link to crime. That a significant correlation existed between poverty and officially measured crime was not seriously questioned by Sutherland. But he was equally impressed that the majority of the poor were not criminal. This fact seemed to suggest to Sutherland that economic explanations of crime were incorrect; that it remained to be discovered why some engaged in crime but not others—at all income levels. In his opinion the best approach to finding an answer to the question was sociological rather than economic. The following passage demonstrates Sutherland's skepticism concerning economic explanations of crime and shows also how he was beginning to apply sociological concepts in the analysis of the poverty-crime relationship:

> Poverty in the modern city generally means segregation in low-rent sections,

where people are isolated from many of the cultural influences and forced into contact with many of the degrading influences. Poverty generally means a low status, with little to lose, little to respect, little to be proud of, little to sustain efforts to improve. It generally means bad housing conditions, lack of sanitation in the vicinity, and lack of attractive community institutions. It generally means both parents away from home for long hours, with the fatigue, lack of control of children, and irritation that go with these. It generally means withdrawal of the child from school at an early age and the beginning of mechanical labor, with weakening of the home control, the development of anti-social grudges, and lack of cultural contacts. Poverty, together with the display of wealth in shop-windows, streets, and picture-shows, generally means envy and hatred of the rich and the feeling of missing much in life, because of the lack of satisfaction of the fundamental wishes. Poverty seldom forces people to steal or become prostitutes in order to escape starvation. It produces its effects most frequently on the attitudes, rather than on the organism. But it is surprising how many poor people are not made delinquents, rather than how many are made delinquents.[72]

Sutherland's aversion to economic theories of crime is somewhat surprising, since his doctorate from Chicago was in sociology *and* political economy. In the early 1920s American criminology relied heavily on biological and psychiatric approaches to the study of crime causation, not on economic approaches. Given Sutherland's outspoken displeasure with what then passsed for criminological theory ("Our literature regarding the causes of crime is more or less interesting, but little of it is of value. . . ."),[73] why then did he not give attention to the development of an economic approach equal to that he had given to a sociological approach?

Snodgrass[74] has suggested that the manner in which Sutherland skirted the whole issue [of economic and class theories of crime] tends to indicate that more than a scholarly objectivism and empiricism determined [his] point of view."[75] Snodgrass believes the "factors of class, wealth and power were simply ideologically untenable forms of explanation, given Sutherland's weltanschauung."[76] Even in his earlier period, Sutherland's attitude toward society was not overly critical of the arrangement of classes and the distribution of wealth. His approach toward America's social and economic ills was essentially reformist, not radical. He believed American society to be basically good. Given his upbringing it seems reasonable that Sutherland had developed such an individualistic personal philosophy, which placed emphasis on hard work, personal integrity, ethical behavior, open and forthright interpersonal relationships, honesty, and lawfulness.

Nor should it be surprising that Sutherland was a supporter of capitalism. Goff reports that Sutherland invested "quite a substantial amount" of his money in the stock market.[77] His defense of free enterprise and his aversion to economic theories of crime may be merely two examples of Sutherland's makeup. Snodgrass writes:

Given his agrarian roots, midwestern origin, provincial affiliations, urban resentments, economic education, and Baptist upbringing, he resembled much more an old-time populist. He shot at corporations [in *White Collar Crime*] from the right hip, not the left. It was precisely because monopolistic corporations were leading America down the road to socialism that invigorated his assault on corporate criminals.[78]

In *White Collar Crime* (1949) and the series of earlier articles on that topic, Sutherland wrote that his major concern was to reform criminology and not American business. And in an interview with Colin Goff, Lois Howard said of Sutherland: "Trying to change society would have been a prostitution of his integrity."[79] While this may have been an overstatement, it probably does reflect Sutherland's conception of himself as a social scientist and his generally unqualified acceptance of American society. His goal as a sociologist was to build up sociology rather than transform society itself.

Weltanschuuang analyses, while helpful in taking the measure of a man whose ideas we wish to understand, fail to explain facts as they were known early in the century to American criminologists. It was these facts, as much as his ideological leanings, which convinced Sutherland that economic theories of crime were flawed. For one thing, while it was generally acknowledged that most conventional offenders came from the lower class, it was also recognized that males rather than females, urban residents rather than rural, and adolescents and young adults rather than their elders were the more criminal. How could a strictly economic theory explain these facts? Also, it was known that some lower-class immigrant groups were criminal, while others were not.[80] Must not this suggest that an adequate theory of criminal behavior take into account the sociological features of these different communities?

Sutherland believed officially recorded criminality appeared to be concentrated primarily in the lower class as a result of biased and therefore unreliable statistics.[81] And criminal statistics are flawed, in part, because those whose responsibility it is to construct them are biased. Sutherland was also aware of how criminal statistics reflected political pressure on criminal justice administrators to foster public belief that crime was being kept in check.

The records of crimes known to the police are apt to be juggled by the police in the effort to protect themselves against criticisms which would be launched if the number of crimes reported as known to them was significantly larger than the number of arrests.[82]

Middle-class and upper-class persons, because of greater wealth or political influence, can more readily escape detection, arrest, prosecution, and conviction and thus escape being stigmatized as "official" criminals.[83] But, as Snodgrass points out, Sutherland could have reached two conclusions based on these facts. First, he could have concluded that the poor and powerless were official criminals because of their circumstances and not because of their behavior. Second, he could have concluded that the official criminality of the middle and upper classes grossly misrepresented the actual amount of criminality prevalent in these more privileged classes.[84]

He chose to believe the second conclusion was correct. He accepted the official criminal justice statistics as being more or less accurate in gauging the extent of criminalty in the lower classes. His complaint was that the official statistics gave an appearance of the concentration of crime in the lower class only because middle- and upper-class crime systematically escaped official notice. The problem with the criminal justice system, then, was the need to reform the police and the courts. In Snodgrass's view, Sutherland's analysis fell short of a thoroughgoing examination of the relationship between social class and political power and the larger issue: the nature of the criminal law itself.

> [Sutherland] would not penetrate the issue and disclose the effects of stratification, not only on the statistics and practical implementation, but on the political process, on the legislature and on the criminal law. Therefore, when fundamental aspects of the institutional order were implicated in the crime problem, Sutherland's analysis was truncated and spent itself on rotten individuals. The problems were in particular men, not the American way.[85]

By choosing to conclude that all classes were roughly equally criminal, the problem for a theory of criminal behavior became one of finding its sociological, rather than economic, explanation. If crime occurs in all classes, and is only weakly correlated, if at all, with the business cycle, it follows that the economic aspects of variables such as social class, wealth, occupation, and political power become secondary to their sociological aspects.

The solution to the problem with the criminal justice system was to reform police and court personnel to the extent that middle- and upper-class persons became "official" criminals in similar proportion to their numbers as did members of the lower class. And the solution to the "problem" with criminological theory, Sutherland held, was to formulate hypotheses that would take into account the sociological features of crime that cut across the social class system.

Dissatisfaction with Instinct

Sutherland shared his colleagues' aversion toward the hypothesis that human "instincts" were the cause of behavior. He earned their support for his criminology textbook by adopting alternative, sociological motivational schemes in his discussion of the causes of crime. W. I. Thomas was one of the leading exponents of such a sociological alternative to biological and Freudian theories of motivation. "The general principle involved in an explanation of crime is that crime is always the joint product of an individual and a social factor, or, as Thomas expresses it, of an attitude and a value."[86] This is how Sutherland introduced his one and one-half page section on Thomas's attitude-value concept as it pertained to crime. While Sutherland was quick to incorporate Thomas's ideas in his explanation of crime, he did not do much with them other than give one or two illustrations of what the attitude-value distinction meant and how it might relate to criminal behavior as a special form of human behavior.

As with Sutherland's treatment of Thomas's attitude-value concept, his treatment of Thomas's "four wishes" is also brief—only four pages (pp. 118-120, 595-597). Early in his career Thomas had been an exponent of human instincts theory, but by 1917 he had introduced a set of instinct substitutes that he labelled the "four wishes"—the wish for new experience, the wish for security, the wish for response, and the wish for recognition.[87]

The four wishes were merely a part of a vigorous, cumulative attack on instinct theory. This attack included Ellsworth Faris's article "Are Instincts Data or Hypotheses?" (1921) and Luther L. Bernard's *Instinct: A Study in Social Psychology* (1924), which Robert E. L. Faris has described as "thorough and definitive in its criticism of all aspects of the concept as applied to the human."[88]

Instinct was the product of fifteen years of research and writing. It surveyed the relevant literature of anthropology, psychology, economics, political science, and sociology to determine the various ways in which the concept of instinct was being used. One of its major accomplishments was to distinguish habitual behavior from that which is purely instinctive, thereby helping to end the exaggerated emphasis on instinct as a social force. As much as anything else, Bernard's motivation to write *Instinct* was a hope of achieving the great popularity that had greeted William McDougall's *Social Psychology* in 1908. McDougall promoted the idea that much of human behavior sprang from quasi-biological instincts. Bernard's book was received very well by sociologists, though less so by psychologists. Most of the participants in this action against instinct theory were Chicago-trained men who Sutherland knew quite well and with whom he was in full accord. "I was especially interested in the four wishes as a substitute for instincts, which were biological and inherited."[89]

Isolation

Criminology contains three and one-half pages (pp. 130-133) that discuss the role of isolation as a cause of crime. This is an interesting section because, as Sutherland wrote in 1942, it is possible to see the seeds of the culture conflict concept being sowed within these pages. In 1922 Sutherland wrote a short article titled "The Isolated Family." He later explained that the motivation for this article was the "dramatic quality of the literature regarding feral men and partly because I worked somewhat intensively on that concept when Burgess asked me to write a paper on 'The Isolated Family' for the Illinois conference of social work."[90] Isolation meant for Sutherland, not necessarily physical separation, but a social distance in which intimate contacts are avoided. Sutherland believed that segregation was the more apt term for physical separation. With this distinction in mind, it is possible to imagine groups that are both segregated and isolated, as blacks are from whites in the United States, and groups that are in physical contact, but isolated.

Sutherland's thesis was that isolation is an important symptom of individual and family maladjustment. Furthermore, this symptom may cause three effects. First, isolation prevents the development of the "distinctively human traits and abilities" when isolation is rather complete. He gave as an instance of this extreme sort of isolation the "authentic records" of feral men who "have been lost and forced to associate with lower animals":[91]

> Such individuals seem to have the habits and intelligence of the lower animals, feel at home with lower animals but not with human beings, eat grass, leaves, roots, berries, bugs and raw flesh, are ignorant of all social customs and are sometimes fierce and untamable.[92]

Second, Sutherland believed that while human traits and abilities are developed in contact with others, they decay and degenerate when individuals are isolated. As an example, Sutherland described the well-known effects of solitary confinement. The prisoner slowly reverts to the condition of a child, and "of course there is moral deterioration attending this."[93]

Third, he believed isolation causes differences in cultural development. This often results in the maladjustment of the individual transferred from one group to another. This last effect of isolation is most relevant to a theory of criminal behavior, and is most readily apparent in the case of the immigrant.

> For the immigrant there is a confusion of standards, the weakening of old standards, and an inadequate development of new standards. When the immigrants come to this country they lose their status. Language, dress, and

customs which gave them asssurance in their home lands of being members of a coherent group are here met with contempt and scorn.[94]

Sutherland believed that the differences in cultural traits resulting from isolation tended to produce even more isolation "from what is regarded as real American culture."[95] In this way, Sutherland suggested, the immigrant is left alone and vulnerable in an alien environment.

> They have a feeling of being lost; they are frequently exploited and treated brutally by police, native-born, and other immigrants. . . . It is not surprising that they give way to their "natural impulses" and commit crimes.[96]

"The Isolated Family" contains an account of a family that had moved from southern Illinois into the "basement of an apartment house in a fairly well-to-do section of a [northern Illinois] city."[97] The husband was the building's janitor. He was illiterate, and his wife was unable to read for lack of proper eyeglasses. They had a twenty-year-old son. There was a great social distance between them and the tenants and neighbors. Their only contacts were the woman's occasional attendance at meetings of the Salvation Army and the couple's formal contacts with their employers. The son was just as isolated from the cultural influences of the neighborhood, although "he has kept up his acquaintance with former neighbors of the negro section [where the family lived upon first arriving in the city]."[98] Sutherland wrote:

> Though this is not intended to be a complete diagnosis, it is sufficient to help us understand why the son has been convicted of various delinquencies and the parents have been occasionally dependent upon charitable agencies. . . .[99]

In the first edition of his textbook, isolation and its opposite, association, were central to Sutherland's ideas about the causes of crime. Each of the subsequent editions reveal modifications of Sutherland's thinking on the exact way in which these twin concepts were related to crime, but the concepts themselves remained the bedrock of his theory of differential association. In the first edition of *Criminology* Sutherland wrote:

> The essential reason why persons become criminals is that they have been isolated from the culture of the law-abiding group, by reason of their residence, employment, codes, native incapacity, or something else. Consequently they are lacking in the experiences, feelings, ideas, and attitudes out of which to construct a life organization that the law-abiding public will regard as desirable. Poverty of ideas and of feelings about people, social relations, codes, and the effect of one's conduct upon others is the difficulty that must be overcome. Criminality . . . is the product of this isolation from

culture. . . . And it is for this reason that reformation depends primarily on contact, either direct or indirect, with people of culture.[100]

It may be that Sutherland's ideas about the relationship of isolation, association, and culture to crime can be traced at least to 1911-1912, when he had served as an investigator for the Chicago Commission on Unemployment. From that experience Sutherland gained firsthand knowledge of the conditions of the unemployed in Chicago's immigrant neighborhoods. On one occasion he helped a Polish laborer from the Chicago stockyards district get to a hospital two miles away. Sutherland was stunned to learn of the isolation that characterized this man's experience in the United States. Ten years later, Sutherland recalled this incident in "The Isolated Family":

> I . . . found that since his arrival about five years before he had never previously been that far from home, that he did not know how to get back home, that he did not know that Chicago is located on Lake Michigan, that he did not know the name of the mayor of Chicago or the President of the United States. Though knowledge of such things does not necessarily imply culture, its absence does imply isolation.[101]

Thus it appears that Sutherland formed certain of his ideas at an early stage—ideas that would continue to form the basis of his theory, not yet explicit in the 1920s.

Public Opinion as a Cause of Crime

Mobility was another of the widely used sociological concepts that Sutherland incorporated in his discussion of the causes of crime in *Criminology*. In 1924 he wrote an article for the *Journal of Applied Sociology* titled "Public Opinion as a Cause of Crime." In it he described how human societies were organized on the basis of primary or face-to-face groups, but had recently become "broken up into departments and different moral areas." Sutherland thought society today is formed by a "great diversity of opinions, standards, and codes."[102] This change has been as thoroughgoing as it has been relatively recent in origin. The factor most responsible for this transformation of human society is mobility.

Robert E. Park expressed the same thought in 1914:

> It is probably the breaking down of local attachments and the weakening of the restraints and inhibitions of the primary groups, under the influence of the urban environment, which are largely responsible for the increase of vice and crime in great cities. It would be interesting in this connection to determine by investigation how far the increase in crime keeps pace with the increasing mobility of the population. It is from this point of view that we

should seek to interpret all those statistics which register the disintegration of the moral order, for example, the statistics of divorce, of truancy, and of crime.[103]

Mobility, for Sutherland, could be either physical or psychological, "but either case means contact with different situations, different traditions, and different standards."[104] As an example, he described how immigrants are arrested, found guilty of crimes, and imprisoned *less* frequently than the native-born population, after correction is made for the differences in their age composition and rural-urban distribution (i.e. immigrants are disproportionately drawn from crime-prone age groups and tend to settle in relatively higher crime rate areas). Not so, however, for their children. Why should this be the case? The reason, Sutherland explained, is that immigrants, in spite of geographical mobility, retain their traditions and standards because they do not come into contact with different standards. "But the childlren of these immigrants come in contact with both sets of codes and a higher criminality rate results."[105]

Later editions of *Criminology* do not contain discussions of mobility or "public opinion as a cause of crime," not because Sutherland rejected the idea but because he incorporated it into more conventional sociological concepts such as culture conflict and social disorganization.

In addition to *Criminology* and articles that Sutherland published during his University of Illinois years, it is instructive to note the unpublished research he conducted. The line of thought he was pursuing, both before and after the publication of *Criminology*, and therefore the direction he might have been expected to follow in the second edition, is clearly indicated by such research. The following is a list that Sutherland compiled in 1927 in response to a questionnaire sent to prominent sociologists of the day by Luther L. Bernard:

> Survey of various things in Champaign-Urbana, Illinois, including negro population, contacts of various groups (telephone operators, school teachers, charity clients), mobility in space of groups (comparison of 100 charity clients and 100 names which appeared consecutively in the city directory), spatial relationship between persons securing marriage licenses (ecological distribution), mobility of residences as shown by comparison of city directories over a period of several years, intensive study of a particular district which was somewhat isolated from the rest of the community and was known sometimes as Criminal Hill, a tabulation of contacts of students over a period of a week.[106]

Here we see a number of ideas which were to remain significant features of Sutherland's approach to criminological theory: mobility, isolation, ecological distribution of human populations, and differential contacts of various groups.

Dissatisfaction at the University of Illinois

Of all the people associated with the University of Illinois department of sociology between 1919 and 1926, perhaps the one who became Sutherland's closest friend was Henry McKay, who himself became a well-known and influential criminologist and whose work continues to be highly regarded. In 1923 McKay began graduate work at the University of Chicago but stayed only a year before leaving to study and work as a teaching assistant at the University of Illinois between 1924 and 1926. As it happened, he did not study with Sutherland at Illinois although his interests were already developing along the lines of his subsequent research on race, nationality, immigration, and delinquency.

Sutherland and McKay maintained their friendship throughout the years they were apart, as when Sutherland was at the University of Minnesota and Indiana University. For five years, from 1930 to 1935, when Sutherland was a research professor at the University of Chicago, they were often in each other's company, sharing ideas, assessing each other's scholarly work, and enjoying the easy sociability the two men found when together. Jon Snodgrass's description of McKay, ". . . the professional scholar and gentleman—polite, kind, thoughtful—an academic out to prove his position with empirical evidence,"[107] could just as easily have been applied to Sutherland. Given similar backgrounds, interests, and temperaments, their friendship seems natural.[108]

Stuart Queen suggests that although Sutherland remained at the University of Illinois for seven years he was not altogether happy there. A good part of his discontent was caused by money or, rather, by the lack of it. When he was at William Jewell College he and Hayes apparently entered into an agreement whereby Sutherland was to receive a larger salary than he actually received once he arrived at the University of Illinois. He was given a starting salary of $2,700 for the 1919-1920 academic year. This experience so outraged Sutherland that he immediately began looking for another position. Throughout his years at Illinois opportunities did present themselves but for a variety of reasons, including his health, Sutherland chose not to relocate. For example, in September 1920 he wrote Luther L. Bernard telling of how he had recently turned down three jobs, all of which would have paid a salary of over $3,500 a year.[109]

By the following year his dissatisfaction had grown to the point where he was now looking more favorably upon other positions.

The salaries here were not raised very much during the war and the faculty have been held with the expectation that a considerable increase would be made when the appropriation by the present legislature came in. Now the assembly seems to be doubtful about giving the money expected, and we are beginning to feel uneasy about the future here. There will certainly be an exodus of the faculty from here if the legislature does not come through with some increases.[110]

Sutherland's relationship with Hayes was in many respects similar to that with his father, George Sutherland, and with Charles Henderson. Sutherland was strongly ambivalent toward authority figures who combined a ministerial background with a confident, outgoing, and self-assured personality. According to Stuart Queen, Sutherland shared Queen's opinion that Hayes was a "terrible department head. He was too much the clergyman, and he couldn't get over it."[111] We can appreciate what Queen meant by noting that Hayes, in his *Introduction to the Study of Sociology*, stated that ethics is the purpose and essential part of sociology. "Sociology aims at nothing less than the transfer of ethics from the domain of speculative philosophy to the domain of objective science."[112]

That Hayes and Sutherland held different views on what sociology was about would not have been important except that Hayes, as department chair, tried to force Sutherland to use *An Introduction to the Study of Sociology* in his introductory course. Sutherland resisted Hayes's pressure on two grounds. [113] First, Sutherland held that it was a matter of academic freedom for a professor to select his own classroom materials. To put undue pressure on a university instructor to do otherwise was a violation of professional ethics. Second, Sutherland simply believed there were better texts available for classroom use.

It is not suggested that Hayes and Sutherland were so much at odds over such matters as textbook selection, conception of sociology (i.e., synthetic versus general), and personal philosophies (i.e., religious versus scientific) that their relationship was only a strained and formal one. The best evidence in support of this conclusion is Hayes's request that Sutherland write a criminology textbook for the Lippincott series. It hardly seems likely he would have given Sutherland this opportunity had he not respected and trusted his intelligence and character.

When Sutherland's *Criminology* was published in 1924 his stock within the profession immediately rose. It was not too long before offers he considered highly attractive began to come his way. In 1926 he left the University of Illinois to accept a position at the University of Minnesota. This move represented a major advance in Sutherland's career, perhaps even greater than that represented by his move from William Jewell College to Illinois. Part of the attraction of the Minnesota position was financial; he was offered a salary of $4,000 a year and a promotion in rank to full professor. While all of Sutherland's biographers recount his modesty, his private correspondence reveals a man who was not indifferent to such public signs of professional recognition as salary and academic rank. In 1927, after he had been at the University of Minnesota for one year, and eight years after his salary dispute with Hayes, Sutherland could still show resentment over the matter in correspondence with Bernard.

> I know the way such stories develop and the way the bargaining is carried on in Illinois. I have a list of at least six cases in which a man has been under the impression that he was offered a certain amount but when the bargain reached the Dean or President they said "Why, no one was authorized to offer such an amount. But we stand ready to give you one half that amount," or some other fractional part of the amount. . . . [Hayes] thinks he should be able to get $6000 for a person whom he is anxious to have there, so he writes a letter of inquiry, asking if that person would be interested in the position at a salary of $6000. Then if the reply is affirmative, he goes to the Dean or the President and they say, "We cannot get that much money for you." Some of the men now in Illinois think that Hayes will not be able to get any one as successor for me, that they found the department could struggle along with a couple of assistants and are going to let it go at that. Most of the influential men in the University of Illinois will do what they can to hold the department down as long as Hayes is there, it seems to me.[114]

Notes

1. Edwin H. Sutherland, Letter to Luther Bernard, 24 November 1912. Luther L. Bernard Papers, Pennsylvania Historical Collections, Pattee Library, Pennsylvania State University, University Park, Pennsylvania.
2. Edwin H. Sutherland, Letter to Luther Bernard, 17 April 1913.
3. Ibid.
4. Floyd Nelson House, *Development of Sociology* (New York: McGraw-Hill Book Company, 1936), p. 334.
5. Colin Goff, "Edwin H. Sutherland and White-Collar Crime" (unpublished Ph.D. dissertation, University of California, Irvine, 1982), p. 130.
6. Ibid., pp. 130-131.
7. Edwin H. Sutherland, Letter to Luther Bernard, 24 November 1912.
8. Edwin H. Sutherland, Letter to Luther Bernard, 17 April 1913.
9. *Bulletin of William Jewell College, 1920-1921*, p. 8, quoted in Colin Goff, "Edwin H. Sutherland and White-Collar Crime," p. 127.
10. Edwin H. Sutherland, Letter to Luther Bernard, 13 November 1913.
11. W. I. Thomas, Letter to Luther Bernard, 16 October 1913. Luther L. Bernard Papers.
12. Edwin H. Sutherland, Letter to Luther Bernard, 7 January 1914.
13. Edwin H. Sutherland, Letter to Luther Bernard, 4 February 1914.
14. Ibid.
15. Colin Goff, pp. 134-135.
16. Edwin H. Sutherland, Letter to Luther Bernard, 11 March 1914.

17. Edwin H. Sutherland, Letter to Luther Bernard, 13 August 1915.
18. Edwin H. Sutherland, Letter to Luther Bernard, 6 July 1916.
19. Edwin H. Sutherland, Letter to Luther Bernard, 6 February 1916.
20. Edwin H. Sutherland, Letter to Luther Bernard, 11 July 1916.
21. Ibid.
22. Edwin H. Sutherland, Letter to Luther Bernard, 10 November 1916.
23. Goff, pp. 128-130.
24. Edwin H. Sutherland, Letter to Luther Bernard, 13 November 1913.
25. Goff, pp. 137-138.
26. Stuart Queen, Interview with Colin Goff, 8 November 1980, quoted in Goff, p. 139.
27. Karl Schuessler, "Introduction," in *Edwin H. Sutherland: On Analyzing Crime*, Karl Schuessler, ed. (Chicago: University of Chicago Press, 1973), pp. xii-xiii.
28. Edwin H. Sutherland, "Development of the Theory," in *Edwin H. Sutherland: On Analyzing Crime*, Karl Schuessler ed. (Chicago: University of Chicago Press, 1973), p. 14.
29. Charles R. Henderson, *The Cause and Cure of Crime* (Chicago: A.C. McClurg and Company, 1914), p. 32.
30. Ibid., pp. 22, 33-34.
31. Stuart A. Queen, "Henderson, Charles Richmond," *Encyclopedia of the Social Sciences*, Vol. 7 (New York: Macmillan, 1932 ed.), p. 320.
32. Don C. Gibbons, "Say, Whatever Became of Maurice Parmelee, Anyway?" *Sociological Quarterly*, 15 (Summer 1974), p. 408.
33. Henderson, pp. 131-132.
34. Ibid., p. 29.
35. Fred Matthews, *Quest for an American Sociology: Robert E. Park and the Chicago School* (Montreal, Canada: McGill-Queen's University Press, 1977), p. 286.
36. Jerome Hall, "Criminology," in *Twentieth Century Sociology*, Georges Gurvitch and Wilbert E. Moore, eds. (New York: Philosophical Library, 1945), p. 345; Gibbons, p. 406.
37. Philip A. Parsons, *Responsibility for Crime* (New York: Columbia University Press, 1909), pp. 29-42.
38. Cesare Lombroso, *L'Anthropologie criminelle*, 5th ed. (Turin, Italy: Bocca, 1896-1897), p. 92, quoted in Parsons, *Responsibility for Crime*, p. 41.
39. Parsons, *Responsibility for Crime*, p. 42.
40. Ibid., pp. 136-137.
41. Ibid., p. 70.
42. Philip A. Parsons, *Crime and the Criminal* (New York: Alfred A. Knopf, 1926), p. vii.
43. Ibid., p. viii.
44. Ibid., pp. 60-64.
45. Gibbons, p. 406.
46. Gibbons, p. 408.
47. Maurice F. Parmelee, *Criminology* (New York: Macmillan, 1918), pp. 32-36, quoted in Gibbons, p. 408.
48. Parmelee, p. 34, quoted in Gibbons, p. 409.
49. John L. Gillin, *Criminology and Penology* (New York: Appleton, 1926), pp. 81-105.

50. Edwin H. Sutherland, *Criminology* (Philadelphia: J.B. Lippincott, 1924), pp. 174-179.
51. Henderson, pp. 22-40; Parsons, *Responsibility for Crime*, pp. 11-45.
52. Gibbons, p. 409.
53. Sutherland, "Development of the Theory," p. 13.
54. Ibid., p. 14.
55. Ibid.
56. Ernest W. Burgess, "Book Review," *American Journal of Sociology*, 30 (January 1925), p. 491.
57. Ibid.
58. Ibid., p. 492.
59. Gilbert Geis, "Editorial," *Criminology*, 14 (November 1976), p. 304.
60. Ibid.
61. Sutherland, *Criminology*, p. 255.
62. Geis, p. 305.
63. Sutherland, "Development of the Theory," p. 14.
64. Ibid., p. 15.
65. Edwin H. Sutherland, "Edward Carey Hayes: 1868-1928." *American Journal of Sociology*, 35 (July 1929), p. 96.
66. Edwin H. Sutherland, Letter to Luther Bernard, 13 July 1927.
67. Sutherland, *Criminology*, p. 72.
68. Ibid., p. 110.
69. Ibid., pp. 170-171.
70. W. I. Thomas, *The Unadjusted Girl: With Cases and Standpoint for Behavior Analysis* (Boston: Little, Brown, 1923), p. 118, quoted in Sutherland, *Criminology*, pp. 170-171.
71. Geis, p. 304.
72. Sutherland, *Criminology*, pp. 169-170.
73. Ibid., p. 72.
74. Jon Snodgrass, "The American Criminological Tradition: Portraits of Men and Ideology in a Discipline" (unpublished Ph.D. dissertation, University of Pennsylvania, 1972), pp. 285-293.
75. Ibid., p. 286.
76. Ibid., p. 291.
77. Goff, p. 236.
78. Snodgrass, "The American Criminological Tradition," p. 229.
79. Lois Howard, Interview with Colin Goff, 15 November 1981, quoted in Goff, p. 197.
80. Sutherland, *Criminology*, p. 99.
81. Ibid., pp. 35-36, 102-106.
82. Ibid., pp. 35-36.
83. Ibid., p. 162; see also, Goff, p. 216.
84. Snodgrass, "The American Criminological Tradition," p. 288.
85. Ibid.
86. Sutherland, *Criminology*, p. 111.
87. W. I. Thomas, *The Unadjusted Girl*, chapter one.
88. Robert E. L. Faris, *Chicago Sociology, 1920-1932* (Chicago: University of Chicago Press, 1967,) p. 94.
89. Sutherland, "Development of the Theory," p. 14.
90. Ibid., p. 15.

91. Edwin H. Sutherland, "The Isolated Family," *Institution Quarterly*, 13 (September-December 1922), p. 189.
92. Ibid.
93. Ibid., p. 190.
94. Sutherland, *Criminology*, pp. 131-132.
95. Ibid., p. 132.
96. Ibid.
97. Sutherland, "The Isolated Family," p. 190.
98. Ibid., p. 191.
99. Ibid.
100. Sutherland, *Criminology*, p. 605.
101. Sutherland, "The Isolated Family," p. 191.
102. Edwin H. Sutherland, "Public Opinion as a Cause of Crime," *Journal of Applied Sociology*, 9 (September-October 1924), p. 51.
103. Robert E. Park, "The City," *American Journal of Sociology*, 20 (1914-1915), pp. 593-609, quoted in Robert E. Park and Ernest W. Burgess, *Introduction to the Science of Sociology*, (Chicago: University of Chicago Press, 1921,) pp. 312-313.
104. Sutherland, "Public Opinion as a Cause of Crime," p. 52.
105. Ibid.
106. Edwin H. Sutherland, Letter to Luther Bernard, 13 July 1927.
107. Jon Snodgrass, "Clifford R. Shaw and Henry D. McKay: Chicago Criminologists," *British Journal of Criminology*, 16 (January 1976), p. 3.
108. Ibid., p. 5-6.
109. Goff, p. 142.
110. Edwin H. Sutherland, Letter to Luther Bernard, 16 March 1921.
111. Goff, p. 141.
112. Edward C. Hayes, *Introduction to the Study of Sociology* (New York: D. Appleton and Company, 1915), quoted in Sutherland, "Edward Carey Hayes: 1868-1928," p. 97.
113. Goff, p. 142.
114. Edwin H. Sutherland, Letter to Luther Bernard, 13 July 1927.

4

Sutherland's Mid-Career, 1926-1929

In this chapter we will see that between 1926 and 1929, while at the University of Minnesota, Sutherland worked hard to solidify his reputation as one of the country's leading criminologists. The articles he wrote during the period promoted sociology as a science. During this brief span he was encouraged by the activity under way at the University of Chicago and at the Institute for Juvenile Research in Chicago. The work of Robert Park, Ernest Burgess, Clifford Shaw, and Henry McKay, members of Sutherland's reference group, is reviewed to allow the reader to appreciate how ideas were borrowed and shared in advancing sociological criminology both theoretically and methodologically. Finally, it will be seen that even though he was growing more and more dissatisfied with multiple factor theory, Sutherland was unable to conceive of a way out of this theoretical impasse.

The University of Minnesota, 1926-1929

When Sutherland moved from the University of Illinois to the University of Minnesota in 1926, he joined a distinguished department of sociology. In the mid-1920s it ranked fourth in the country after the University of Chicago, Columbia University, and the University of Wisconsin. He entered a department in which scholarly productivity was both encouraged and expected. A number of people there produced such outstanding work that their names are still remembered today: F. Stuart Chapin, Pitirim Sorokin, Malcolm Willey, and Carle Zimmerman.[1]

One might be inclined to think that Sutherland would have felt a warm glow of satisfaction while being part of such a distinguished faculty. As a full professor, he now had greater freedom to teach courses of his own choice than at the University of Illinois. In addition to criminology, he taught courses on the sociology of conflict, modern social reform movements, the family, methods of social investigation, and a seminar in applied sociology.[2] However, Sutherland soon discovered that he had entered a hornet's nest. Martindale reports that from the moment Sorokin arrived in 1924 until six years later when he departed for Harvard University, he was an "intense competitor."[3] Sorokin was deeply embittered that he had been hired as a full professor at a yearly salary of $2,000 while Chapin was receiving $5,500 and the budget provided for another full professorship at $4,000. Manuel C. Elmer, an associate professor, was receiving $3,300. The manifest injustice of this rankled Sorokin and poisoned the collegial relationships that Sutherland must have hoped for at this prestigious department. Tension was high and relationships strained, as the "strong individuality manifest in Sorokin was also present in other staff members who were also inclined to give first priority to their professional careers."[4] These memories were still so fresh in the early 1950s that George Vold and Elio Monachesi, who had been graduate students some thirty years earlier, could tell Martindale that "there was much back-biting and a tendency to punish each other's students."[5]

Department chair Stuart Chapin took a two-year leave of absence in 1928 to serve in New York as editor of *Sociological Abstracts*. In the interim, Sutherland was named to assume the position of chair pending Chapin's return. The choice of Sutherland reflected the trust and confidence that Chapin had in him. Chapin must have hoped that Sutherland, as one who was held in respect by his colleagues, would be able to control the underlying tensions within the department. Unfortunately, the combination of Sutherland's mild temperament and relative lack of political adroitness resulted in intensified infighting. Malcolm Willey and Sorokin emerged during this time as heads of "warring factions."[6] By 1929, his patience worn thin, Sutherland took a leave of absence to work at the Bureau of Social Hygiene in New York. When Chapin returned in 1930 he confronted a department in complete disarray. Sorokin departed in 1930 for Harvard, with Carle Zimmerman joining him the next year. Chapin was then faced with the task of rebuilding the department, with Willey as the lone holdover of the department's major sociologists.

In spite of the intense competition within the department, or perhaps because of it, Sutherland was very productive during these three years. Due to the time lag between the completion of an article and its actual publication, it is difficult to say with certainty how many of his published works were actually researched and written at Minnesota. If we rely on publication dates alone, however, it is clear that this period was one in which he was striving to solidify his reputation as a leading American criminologist. The period marked the point in Sutherland's career when his professional identity crystallized, with criminology as the nucleus. He no longer thought of himself as a sociologist/political economist. Criminology replaced forever his previous interests in trade unions, farmers' organizations, and socialism. As the decade passed, he became increasingly involved in the professional activities of sociology. His willingness to assume the position of chair of the department of sociology at the University of Minnesota during Chapin's absence suggests he was responsive to the organizational as well as the intellectual requirements of sociology.

During this period at Minnesota, beginning with "Capital Punishment" in *Nelson's Encyclopedia* in 1926 and continuing through "Edward Carey Hayes: 1868-1928" in the *American Journal of Sociology* in 1929, Sutherland wrote eleven articles. With the exception of the memorial piece on Hayes and one short article on social work, "Is Experimentation in Case Work Processes Desirable?" (1928), each of his publications concerned criminology.

The quality of these articles varies with the importance of their topics. Some are essential to understanding Sutherland's approach to criminological theory, while others are only of passing interest. An additional problem facing the modern reader who wants to assess the merit of these articles is inherent in the fact they were written over fifty years ago. For example, in "Biological and Sociological Processes" (1926) Sutherland had attempted to sort out the proper relationship of biology and sociology. He had argued that "biological pocesses and sociological processes are on different planes"[7] and are therefore incommensurate. Thus, he had presented the case against a reductionist sociology that conceived of sociology as merely a part of biology, or chemistry, or physics.

> Within the last generation many sociologists have concluded that the proper method of explaining a process is by describing what is going on in that process rather than by trying to relate something in the process to something outside of the process. . . . Thus, at one time crime was explained as due to biological equipment. Now it is rather generally agreed by sociologists that we have practically no explanation of crime in terms of biology.[8]

This was not a new argument, merely a new application of it to Sutherland's particular field within sociology. During this time he was a true believer in the desirability and possibility of a scientific sociology, and many of his articles called for the application of science to the perplexing problems of human behavior and social control. In his review (1927) of William Healy and Augusta Bronner's *Delinquents and Criminals: Their Making and Unmaking*, for example, he concluded: "This book should be commended especially to members of crime commissions. In the long run the only efficient method of dealing with the problem is a demonstration of the possibility of solving this problem in human engineering just as problems in any other field of engineering are solved, by the method of science."[9]

In another article from this period, "Social Aspects of Crime" (1927), he wrote:

> We seem to have reached the point of understanding that behavior has a cause, that we cannot adequately control the behavior without understanding the cause, and that we do not sufficiently explain the behavior when we say that an individual commits a crime because he wishes to do so.
>
> Science is the basis upon which our whole material civilization has been built and likewise the basis upon which a culture adapted to modern conditions of life must be built. Science does not determine ultimate values but does have the possibility of developing the techniques by which the values may be realized.[10]

Most of the articles written by Sutherland while at Minnesota not only beat the drum for a scientific sociology but expanded on themes contained in his *Criminology*. Thus, in "The Person versus the Act in Criminology" (1929), he stressed the need for scientific analysis to replace fear and hatred if society was to make headway in the social control of crime. Treatment and prevention received prominent attention, while the subject of punishment was treated with relative neglect. Treatment and prevention, of course, were two of the themes given most attention in *Criminology*. For more than two-thirds of the book Sutherland developed simultaneously a critique of the current practices of the criminal justice system and a program for its improvement. The linchpin of his analysis and program was the idea of individualization, which in turn, rested on indeterminate sentencing.

In Sutherland's opinion, when criminal justice personnel form judgments as to the proper disposition of particular offenders they ought to consider, in addition to the criminal acts for which the offenders are convicted, their personalties and social backgrounds in their entirety.[11]

> The court [should] consider everything relating to the person or his social situation that may appear to be significant, taking into account sex, age, health, mentality, emotional control, school record, recreational interests, previous behavior, the character of his home, neighborhood, and playmates, and a variety of other things. The best juvenile courts do not feel competent to deal with complicated cases without complete pictures of the personality and the circumstances of the delinquent.[12]

In another article from this period, "Is There Undue Crime Among Immigrants?" (1927), Sutherland began his analysis with an honest admission in answer to the question posed in the article's title: "I am not sure but that the best way to answer this question is to say that I do not know; you do not know; nobody knows; nobody can know in the present state of our statistics of crime. If you want to guess at the answer it would be better to guess from general observations rather than from the available statistics."[13] However, relying in part on the sparse and wholly inadequate statistics that could be secured, but mostly on rigorous logic and cautious inferences based on what secure knowledge existed at the time, Sutherland concluded: "No, immigrants were not 'unduly' criminal."[14] This generalization, however, was hemmed about with exceptions that Sutherland admitted forthrightly. He used the same ideas found in *Criminology* to analyze this question: mobility of the immigrant, conflicts in cultural values, the primary group, disruption of old habits, isolation from the "best" elements of the native population, and social disorganization.

While it is true that Sutherland's analysis of the criminality of the immigrant was based on the concepts he had used earlier in *Criminology*, this is not to suggest that his use of those concepts was unchanged. "Is There Undue Crime Among Immigrants?" reveals that Sutherland was sharpening his perspective, fitting it more closely to the facts on the social and geographical distribution of crime from the studies of the urban sociologists at Chicago, and rendering his analysis in more concrete language than was the case in *Criminology*.

> It has been found in Chicago that the highest rates of juvenile delinquency are not in the heart of a particular foreign section but on the borderline between sections. . . . This, in fact, seems to be the fundamental or basic factor in the explanation of crime in general. . . . In the preliterate community the population was uniform; the codes, techniques, and ideals were harmonious. An even pressure was exerted upon every child to develop in accordance with the traditions and standards of the group. . . . But in modern life children get away from ancestors at an early age and the ancestors soon become a dim memory. The solidarity of general community life has been reduced by the general mobility, by the detachment of people from any particular group, by the rapidly shifting membership of groups, and by the conflict of cultural values. The spontaneous and natural pressures have been weakened, and the consequence is we have an immense amount of law to take the place of the spontaneous control, but the law does not have the support of the group interests and evaluations.[15]

The Chicago School: Sutherland's Reference Group

At the same time Sutherland was solidifying his reputation as a criminologist, there were others in the field who were also trying to develop a sociological understanding of delinquency and crime. Most were associated, either as faculty or as students, with the University of Chicago; these people constituted an important reference group for Sutherland. He followed their research closely and with great interest. Even though Sutherland was not especially impressed with the quality of his education in the sociology department between 1906 and 1913, he increasingly came to value his association with the world's leading center of sociological teaching and research.

The same year (1927) Sutherland wrote "Is There Undue Crime Among Immigrants?" Frederic Thrasher's Ph.D. dissertation, *The Gang: A Study of 1,313 Gangs in Chicago*, was published by the University of Chicago Press. Thrasher introduced a useful concept—interstice—that had direct relevance for Sutherland's theory of criminal behavior. Interstice could refer to *time*, as in "[t]he gang is largely an adolescent phenomenon . . . an interstitial group, a manifestation of the period of readjustment between childhood and maturity. . . ,"[16] and to *place*, both geographical and social.

> The most important conclusion suggested by a study of the location and distribution of the 1,313 gangs investigated in Chicago is that *gangland represents a geographically and socially interstitial area in the city*. Probably the most significant concept of the study is the term *interstitial*—that is, pertaining to spaces that intervene between one thing and another. In nature foreign matter tends to collect and cake in every crack, crevice, and cranny—interstices. There are also fissures and breaks in the structure of social organization. The gang may be regarded as an interstitial element in the framework of society, and gangland as an interstitial region in the layout of the city.[17]

Not all of the gangs Thrasher studied were delinquent. Some could simply be called play groups, while others were clearly criminal organizations. But the idea of interstice was common to all gangs. As he roamed Chicago, Thrasher observed that most gangs were found in "that broad twilight zone of railroads and shifting populations, which borders the city's central business district on the north, on the west, and on the south."[18] Gangs served to ease the passage to new social status that adolescents must make as they move into young adulthood. And, importantly, Thrasher "found the boys to be psychologically normal, and the phenomenon of gang formation to be a natural sociological development."[19] Active, sociable, and psychologically healthy boys formed gangs as a way to cope with their ambiguous social status. And if some of these gangs became delinquent, then Thrasher believed it was due to the inability of weakened communities to curb the boys' illegal behavior. Certain types of communities were less able to exert steady social control over their youngest members. Thrasher believed the common denominator of these weakened communities was their frontier-like quality. "That the conception of the gang as a symptom of an economic, moral, and cultural frontier is not merely fanciful and figurative is indicated by the operation of similar groups on other than urban frontiers."[20]

On the urban frontiers of Chicago, which the University of Chicago sociologists called the "zone of transition," transitional and marginal ethnic communities struggled to establish themselves economically and socially. In this setting youths faced a moral frontier as well. Unlike their parents, whose moral selves were formed in the Old World, most likely in small villages where they were surrounded by consistent expectations from birth onward, immigrant children found themselves trapped between Old World parental traditions and the formative culture of urban America. Thus they turned to the gang for support and guidance along the tumultuous path to young adulthood. But in such unstable communities the gang could easily drift into delinquency.

> The gang in Chicago is primarily a phenomenon of the children of foreign-born immigrants. The child of the immigrants tends to escape parental control and become superficially Americanized. The normally directing institutions of family, school, church, and recreation break down on the intramural frontier of gangland and the gang arises as a sort of substitute organization.[21]

Because these gangs of second generation immigrants encouraged truancy and passed on to their newest recruits the techniques and values of delinquency, which often led to criminalty, Thrasher saw them as an important factor in the support of organized crime.[22]

In the years following the First World War Thrasher's research on gangs suggested an analysis that was contrary to conventional wisdom. Most students of delinquency at the time viewed gangs as an effect, rather than as a cause. Most social workers and probation officers held the view that delinquency was the result of poverty or genetic inferiority. Dr. William Healy minimized the gangs' importance to an understanding of delinquency.[23]

Most of the research on delinquency and crime conducted in the 1920s emanated from the department of sociology at the University of Chicago and from Chicago's Institute for Juvenile Research. Both were leading centers of the social science movement known as the "social ecology school." Sutherland learned much from those at the university and the institute who were developing their own sociological theories of crime causation.

Robert E. Park and Ernest W. Burgess were the principal figures of the movement within the university, and Clifford R. Shaw and Henry D. McKay, who formed a highly productive research team at the institute for nearly thirty years, were its chief exponents there. Shaw was appointed director of the new sociology research section at the institute in October 1926, probably on the recommendation of Burgess.[24] McKay, Sutherland's friend from the University of Illinois, joined Shaw as a clerical research assistant in January 1927.

Shaw and McKay, through their work at the Institute for Juvenile Research, conducted research that made them well known in the field of criminology. It is probably no exaggeration to say that Shaw and McKay were the first to conduct systematic, empirical sociological research on delinquency in the twentieth century. However, this statement requires clarification. First, it is true that W. I. Thomas and Robert Park developed ideas on delinquency, but they were not particularly interested in personally conducting such research, as their ideas suggested. Both men's strong suit was in laying out broad conceptual frameworks to be followed by their graduate students. Second, empirical sociological research on delinquency conducted before Shaw and McKay, such as Thrasher's study of gangs, tended to be unsystematic and unfocused, hallmarks of research not firmly grounded in a body of theory. While Thrasher conducted his research from the standpoint of human ecology as developed by Park and Burgess, that theory was in its infancy when Thrasher began his research in 1918.[25] Third, Alfred Lindesmith and Yale Levin (1937) have argued persuasively that

> an extensive literature upon juvenile delinquency, professional crime, crime causation, and their aspects of criminology was already in existence when Lombroso began his work. The use of autobiographical documents, the employment of official statistics, *the ecological approach*, and the study of the criminal "in the open," were understood and applied long before the time of the Italian school. The eclipse of the earlier work may perhaps best be explained as a result of . . . the importation of social Darwinism into the social sciences, with the growing popularity . . . of psychiatric and other individualistic or biological theories, and with the isolation of American criminology from earlier European developments (emphasis added).[26]

Given the "isolation of American criminology from earlier European developments," the work of Shaw and McKay was "unprecedented" in the sense that they seem to have been unaware of the earlier work conducted along similar lines by Andre-Michel Guerry (1802-1866) and Lambert A. J. Quetelet (1796-1874) in Europe. One hundred years before the University of Chicago established the Local Community Research Committee to stimulate interdepartmental studies of the "spatial patterns and forms of cultural life—modes of living, customs, and standards"[27] within Chicago—Guerry first made use of shaded maps to represent urban crime rates. In

1833 Guerry used his "cartographic method" to try to isolate causal relationships affecting crime rates, just as Shaw and McKay were later to do in the urban America of the 1930s.[28]

Cut off from history, American criminology had to reinvent its lost legacy. With Shaw and McKay's studies, empirical criminology was no longer limited to an exclusively psychological interpretation of juvenile delinquency. As Shaw wrote in *Delinquency Areas* (1929):

> Although the individual delinquent has been studied intensely from the standpoint of psychological tests, biometric measurements, and emotional conditioning, comparatively little systematic effort has been made to study delinquency from the point of view of its relation to the social situation in which it occurs.[29]

From the late 1920s on, Shaw and McKay and other sociological criminologists, including Sutherland, promoted the idea that delinquency and crime should be seen "from the point of view of its relation to the social situation in which it occurs."

In a series of books and articles from the 1920s to the 1940s, Shaw and McKay documented and expanded the fruitfulness of this perspective from two vantage points. First, they located delinquency geographically in certain neighborhoods in the city, called "natural areas," as revealed by official statistics. From this followed the laborious job of constructing spot maps of male delinquents' home addresses; rate maps that showed the number of delinquents in a census area per hundred persons controlling for age; a radial map, which was a gradient of declining rates along lines extending from the city's central business district; and a zone map, which showed crime rates by zones that concentrically encircled the central business district. The pattern that Shaw and McKay found—decreasing rates of officially recorded delinquency as distance from the central business district increased—conformed to what was later called Burgess's "zonal hypothesis."[30]

Shaw and McKay discovered that delinquency rates remained more or less constant in certain neighborhoods, those like Thrasher's "interstitial areas," while their populations changed with the influx of new waves of immigrants from Europe and the southern states. Regardless of what group was living there—Irish, Polish, Italian, Black—the delinquency rates held steady, this in spite of their further finding that group delinquency rates gradually declined as groups became economically and socially established and began to move to more desirable neighborhoods farther from the urban center.

Shaw and McKay concluded that the cause of delinquency is located in social disorganization, which Thomas and Znaniecki defined in *The Polish Peasant* as a "'decrease of the influence of existing social rules of behavior upon individual members of the group."[31] They believed that social disorganization, in turn, was caused by "crisis," be it technological, political, social, or personal.[32]

Shaw and McKay's idea, then, was that bad housing, inadequate schools, mental illness, alcoholism, poor health, and poverty did not directly cause high rates of delinquency. These and other indices of social and personal pathology were relevant to an explanation of crime rates only insofar as they influenced the effectiveness of social norms. Delinquency was not believed to be the result of biological or psychological abnormality, but rather the consequence of an absence of effective mediating community institutions for linking the individual to the larger society, with its presumably integrated value system. Shaw and McKay expressed W. I. Thomas's ideas in these words in *Delinquency Areas*:

> Under the pressure of the disintegrative forces which act when business and industry invade a community, the community thus invaded ceases to function effectively as a means of social control. Traditional norms and standards of the conventional community weaken and disappear. Resistance on the part of the community to delinquent and criminal behavior is low, and such behavior is tolerated and may even become accepted and approved.[33]

The second vantage point Shaw and McKay used to demonstrate the utility of seeing crime "from the point of view of its relation to the social situation in which it occurs" was the delinquent's own definition of his behavior. Beginning with *The Jack-Roller: A Delinquent Boy's Own Story* (1930), Shaw and McKay embarked on an ambitious program of soliciting delinquent boys to write their "life-histories." Shaw believed the life history to be the best vehicle for uncovering the subjective aspect of juvenile delinquency, for revealing the meaning that the delinquent placed on his own experiences. "So far as we have been able to determine as yet, the best way to investigate the inner world of the person is through a study of his revelation of himself through a life-history."[34]

Roughly coincident with the initial publication of Thomas and Znaniecki's *The Polish Peasant* (1918-1920), Sutherland's interest in social theory was renewed and Shaw and McKay were absorbing Thomas's ideas on social change, including as they did his notion of social organization, disorganization, and reorganization. Louis Wirth expressed his opinion on the importance of this theory of social change for sociological criminology in the 1920s and 1930s in these words:

> It is my belief that the notion of disorganization as a phase of reorganization

in a new culture, and the putting of the personality into the context of a social milieu, of a cultural matrix, which is in a state of transition, has had a profound impact upon the mentality of people working in the field of crime.[35]

While Thomas is not generally remembered for his work on delinquency or crime, and there exists no book by him addressed exclusively to these topics, his ideas were the basis of much of the research and theory that emerged between the two world wars.

As is often the case, influence runs in both directions and two scholars mutually support and enrich each other's work. In Thomas's books *The Unadjusted Girl* and *The Child in America* (coauthored with Dorothy Swaine Thomas) he often quotes Shaw. And in an autobiographical sketch prepared for Luther L. Bernard in 1927 Thomas wrote:

> I have now lived to the point where my most stimulating contacts are with the younger sociologists, such as Bernard, Burgess, Thrasher, Zorbaugh, and Shaw, some of whom have been my pupils.[36]

When Shaw enrolled at the University of Chicago in 1919, W. I. Thomas had already departed, but Park and Burgess were advancing the sociological perspective Thomas had established during his last ten years at the university.

Thomas was fifty-five years old when he was dismissed from the University of Chicago. He had completed his major piece of research, *The Polish Peasant*, and never again held a regular university appointment. However, one must avoid the conclusion that he ceased to exert influence on his contemporaries, including the younger Chicago-trained sociologists. Although he lived in New York during the 1920s, he returned to Chicago occasionally to visit his old friends and to meet with the junior sociologists in attendance there. It was during one such visit in the early 1920s that Shaw first met Thomas:

> Thomas was gone, but used to come back once in a while and when he came back, Louis Wirth would get up a meeting and we'd go and meet him and we'd all get out our little notebooks and somebody would ask him, "Now which set of four wishes do you believe in?" and he'd say, "What are they?" And he said, "Oh well, Florian Znaniecki made me put that in." And then he would talk. Fascinating! But he had been thrown out. It was customary in those days to throw people out for women trouble. The only difference about the University of Chicago was that more of them had women trouble, or at least admitted it.[37]

Thomas's ideas quoted below take on added meaning in the light of how

Shaw and McKay and Sutherland applied them to the understanding of delinquency in the following few years:

> The "human document," prepared by the subject on the basis of the memory, is one means of measuring social influence. It is capable of presenting life as a connected whole and of showing the interplay of influences, the action of values on attitudes. It can reveal the predominant wishes in different temperaments, the incidents constituting turning points in life, the processes of sublimation or transfer of interest from one field to another, the effect of other personalities in defining situations and the influence of social organizations like the family, the school, the acquaintance group, in forming the different patterns of life-organization. By comparing the histories of personalties as determined by social influences and expressed in various schemes of life we can establish a measure of the given influences. . . . It will be found that when certain attitudes are present the presentation of certain values may be relied upon to produce certain results.[38]

One may think of Park, Burgess, McKay, and Shaw as occupying different positions along a continuum "from the ivory tower of academia to the workaday world of high crime-rate neighborhoods where events obscure abstract causal patterns."[39] By the time Park's career brought him to the faculty at Chicago he had found his greatest satisfactions in "developing broad conceptual frameworks and generating new problems for inquiry."[40] Park was truly dedicated to putting sociology on a sound scientific footing, and little concerned with solving social problems. At best, his theory of social change implied a highly qualified optimism for the future. Influenced by William Graham Sumner's evolutionism, Park had a keen sense of the limits on reform intervention. He believed the basic processes of social change lay beyond legislation and that there was a strong element of inevitability in society. This view of social change was not entirely fatalistic, however. Park did believe in science as the best means for developing the possibility of rational control over social behavior. His skepticism concerned the method by which progressive social thought could be meaningfully introduced into the competitive ecological struggles of social groups.[41]

Glaser wrote that it was not only Park who was influenced by William Graham Sumner, but also Shaw and McKay who had felt the power of his ideas.[42] While Folkways was first published in 1906, it continued to be the most influential book in "making people think sociologically throughout the 1920s and 1930s,"[43] notwithstanding the fact that Sumner was an archconservative whose ideas ran counter to the social reformism about which sociology students felt so strongly in the 1930s. Folkways was the first and the longest-running best seller of American social science in this century. The book advanced the idea of cultural determinism in a way that even Sumner may not have fully appreciated.

Sumner's assertion that "the mores can make anything right," buttressed by his evidence on the multiplicity of creeds, moral standards, taboos, and tastes in the world, meant that the status quo was not sacred and that customary beliefs could be questioned. Indeed, his sloganistic phrases became sociological foundations for challenging prior verities and for explaining deviance, especially that which Chicago researchers were finding disproportionately concentrated just outside the business areas of the city.[44]

Cultural determinism and cultural relativity are ideas that are much less frequently used today to analyze and understand crime and delinquency. But during the 1920s and 1930s they "preoccupied"[45] sociological thinking. It was basic to the sociological analysis of the period to view the world in terms of culture. Sociologists were alive to culture's ability to determine what people regard as proper or improper behavior. They appreciated the changeable nature of culture and recognized that it is acquired through social contact. Glaser suggests that this view of culture "implies a basic law of sociology and anthropology: social separation produces cultural differentiation."[46]

Ernest Burgess is also remembered as an academician—slight of stature, with the "pallor of a man who spent most of his time indoors."[47] He had a prodigious capacity for work. His lifelong bachelorhood permitted him to put in very long days, and he and Park, with whom he shared an office for a number of years, frequently talked through the afternoon and dinner hour as they worked out their ideas on a problem. The university was Burgess's base for thinking and writing. Despite his sedentary life he outlived his colleagues by many years, continuing to be productive well into retirement. However, unlike Park, Burgess did not scoff at the social workers and other "do-gooders." He was actively associated with social action and social reform organizations, most particularly with Shaw and McKay's Chicago Area Project.

Henry McKay was perhaps, as Snodgrass has described him, the "cool researcher," responsible for "correspondence, memoranda, progress reports and their written material (including the books), many of which were for Shaw's signature or presentation."[48] Compared to Shaw, McKay appears to have more closely resembled the "academic out to prove his position with empirical evidence."[49] Yet his involvement with the Chicago Area Project suggests that he was not entirely removed from the practical application of social science research.

Clifford Shaw stands at the other end of the continuum from Park. By all accounts he was "talkative, friendly, personable, persuasive, energetic and quixotic—out to make his case through action and participation."[50] He was especially preoccupied with the organization of action. McKay recalls:

Shaw was a great organizer. He kept a research department alive throughout a long depression, and a great war, which is no mean achievement. First as a participant in the Behavior Research Fund and later as director of the Chicago Area Project he developed private sources of support which were coupled with the State facilities with which both of us were connected. Clifford coupled charisma with organization talent with very interesting results.[51]

As Shaw and McKay began mapping Chicago's delinquency rates in the 1920s they naturally turned to the sociological concepts of the day around which to organize their data. Confronted by distinct "delinquency areas," they asked themselves why these neighborhoods should so consistently manifest high rates of delinquency. The answer that hung in the air was "social separation leads to cultural differentiation." The life histories they were eliciting from delinquent boys described the processes by which criminal traditions or criminal cultures were passed from one generation to another.

> What fostered persistently high delinquency rates in these areas of first settlement for new and poor immigrants was social separation from children and adults elsewhere. In the streets, schools, and youth hangouts of neighborhoods that had long had high delinquency rates, as well as in the hangouts of adults who had grown up in these neighborhoods, there was continuity in the diffusion of norms, values, and rationalizations conducive to delinquency and crime, just as there was continuity in the contrasting cultures of youth and adults in suburban and rural communities.[52]

In *Delinquency Areas* (1929) Shaw and McKay used these words to express the principle that Glaser calls the "law of sociocultural relativity":

> Delinquency and criminal patterns arise and are transmitted socially just as any other cultural and social pattern is transmitted. In time these delinquent patterns may become dominant and shape the attitudes and behavior of persons living in the area. Thus the section becomes an area of delinquency.[53]

It would be no mean feat to overemphasize the degree to which Shaw and McKay were influenced by Thomas and Park. As Kobrin wrote more than a decade ago, Shaw and McKay's "approach to the problem [of delinquency] was guided by ecological and social psychological theory, the former derived from the writings of Robert E. Park, the latter from those of W. I. Thomas."[54] All of these scholars were concerned with attaining an abstract understanding of social change, the preeminent social reality facing the modern world. Thomas's ideas on social change may have influenced Shaw and McKay even more than Park's, for Thomas put special emphasis on the idea that the study of society should be concerned with the individual's subjective definition of the situation, as well as the structural aspects of society.

> If social theory is to become the basis of social technique and to solve these problems really, it is evident that it must include both kinds of data involved in them—namely, the objective cultural elements of social life and the subjective characteristics of the members of the social group—and that the two kinds of data must be taken as correlated.[55]

Beginning with *The Polish Peasant* this was the message contained in nearly all of Thomas's subsequent work. The "Methodological Note" repeatedly stressed the need to study the relationship of attitudes, the subjective motivational element, and values, the objective cultural elements that confronted the individual.

> The cause of a social or individual phenomenon is never another social or individual phenomenon alone, but always a combination of a social and an individual phenomenon.[56]

Shaw and McKay readily accepted Thomas's description of the processes of social disorganization and reorganization as being highly appropriate to Chicago. As wave after wave of immigrants "invaded" the city, the pair plotted the groups' experience of disintegration and reintegration as measured in the delinquency rates of each group as it passed through the spatial grid of Chicago.

In their homelands the peasants experienced relative stability. The old traditions, habits, and standards held sway and the rate of social change was such that new elements could be incorporated into the existing cultural fabric without widespread demoralization and its consequent social deviance. In modern society, however, the primary group was overwhelmed by mass society's various and conflicting definitions of situations. Group solidarity declined and the individual was cast adrift to be pushed and pulled in all directions. Social disorganization had set in. The younger generation was no longer exposed to the unwavering, uniform social control its parents had experienced in the old country. Instead, the children faced one set of seemingly irrelevant norms and values at home and another, often antithetical set in the streets of their neighborhoods. The only solution for this problem was a complete "social reconstruction" in which emerge wholly new values, codes, standards, and institutions, adapted more readily to the changed conditions of life.

Shaw and McKay's work reflected Thomas's belief that all social phenomena may be viewed from two aspects, the individual and the group. In this regard Thomas sought to merge the sociological and the social psychological perspectives. Shaw and McKay, as did Sutherland, accepted Thomas's idea that a theory of behavior needed to encompass epidemiology, or the "statistical distribution of the behavior in time and space. . . ," and etiology, "the process by which individuals come to exhibit the behavior in question".[57]

At the sociological, or group, level, they accepted Thomas's view that social change was a process in which relations between individuals and groups underwent a constant process of realignment. As Shaw and McKay at Chicago plotted their maps of social disorganization with its "pathological fallout," they calculated rates measuring the natural history of immigrant groups' competitive struggles for survival and dominance. Their focus was on the complex interaction of cultural, social, and spatial processes.

At the social psychological, or individual, level, they collected life histories by which to understand the process of becoming delinquent.

> This process was viewed as the individual counterpart of the process of social disorganization. At this level it was assumed that social disorganization would be manifested as a breakdown in communication and understanding between youth and adult representatives of conventional institutions, such as parents, teachers, and judges. As [this breakdown in communication progressed] the individual inevitably worked free from the controls exercised by such conventional ties and became a candidate for novel relationships, novel forms of experience, and the assimilation of novel ideas.[58]

The influence of Thomas, Znaniecki, Park, and Burgess was felt by virtually all American sociologists, not Shaw and McKay alone. Sutherland, too, was stimulated by *The Polish Peasant's* call for an empirical sociology, by its plea for an understanding of social processes and mechanisms, by its emphasis on the desirability of merging sociology and social psychology, and by its stress on the importance of developing a general theory of behavior.

Sutherland's Theoretical Impasse

In addition to the published articles discussed earlier, Sutherland worked on other, unpublished projects between 1926 and 1929 while at the University of Minnesota. In 1927, for example, he began a study of homicides and suicides in Minneapolis and St. Paul between 1908 and 1927. His study examined their "ecological distribution, composition of groups affected, [and] variations in rates."[59] This research was to have been the first step in a more general study of the Twin Cities whose particular purposes would be locating "cultural areas and studying processes of a social nature."

That same year he also began an ambitious project in collaboration with Samuel C. Ratcliffe and Ernest T. Hiller, his former colleagues at Illinois. Sutherland was very much impressed with Park and Burgess's *Introduction to the Science of Sociology* (1921). Of course, he was not alone in his high regard for this book. It became referred to as the "Green Bible" among sociologists for the color of its binding and especially its importance.[60] Faris wrote that the Park and Burgess text set the "direction and content of American sociology after 1921."[61] This book was a magisterial tome of over one thousand pages. It was organized by topics, each introduced by Park or Burgess and followed by conceptual readings. By 1927 Sutherland had been at work for three or four years in an attempt to develop a "case book" in sociology. He had envisioned a format similar to that used by Park and Burgess, but having "amassed thousands of cases" he proceeded instead to illustrate the topics with concrete cases. As it happened, Sutherland, Ratcliffe, and Hiller did not produce such a book. Sutherland also considered writing a "general book in criminology, treating the subject as a process of conflict."[62] It was an idea that never advanced beyond the planning stage, yet the theme of conflict was to remain prominent in all of his future writings on crime causation.

By 1929, Sutherland's last year at the University of Minnesota, he had achieved the kind of professional recognition that he could only have dreamed about at William Jewell College. Between 1924, the year *Criminology* was published, and 1929, he rose in rank from assistant professor at Illinois to full professor at Minnesota, a member of the fourth most prestigious sociology department in America. He was in the kind of intellectual environment in which he could be productive, and his publications demonstrate the point. Yet, for all that, his greatest accomplishments still lay ahead. Goff has nicely summarized this stage of Sutherland's intellectual development and the significance of his work to that date.

> Sutherland's work during this time can best be described as following the major themes and issues which were then in vogue among sociologists and criminologists. He wasn't a "trailblazer" or an original thinker; his work at the University of Illinois, for example, made extensive use of the notion of "social process," a concept then favored by many of his colleagues. Similarly, in the late 1920's, when the concepts of "culture" and "culture areas" were popular ... Sutherland utilized them in many of his articles. The basis of Sutherland's work during these sixteen years reflected the ideals with which he had been indoctrinated as a graduate student at the University of Chicago.[63]

In other words, Sutherland was an apt student of sociology and his work incorporated concepts then popular within the field. While he was incorporating conventional sociological concepts into his analysis of crime causation, his other writings show him still wedded to the idea of multiple factor theory. In "Social Aspects of Crime" (1927) Sutherland wrote:

> Studies show that no one thing taken by itself is very important as a cause of crime. Mentality, economic conditions, nativity, heredity and other things have been claimed by various investigators to be the important cause of crime, but further investigation reduces the significance of every such factor, when considered by itself. . . . [C]rime is always due to multiple factors, and that any trait of the person, whether it is good or bad, and any condition of the environment, whether it is good or bad, may enter into the total set of factors which is instrumental in producing the crime.[64]

At this point in his career Sutherland was unable to make the distinction between multiple causes or "factors" and multiple factor theory. Because he did not recognize the difference between a single theory that incorporated multiple factors within it and what was called multiple factor theory, he was unable to see that he was on the verge of developing a broad generalization that would explain the criminal behavior of individuals.

Notes

1. Don Martindale, *The Romance of a Profession: A Case History in the Sociology of Sociology* (St. Paul, Minnesota: Windflower Publishing Company, 1976), p. 60.
2. Edwin H. Sutherland, Letter to Luther Bernard, 13 July 1927. Luther L. Bernard Papers, Pennsylvania Historical Collections, Pattee Library, Pennsylvania State University, University Park, Pennsylvania.
3. Martindale, p. 61.
4. Ibid., p. 62.
5. Ibid.
6. Ibid.
7. Edwin H. Sutherland, "The Biological and Sociological Processes," *Papers and Proceedings of the Twentieth Annual Meeting of the American Sociological Society*, 20 (1926), p. 58.
8. Ibid., p. 62.
9. Edwin H. Sutherland, "Review of *Delinquents and Criminals: Their Making and Unmaking*, by William Healy and Augusta F. Bronner," *Harvard Law Review*, 40 (March 1927), p. 800.
10. Edwin H. Sutherland, "Social Aspects of Crime," *Proceedings of the Conference of the National Crime Commission* (Washington: U.S. Government Printing Office, 1927), p. 156.
11. Edwin H. Sutherland, "The Person versus the Act in Criminology," *Cornell Law Quarterly*, 14 (February 1929), pp. 159-167. Reprinted in *Edwin H. Sutherland: On Analyzing Crime*, Karl Schuessler, ed. (Chicago: University of Chicago Press, 1973), pp. 149-159.
12. Ibid., p. 154.
13. Edwin H. Sutherland, "Is There Undue Crime Among Immigrants?" *National Conference of Social Work*, 1927, p. 572.
14. Ibid., p. 579.
15. Ibid., p. 578.

16. Frederic Milton Thrasher, *The Gang: A Study of 1,313 Gangs in Chicago* (Chicago: University of Chicago Press, 1927), p. 36.

17. Ibid., p. 22.

18. Ibid., p. 3.

19. Quoted in James Bennett, *Oral History and Delinquency: The Rhetoric of Criminology* (Chicago: University of Chicago Press, 1981), p. 160.

20. Thrasher, p. 41.

21. Robert E. L. Faris, *Chicago Sociology, 1920-1932* (Chicago: University of Chicago Press, 1967), p. 74.

22. Thrasher, pp. 367-368.

23. Bennett, p. 159.

24. Ibid., p. 166.

25. Faris, p. 52.

26. Alfred Lindesmith and Yale Levin, "The Lombrosian Myth in Criminology," *American Journal of Sociology*, 42 (March 1937), p. 653.

27. Faris, p. 54.

28. Lindesmith and Levin, pp. 654-657.

29. Clifford R. Shaw, with the collaboration of Frederick M. Zorbaugh, Henry D. McKay, and Leonard S. Cottrell. *Delinquency Areas: A Study of the Geographic Distribution of School Truants, Juvenile Delinquents, and Adult Offenders in Chicago* (Chicago: University of Chicago Press, 1929), p. ix.

30. Bennett, pp. 168-169.

31. W. I. Thomas and Florian Znaniecki, *The Polish Peasant in Europe and America*, 2 (New York: Dover Publications, 1958 ed.), p. 1128.

32. Morris Janowitz, Introduction to W. I. Thomas," in *On Social Organization and Social Personality*, Morris Janowitz, ed. (Chicago: University of Chicago Press, 1966), p. xxxii.

33. Shaw et al., pp. 204-205.

34. Ibid., p. 9.

35. Herbert Blumer, *An Appraisal of Thomas and Znaniecki's "The Polish Peasant in Europe and America,"* (New York: Social Science Research Council, 1939), p. 130, quoted in Bennett, p. 167.

36. W. I. Thomas, Letter to Luther Bernard, 13 July 1927. Luther L. Bernard Papers.

37. Lyn H. Lofland ed., "Reminiscences of Classic Chicago: The Blumer-Hughes Talk," *Urban Life*, 9 (October 1980), p. 256.

38. W. I. Thomas, *The Unadjusted Girl: With Cases and Standpoint for Behavior Analysis* (Boston: Little, Brown, 1923), pp. 249-250, quoted in Bennett, pp. 131-132.

39. Daniel Glaser, "Marginal Workers: Some Antecedents and Implications of an Idea from Shaw and McKay," in *Delinquency, Crime, and Society*, James F. Short, Jr., ed. (Chicago: University of Chicago Press, 1976), p. 255.

40. Bennett, p. 157.

41. Berenice Fisher and Anselm Strauss, "The Chicago Tradition and Social Change: Thomas, Park and Their Successors," *Symbolic Interaction*, 1 (Spring 1978), pp. 9-10.

42. Glaser, pp. 256-259.

43. Ibid., p. 257.

44. Ibid.

45. Ibid.

46. Ibid.
47. Faris, p. 27.
48. Jon Snodgrass, "Clifford R. Shaw and Henry D. McKay: Chicago Crimi-nologists," *British Journal of Criminology*, 16 (January 1976), p. 6.
49. Ibid., p. 3.
50. Ibid.
51. Henry McKay, Letter to Jon Snodgrass, 3 March 1971, quoted in Snodgrass, p. 6.
52. Glaser, p. 258.
53. Shaw et al., p. 206.
54. Solomon Kobrin, "The Formal Logical Properties of the Shaw-McKay Delin-quency Theory," in *Ecology, Crime, and Delinquents*, Harwin L. Voss and David M. Petersen, eds. (New York: Appleton-Century-Crofts, 1971), p. 103.
55. Thomas and Znaniecki, I., p. 20.
56. Ibid., p. 44.
57. Donald R. Cressey, "Epidemiology and Individual Conduct: A Case from Criminology," *Pacific Sociological Review*, 3 (Fall 1960), p. 47.
58. Harold Finestone, "The Delinquent and Society: The Shaw and McKay Tradi-tion," in *Delinquency, Crime, and Society*, James F. Short, Jr., ed. (Chicago: University of Chicago Press, 1976), p. 29.
59. Edwin H. Sutherland, Letter to Luther Bernard, 13 July 1927.
60. Bennett, pp. 157-158.
61. Faris, p. 37.
62. Edwin H. Sutherland, Letter to Luther Bernard, 13 July 1927.
63. Colin Goff, "Edwin H. Sutherland and White-Collar Crime" (unpublished Ph.D. dissertation, University of California, Irvine, 1982), pp. 157-158.
64. Sutherland, "Social Aspects of Crime," pp. 156-157.

5

The Emergence of the Theory

This chapter covers Sutherland's career from 1929, when he worked at the Bureau of Social Hygiene, until 1935, when he was forced to leave the University of Chicago. It chronicles four events important in the development of the theory of differential association. First, the publication of the Michael-Adler Report, which criticized contemporary criminological theory and research, goaded Sutherland to develop a scientific theory of criminal behavior. Second, a meeting called by Dean Beardsley Ruml of the University of Chicago to ascertain the current status of criminological knowledge forced Sutherland to conclude that positive generalizations about the cause of crime could not be stated with any confidence. This admission embarrassed him and he resolved to do something about it. Third, his work on *The Professional Thief* helped him to see a common process present within all crime. And fourth, Sutherland discovered the value of using Charles H. Cooley's work on social process as an approach by which to formulate a tentative explanation of criminal behavior. These events and their consequences led Sutherland to form the first approximation of a theory of crime causation, the theory eventually to become known as differential association.

The Michael-Adler Report

When F. Stuart Chapin took a two-year leave of absence in 1928 to become editor of *Sociological Abstracts*, Sutherland was appointed acting chair of the department of sociology at the University of Minnesota. The next summer, however, he took a one-year leave of absence to conduct research for the Bureau of Social Hygiene in New York. He intended to return to Minnesota the next year but, as it happened, he did not.

The Bureau of Social Hygiene was established in 1913 by John D. Rockefeller, Jr., and other philanthropists for the purpose of the "study, amelioration, and prevention of those social conditions, crimes, and diseases which adversely affect the well-being of society."[1] While the name "Bureau of Social Hygiene" may sound a bit odd to today's reader, during its span of twenty-seven years (1913-40) the bureau was a highly respected research institute. It attracted well-known scholars, among them Sutherland, to work with its professional staff on such problems as narcotics, juvenile delinquency, birth control, sex education, maternal health, and criminology. It carried out studies of probation, parole, and prison systems. The bureau also investigated topics, such as white slavery and eugenics, which today are of little or no interest to scholars.

Sutherland was hired to conduct two major studies. The first was to explore the causes of the declining prison population in England, with the goal of learning in what ways the English experience might be instructive to the American penal system.[2] The second was to determine whether there was a need for an institute of criminology in the United States, and if so, how it should be staffed and organized to carry out its mission.

The first study was the basis of Sutherland's article "The Decreasing Prison Population in England" (1934), which was published in the *Journal of Criminal Law and Criminology*. Sutherland's conclusion is contained in the following passages.

> Prisons are being demolished and sold in England because the supply of prisoners is not large enough to fill them. The number of prisoners in custody in England in 1930 was less than half the number in 1857, though the population of England was twice as large. This decrease was not a direct result of a reduction in the general crime rate, but rather of changes in penal policies.[3]

And:

> The general positive conclusion from the preceding analysis is that the reduction in the prison population of England is due to two factors, first, to the development of probation and of the provision for time in which to pay fines; second, the reduction in intoxication. The general negative conclusion is that the reduction was not a direct effect of changes in crime rates. . . . Also the prison population has been reduced in Scotland, Ireland, Sweden, Germany and other continental countries. This movement probably spreads wherever the crime rates do not produce a feeling of insecurity.[4]

Of the other major study Sutherland was hired to conduct—on the need and feasibility of an institute of criminology—Goff writes that "there is no evidence in the BSH files that he was ever involved with [such] an investigation."[5]

Between 1932 and 1933, however, Sutherland did write an unpublished paper titled "The Michael-Adler Report." In it he responded to a sharply critical report on the current state of American criminology and the criminal justice system written by Jerome Michael and Mortimer Adler and published in 1932 under the title "Crime, Law, and Social Science." Schuessler writes that the Michael-Adler report was prepared for the Bureau of Social Hygiene under the auspices of the Columbia University School of Law.[6] It would be interesting to know why the bureau selected two men outside the discipline of criminology to answer their questions on the need and viability of an American institute of criminology. Perhaps the bureau simply wanted to first secure an appraisal that was not constrained by ties of professional loyalty to colleagues whose work might justly be open to severe criticism. Schuessler writes:

> in the ... "Development of the Hypothesis of Differential Association," Sutherland candidly admits that ... he was greatly influenced by the Report. In informal discussions he often agreed that the negative evaluations of criminological research in the [Report] were essentially correct ... and that the Report exerted an important influence upon him in turning his attention to abstract generalization.[7]

It does not appear that the bureau intended its work to be critical in only the negative sense. For after receiving the report, the bureau submitted it to the Social Science Research Council, "indicating that it would be most interesting and helpful to have an expression of the views of the Council."[8]

What was the thrust of the Michael-Adler report? Sutherland summarized its general argument as follows:

> (1) Criminological research has been futile. (2) The reason for the futility of research in criminology is the incompetence of criminologists in science. (3) The current methods of criminological research should be abandoned, and scientists should be imported into criminology from other fields.[9]

Schuessler writes that Sutherland's statement was written shortly after the report appeared and, in the "framework of controversy" that surrounded the Michael-Adler assessment of American criminology, his tone was generally critical and negative. It was only later—"after his first reaction of emotional antagonism had worn off"[10]—that Sutherland was able to grant the validity of much of what Michael and Adler had written.

The Michael-Adler report proposed that the institute of criminal justice have two separate divisions: a division of criminology and a division of criminal justice. The division of criminology was to be staffed with a logician, a mathematician, a statistician, a theoretical physicist, an experimental physicist, a mathematical economist, a psychometrist, and a criminologist. As to the criminologist, Michael and Adler preferred one who had *not* engaged in criminological research. Presumably, this would insure that the person had not acquired any bad research habits along the way.[11]

At the conclusion of his year at the Bureau of Social Hygiene, Sutherland accepted a position as research professor at the University of Chicago. He was interested in this position because it would provide "the opportunity to specialize in criminology and [because of] the unusual financial and other resources for research work in criminology." Sutherland thought that by devoting his full time to criminological research he would be able to make substantial headway in advancing a scientific analysis of crime. He believed this goal would be attainable because Chicago had "secured large grants from various foundations for research work in the social sciences and at present no other institution is able to approach Chicago in its facilities in this field."[12] Perhaps the most attractive feature of the position was that it was at the University of Chicago. Chicago was still the top-ranked department of sociology in the nation and, of course, the university from which Sutherland had received his doctorate. He was excited by the prospect of working with those whose ideas had helped to shape his own work: Park, Wirth, Burgess, and McKay (at the Institute for Juvenile Research). Chicago's offer, therefore, was highly attractive, notwithstanding the fact that he "loathed Chicago as a place in which to live almost as much as I do New York City."[13]

Another reason it may be assumed that Sutherland was eager to get back to Chicago was his desire to be closer to his friends. Schuessler has written: "[Sutherland] covered no great distance and remained within a rather restricted geographical area throughout his academic career. This pattern is of no special significance, except that it kept him within easy distance of his friends in Chicago (McKay, Ogburn, and Hughes) and relatively distant from sociologists outside the Midwest."[14]

When Sutherland considered the relative advantages of working at the University of Chicago he was referring to changes at the university during the middle and latter part of the 1920s that put Chicago head and shoulders above its competitors in the social sciences. In 1923 the Social Science Research Committee was formed to coordinate multidisciplinary research conducted by the departments of political science, sociology and anthropology, political economy, history, philosophy, and social service administration. The committee received its funding from outside the University of Chicago, primarily from the Laura Spelman Rockefeller Memorial. Beginning with a grant of $21,000 in 1923, this Rockefeller family trust increased its contribution to $75,000 in 1924 and augmented it again in 1927. By the end of the 1920s the committee had over $100,000 a year for the support of research activities within this group of academic departments. Martin Bulmer has described the main tasks of the committee in these words:

> The main characteristics of the [committee] as a form of support for social science research were those of a network which held together disparate parts of the Social Science group, encouraged their research activities, and provided concrete help in the form of clerical assistance, statistical and computational facilities, typing of manuscripts, and a medium of publication in the University of Chicago Press "Studies in Social Science" series which the [committee] created and subsidized.[15]

The memorial fund enabled the committee to bring together, as never before, established scholars, research supervisors and assistants, graduate students, and clerical, secretarial, and statistical support, all to encourage the development of empirical social science. Beginning in 1927, Rockefeller memorial grants made research professorships possible for the first time at the University of Chicago.

Sutherland's rank at Chicago was professor of sociology, and he taught during each quarter that he remained there. For the first two years (1930-32) he taught a quarterly seminar, "Research in Criminology." In 1932, when Ernest Burgess took a sabbatical leave, Sutherland taught a number of his courses: "Social Pathology," "Crime and Its Social Treatment," "Research in Criminology," and "Field Studies in Criminology." The next year, with Burgess back in the classroom, Sutherland taught "Theories of Criminality" and "Organized Crime and Criminal Culture." He taught these two courses his final year at Chicago in addition to "Methods and Theories of Punishment."[16]

But it was primarily as a researcher that Sutherland was hired by the University of Chicago. "In announcing his appointment, President Robert M. Hutchins stated that the step was taken to strengthen the university's crime-study program."[17] Hutchins had been appointed president of the University of Chicago just the year before, making him, at age twenty-nine, a dynamic force for change at Chicago. As the world reeled from the collapse of the financial markets and began to slide into a debilitating depression, the university's faculty braced itself for the unfamiliar experience of diminished resources and heightened job insecurity. In that context Sutherland pinned his professional aspirations on an untenured position at Chicago. Had he chosen to, he could have stayed on at the Bureau of Social Hygiene. Goff reports that the "administrators at the BSH were satisfied with Sutherland's work; in 1931, they unsuccessfully tried to lure him back to New York City from Chicago with an attractive offer, including the promise of a permanent position."[18] The University of Chicago's allure was too strong, however, and Sutherland elected to accept the professional judgment of numerous administrators, including Ellsworth Faris, the department of sociology's chair between 1925 and 1936. Sutherland's decision to remain in a tenuous position at Chicago rather than accept a guarantee of secure employment with the Bureau of Social Hygiene suggests the powerful hold the University of Chicago had over him.

Sutherland's productivity as a researcher between 1930 and 1935 is open to varied interpretations. For example, Goff renders this judgment of Sutherland during his Chicago years:

> That Sutherland completed only a few research projects during the five years he was at the University of Chicago offers a revealing insight into his role as a professional sociologist. That he received funding for ten research projects but finished only three is a striking commentary on the work pattern of the individual who was to have the greatest influence upon American criminology during the twentieth century. Further, all three of the completed projects involved a collaborator. . . . Perhaps this inability to complete his research assignments reflected the fact that he allotted only so much time to the different activities he pursued during the day. . . . Each evening, for example, usually he would either read the *Saturday Evening Post* or play bridge. The highly structured lifestyle with no time given to evening work that Sutherland followed no doubt mitigated [*sic*] against the completion of his research projects and restricted his intellectual activities and output. He relied on others for much of his work in this period; Sutherland was the catalyst, the individual who could develop the conceptual schema, but he appeared to lack the technical skill to finish research projects.[19]

The ten projects Goff refers to were all funded by the Social Science Research Committee. As indicated, Sutherland worked closely with a collaborator on three of the projects. He operated as a single researcher on the remainder, although at least one of them placed him in the role of principal investigator for one phase of a larger, more inclusive project.

While it is true that he completed only three of the ten research projects funded by the Social Science Research Committee, one should avoid the inference that Sutherland was not productive during his years at Chicago. Besides revising his criminology textbook and conducting research that later resulted in *Twenty Thousand Homeless Men* (with Harvey J. Locke) and *The Professional Thief* (with Broadway Jones), Sutherland also wrote seven articles and three book chapters and (with Thorsten Sellin) edited a volume of *The Annals of the American Academy of Political and Social Sciences* titled *Prisons of Tomorrow*.

It is hard to imagine how Sutherland could have accomplished all this if he had cultivated poor work habits, as Goff claims. If Sutherland can be faulted, it is for allowing himself to become so overextended that he was unable to complete every project which he had begun. Given his disposition to please others, one imagines him agreeing to participate in more research projects than he could reasonably be expected to finish. In addition, he probably assumed he would remain at the University of Chicago for many more years, with the opportunity to bring to fruition some of the projects that were unfinished in 1935.

In 1930 Sutherland and Ernest Burgess worked independently on a study of the possible relationship between insanity and crime. Burgess "was to study the extent to which the traditional ethnic family shaped the personalities of its children and the degree to which the success or failure of child training was correlated with the incidence of crime and insanity."[20] Sutherland's task was to focus on four immigrant groups in the Chicago metropolitan area—Swedes, Germans, Italians, and Irish. Working with published crime reports from police departments, criminal courts, and correctional institutions, he was to determine whether physical characteristics, cultural traits, family organization, and differential group experience with respect to assimilation to American culture and society were correlated with the crime rates for these specific ethnic groups.

By the end of the 1930-1931 academic year Sutherland had collected a number of case histories of incarcerated immigrant criminals, had "almost finished"[21] a statistical analysis of immigrant prisoners in local correctional institutions, and had analyzed the crime reports concerning immigrants from criminal justice agencies in the Chicago area. He then decided to wait until he could analyze the 1930 census data before proceeding, but, as these data were not published until 1934, he failed to complete the project before leaving Chicago in 1935. One does not know whether to fault Sutherland for his failure to finish the project because of dilatory work habits, as Goff suggests, or because he had made a research judgment based on a miscalculation of government printing schedules.

Other research projects Sutherland began but did not complete between 1930 and 1935 included a study of fining practices in Chicago, a study of the "fix" (i.e., arranged immunity for a thief on a criminal charge), an "analysis of crime and delinquency in selected delinquency areas of Chicago," a study of the value of predictive tests for paroled inmates, and a study to investigate the feasibility of establishing a library of case studies of juvenile delinquents.[22]

Even though Sutherland did not complete these projects for the committee in the sense of presenting a monograph or other finished project, he did incorporate some of this work in other scholarly materials later published either as books or articles. For example, *The Professional Thief* (1937) contained a chapter entitled "The Fix" (pp. 82-118). In January 1931 Sutherland received funds from the committee to conduct research on the reliability of criminal statistics. He collaborated with C. C. Van Vechten,

Jr., and their findings were published in the *Journal of Criminal Law and Criminology* in the May-June 1934 issue.

During the 1934-1935 academic year Sutherland worked closely with Harvey J. Locke to produce *Twenty Thousand Homeless Men: A Study of Unemployed Men in the Chicago Shelters*. The Illinois Emergency Relief Commission authorized this study on January 15, 1934. Fieldwork in the Chicago shelters of the Service Bureau for Men (a division of the Illinois Emergency Relief Commission) was begun shortly thereafter and continued until the spring of 1935. This was a fairly large research project, including eight sociologists, four psychiatrists, four psychologists, two statisticians and nine clerks and stenographers. The Illinois Emergency Relief Commission paid the salaries of the staff members. The remaining expenses of the project were paid by the Social Science Research Committee. Sutherland was the project director.[23]

Twenty Thousand Homeless Men was based on the use of informal conversations with the shelter men in order to elicit their life histories and attitudes. In some ways the book resembles the "own story" format employed by Dr. William Healy and Clifford Shaw a few years earlier. All members of the research staff used the interview method, and six research workers actually lived in the shelters as shelter clients for periods ranging from one week to several months. In the preface Sutherland and Locke wrote: "Because verbatim reports are an indispensable means of securing insight into attitudes, such records occupy a considerable part of this book. The portions of the book which are not of that nature are principally inferences from or summaries of such conversations."[24]

By design, *Twenty Thousand Homeless Men* was descriptive rather than analytical, and the authors offered no solutions to the problems of the shelter men. Sutherland and Locke titled one chapter "Four Vices"— "excessive drinking, gambling, irregular sex practices, and begging"—leading one to wonder whether it was not a sly allusion to Thomas's "four wishes."[25] Another chapter, "The Process of Shelterization," described a process very similar to what Donald Clemmer would call prisonization in his study of the prison in Menard, Illinois, published in 1940. The value of *Twenty Thousand Homeless Men* is suggested by the decision of the Arno Press and *The New York Times* to reissue it in 1971 as part of a series entitled *Poverty U.S.A.: The Historical Record*, edited by the historian David J. Rothman. In summary, then, Sutherland and Locke produced a book that vividly described a social problem but made no attempt at suggesting a policy for its solution.

During Sutherland's last year at the University of Minnesota he began to investigate what he later termed "white-collar crime," exploring the relationship between crime and poverty.[26] At Chicago, he was given funds in

1933 by the committee to study white-collar crime in greater detail. The fruit of this research became evident only at the end of the decade when, as president of the American Sociological Society, he made his first major presentation on the subject in his presidential address at Philadelphia in December 1939.

The Professional Thief: The Theory Emerges

The final research project for which Sutherland obtained funds from the Social Science Research Committee was an investigation of the professional thief. Sutherland "wrote" his book of that title (a classic in criminology) in the same sense that Clifford R. Shaw is said to have "written" *The Jack-Roller:* each sociologist sat his subject down with pen and paper and encouraged him to tell about his personal experiences. In the case of *The Jack Roller*, Shaw worked with "Stanley" to draw out the young man's "own story." Sutherland used "Chic Conwell," not to create an autobiography, biography, or case study, but to produce a "monograph which tells how groups of men made a living by stealing, primarily by picking pockets, shoplifting and operating confidence games. It is not a personal account of [the thief's] career; it does not concern his life-history and causal entry into the world of crime."[27]

Sutherland described his book this way: "This document is a description of the profession of theft as experienced by one professional thief."[28] Sutherland wanted to insure that the thief's description was not simply one man's limited and biased view of the world of the professional thief:

> [Sutherland] submitted the manuscript to four other professional thieves and to two former detectives. Without submitting the manuscript, I discussed the ideas and problems with several other professional thieves, with several other representatives of municipal and private police systems, and with clerks in stores.[29]

The most complete source of information on the history of *The Professional Thief* is Jon Snodgrass's article "The Criminologist and His Criminal: The Case of Edwin H. Sutherland and Broadway Jones" (1973). According to Snodgrass, Sutherland began working on this book in 1932, when Broadway Jones (the man behind Sutherland's pseudonymous "Chic Conwell") was released from the U.S. penitentiary at Leavenworth, Kansas. The record is unclear as to how Sutherland first met Jones. Snodgrass suggests that Dr. Ben L. Reitman brought the two together.[30] However, Herbert Blumer claims the distinction for himself.

> Ben Reitman . . . was a specialist in venereal diseases—or rather, he handled

venereal diseases ... I won't pass upon the solidity of his medical background. ... But he was treating venereal disease among the underworld, that was his clientele: prostitutes, pimps, petty gamblers and thieves, robbers, and safe-crackers—that whole world—and if they or their women had any difficulty along the line of venereal infection, they'd go to Ben. ... You've all heard of *The Professional Thief,* a book that appears under the name of Sutherland, which Sutherland did not write. The book was written by a most interesting person, a very close friend of mine, who, incidentally, I introduced to Sutherland under the moniker of Broadway Jones—a professional thief par excellence—who really provided that material for that book.[31]

Snodgrass reports that Reitman and another, unknown physician offered a research grant of $150 (which the Social Science Research Committee matched with $200) for Sutherland to use Jones in any capacity he chose. He put Jones to work writing about his experiences with professional thieves, at the rate of $100 per month for three months. They began their collaboration in November 1932, and five years later the University of Chicago Press published *The Professional Thief.*[32]

Although Sutherland did not expect the book to remain long the "most authoritative statement on the subject of stealing as an occupation,"[33] Snodgrass quotes Ned Polsky as writing, thirty years after its initial appearance, "[c]riminologists can tell you about Sutherland's 'Chic Conwell'; but they can't give you comparable data on professionals of today. . . ."[34]

Snodgrass writes that "*The Professional Thief* was not an etiological work, at least not in an overt sense. But it did have strong implications for contending causal theories."[35] This statement is both correct and misleading. The thief's description of the planning that went into the commission of his crimes, the technical skills (picking pockets, shoplifting, stealing from jewelry stores by substitution of fakes, confidence games, passing illegal checks), the social skills ("approach, front, honesty, reliability, wit, and . . . talking ability"), the codes of ethics, organization ("mob, troup, or outfit"), and the political acumen (the "fix") all had the effect of countering theories of criminality which "maintained that criminals were mentally abnormal, or feeble-minded, or constitutionally inferior."[36]

Sutherland wanted the thief's description of his criminal world to make another point as well. "Chic Conwell" was represented by Sutherland as a man born to a family "in comfortable circumstances."[37] Jones's reluctance to talk about himself, and especially his early life, together with what Sutherland was able to learn from a social background investigation prior to Jones's parole from Leavenworth, led him to conclude that Jones was the son of a prominent shipbuilder and real-estate investor and "in some way connected with the Harvard Law School."[38]

In the early 1970s Snodgrass tried to follow these leads to see whether Jones in fact came from a "financially comfortable family" in an "excellent neighborhood" near Harvard University in Cambridge, Massachusetts. He was unable to do so and concluded that the facts were just the opposite. Not only was Jones's father not well-off, "he was probably either an electric or a horse-drawn trolley car operator."[39] The question of Jones's class origin is important because Sutherland seemed to give it significance when he asserted that "[the] professional thief in America feels that he is a social outcast. This is especially true of the professional thieves who originated in middle-class society, as many of them did."[40] If this assertion of middle-class origins was also a fact, it struck a blow against theories of criminality that used social class or poverty as the major causal agent. Thus, Snodgrass is correct when he writes that *The Professional Thief* had strong implications for contending causal theories of crime.

But Snodgrass is wrong when he suggests *The Professional Thief* is not an etiological work:

> Sutherland also interpreted professional stealing as the product of differential association. *The Professional Thief* has often been cited as another case, along with *White Collar Crime* (1949), in which Sutherland tried to demonstrate his theory of differential association. This citation overlooks the fact that *The Professional Thief* was published two years before the theory. Careful attention to the way differential association is used in *The Professional Thief* indicates that it meant different social contacts and interactions, not a network of learning experiences through which an individual was inducted into a criminal way of life. The learning that was required to become a professional thief was certainly emphasized, but it was not called differential association.[41]

Snodgrass's remarks suggest that he is equally guilty of overlooking the facts. First, *Principles of Criminology*, the title given to the second edition of Sutherland's criminology textbook in 1934, contained an inchoate—yet discernible—version of differential association theory.[42] While it is true that Sutherland did not call his hypothesis "differential association theory" in the 1934 edition, it was nonetheless a theory of criminality which relied on ideas that were expanded and sharpened in the third and fouth editions of the Sutherland text. Consider his theory in the 1934 edition:

> The hypotheses of this book are as follows: First, any person can be trained to adopt and follow any pattern of behavior which he is able to execute. This pattern may cause him to suffer death, physical injury, economic loss, sacrifice of friendship, and any other type of loss, but [will] be followed nevertheless even with joy, provided it is accepted as the thing for him to do. Second, failure to follow a prescribed pattern of behavior is due to the inconsistency and lack of harmony in the influences which direct the individual. Third, the conflict of cultures is therefore the fundamental principle in the

explanation of crime. Fourth, the more the cultural patterns conflict, the more unpredictable is the behavior of a particular individual.[43]

It would be unfair to criticize Snodgrass too harshly for overlooking the existence, even in rudimentary form, of the theory of differential association before *The Professional Thief* was published. In truth, Sutherland himself was unaware of its existence even as he wrote the words! Years later he wrote:

> I assure you that I was surprised to learn [from Henry McKay in 1935] that I had stated a general hypothesis regarding criminal behavior. . . . My thinking was compartmentalized rather than integrated. . . . In spite of [McKay's] statement about the hypothesis, if anyone had caught me in my usual frame of mind and asked me what my theory of criminal behavior was, I would have answered, "The multiple-factor theory."[44]

This statement should be taken both as the truth and as a demurrer that reflects Sutherland's inherent modesty.[45] Not only were the ideas contained in these hypotheses carried over to the 1939 edition, but much of the language is identical. That the theory of differential association was first made explicit in 1939 (two years after *The Professional Thief* was published) offers by itself no evidence, contrary to Snodgrass, that it could not have been Sutherland's explanation of the thief's criminality.

Second, when Snodgrass writes that "[c]areful attention to the way differential association is used in *The Professional Thief* indicates that it meant different social contacts and interactions, not a network of learning experiences through which an individual was inducted into a criminal way of life,"[46] he makes a common error in failing to recognize how the theory of differential association changed between the 1939 statement and the 1947 statement. When Sutherland was writing *The Professional Thief* (1932-1937) he conceived of differential association in terms of contacts and interactions with persons and *not* networks of learning experiences. The second proposition in the 1939 version reads "systematic criminal behavior is determined in a process of association with those who commit crimes, just as systematic lawful behavior is determined in a process of association with those who are law-abiding."[47] He went on to write: "[Any person] inevitably assimilates such behavior from the surrounding culture. . . . Since criminal behavior is thus developed in association with criminals it means that crime is the cause of crime."[48] Therefore, "different social contacts and interactions" and *not* a "network of learning experiences" was what differential association was in the 1930s.

In 1934 Sutherland published the second edition of his criminology textbook, *Principles of Criminology*. Goff writes that the new edition "virtually remained unchanged in its orientation. This is particularly true of those sections which dealt with the treatment of the criminal offender and the reform of the criminal justice system, with several chapters being reprinted word-for-word."[49] The new edition no longer had chapters on "The Victims of Crime," "Popular Justice," and "Composition of the Criminal Population," and Sutherland added a number of chapters on the causes of crime. But these changes did not greatly expand the number of pages devoted to the question of crime causation. More importantly, the treatment of crime causation did not change much even though the theory of differential association was implicit in this edition. Sutherland still embraced multiple factor theory:

> *The* theory of criminality which may be derived finally [from biological, personality, primary social groups, and broader social processes] will proba- bly weave these various elements into an integrated and compact system of thought. . . . It seems probable that in a situation where all the influences point consistently in one direction, all persons will act in the same manner.[50]

Just as in the first edition, Sutherland incorporated concepts that, in rela- tion to the understanding of crime, found wide circulation within general sociology: W. I. Thomas's theory of social change, social and geographical mobility, culture conflict, and culture areas.

In the chapter titled "Crime and Social Processes" he used Thomas's theory of social change to illuminate the historical and economic forces at work within the Western world from about the time of America's coloniza- tion, forces that had weakened the fabric of society and made social control increasingly problematic. He explained how the colonization of America "threw the Old World out of economic balance." The old economic, social, and political order began to give way to the forces for political and religious democracy. The Industrial Revolution spawned increased social interac- tion, increased economic competition, economic and political individu- alism, and the "ambition for luxury standards of life and for easy money. . . ."[51]

Sutherland also thought he saw forces working to establish social recon- struction. He believed that within the recent past there had emerged three tendencies which, taken together, might reunify society. The first of these centripetal forces was an increased uniformity of thought fostered by the mass media, theaters, and public education, another was "gropings toward social organization to replace the individualism which has broken down or is breaking down economically, legally, and politically."[52] Examples of such "gropings toward social organization" in the Western world were "the Nazi regime in Germany, fascism in Italy, sovietism in Russia, dictatorships in other countries ... [and] the New Deal in the United States. . . ."[53] (Of course, when Sutherland wrote this in 1934, he, like most Americans, did not understand the true character of Nazi Germany, fascist Italy, and the Soviet Union.) The third of the unifying forces was the "development of scientific activities and the tendency toward intellectual honesty."[54] It was in forces such as these, more than anything else, that Sutherland placed his greatest faith for the long-term control of crime. While he is often thought of as more social-psychological than sociological in his approach to crime causation, Sutherland would have disputed such a view of his perspective.

Social Process and Differential Association

Of all the materials that Sutherland produced during the first half of the 1930s, his article "Social Process in Behavior Problems" (1932) is most closely related to the development of the theory of differential association. This is not to say that the article was profound or broke new ground. However, it does suggest that Sutherland was on the verge of a theoretical breakthrough. In this article he explored the relevance of Cooley's use of the concept of social process as a method of explaining current behavior. Used in this way, "method of explaining" is synonymous with causation. Sutherland wrote:

> [Social process] differs from many methods of explanation in its insistence on including a wide range of facts, a sequence of events, actions, and situations in which some order has been found by reflection.[55]

In recognizing that social process is a method of explanation that insists "on including a wide range of facts," Sutherland began to appreciate the difference between integrated *theory* and multiple *factors*. That is, he appreciated Cooley's point that a method of explanation (i.e., a theory) has the power to order a "sequence of events, actions, and situations in which some order has been found."

Social process as a method of explanation carries a personal reference in some instances and an impersonal reference in others. When used in reference to a *person*, "it is a collection of social mechanisms [such as imitation, definition of the situation, or conception of one's role] involved in the development of a pattern of behavior of a particular person."[56] It was Sutherland's goal to use social process as an explanation of individual behavior. When used in reference to *impersonal functional forms* (such as fashion, language, or myth), "it does not grow merely as the result of rational plans of the persons involved in it, for the persons are often unconscious of the changes taking place and do not understand that the social organism is changing. The growth occurs by a tentative method, by feeling its way, by experimenting, as a means of adapting to a situation."[57] Cooley had used social process only in reference to impersonal functional forms.

The use of social process in reference to an individual leads one to pose the question, What is the social process by which a person develops a delinquent behavior pattern? Sutherland wrote:

> One of the significant conclusions derived from the study of delinquents from the point of view of social process in this sense is that the social process by which delinquent behavior develops is the same as the social process by which non-delinquent behavior develops. . . . The variant is not in the social process. . . . Consequently social process may be a valuable step in the direction of explanation of delinquent behavior but it does not in itself contain the explanation of delinquent behavior as contrasted with non-delinquent behavior, since the process is the same in each. The empirical facts regarding the situation must be taken into account in each case in connection with the mechanism.[58]

Sutherland was confident that one individual became delinquent through the same social process by which another became non-delinquent (i.e., the "variant is not in the process"). What he did *not* understand was the precise social mechanism—such as imitation, definition of the situation, conception of one's role, or something else—that conveyed delinquency through social process. Not only was he unaware of the precise social mechanism conveying delinquency, he thought that such knowledge would *never* be sufficient to explain why a particular individual became delinquent.

> The empirical facts regarding the [particular] situation must be taken into account in *each case* in connection wth the mechanism. The mechanism is a generalization but the empirical facts are not. Consequently generalized explanations of delinquency have not resulted from the use of social process in this manner[59] (emphasis added).

He accepted the conventional wisdom of the time that bad housing, mental deficiency, alcoholic parents, bad associates, poverty, broken homes, or some combination of these or other factors might, *in any given case*, cause delinquency. In 1932 he was still an adherent of multiple factor theory, yet he felt it intellectually unacceptable to believe that a generalized explanation of individual delinquency might forever be elusive.[60] The research he conducted in the late 1920s and early 1930s on such alleged causes of crime as mental deficiency and bad housing (see, for example, "Mental Deficiency and Crime" [1931] and "Housing and Delinquency" [1932]) increased his skepticism that factors were causes. He wrote:

> I had long felt dissatisfied with work which consisted in finding a high correla-
> tion, say .72, and then regarding that problem as solved and passing to
> another problem. . . . [Later] I became acquainted with [Alfred Lindesmith's]
> conception of methodology as developed in his study of drug addiction.
> According to this conception, an hypothesis should fit every case in the
> defined universe. . . .[61]

Sutherland was writing "Social Process in Behavior Problems" when the
Michael-Adler report was published. Its assertion that American criminology was prescientific and unschooled in the philosophy or methods of
science goaded Sutherland to search for a positive generalized explanation
of delinquency. Also about that time:

> Dean Ruml of the University of Chicago called together several persons
> interested in criminology and asked us, "What do you know about criminal
> behavior?" The best I could say was that we had certain facts about the
> incidence of high crime rates and that we had proved that certain proposi-
> tions were false. I could state no verified positive generalizations.[62]

We can assume that Dean Beardsley Ruml's question was asked quite
ingenuously. But we may also surmise the criminologists' unease as they
shifted in their chairs and sought an equally candid and straightforward
answer. Sutherland was too proud and too honest a professional to accept
his own response as satisfactory. In the 1930s he began to search single-
mindedly for a scientific explanation of crime causation.

Beardsley Ruml's question was bound to carry considerable weight. In
addition to his post as dean of the division of social sciences and professor
of education at Chicago, Ruml had been director of the Laura Spelman
Rockefeller Memorial from 1921 to 1931. In that position he was one of the
most influential forces in providing financial support for basic work in the
social sciences through the memorial's funding of the Social Science Research Committee. It also should be remembered that the committee un-
derwrote a number of Sutherland's research projects at the University of
Chicago.

Sutherland asked himself hard questions about the state of knowledge of
American criminology in the 1930s. Cooley's use of the concept of social
process, for all its problems, seemed promising to Sutherland. He thought
it would be useful in developing a theory of criminal behavior, if only he
could devise a way to organize the multiple factors in relation to each other,
or to abstract certain common elements from them.[63] He also believed
social process might be useful in developing a theory of criminal behavior
that avoided what Albert Cohen later called the "evil-causes-evil fallacy."

This fallacy is that "evil" results (crime) must have "evil" precedents (broken homes, psychopathic personality, and so on). Thus, when we "explain" crime or almost any other social problem, we tend merely to catalog a series of sordid and ugly circumstances which any decent citizen would deplore, and attribute causal power to those circumstances.[64]

   Sutherland sought a theory of crime causation that "contrasted . . . with the interpretation of behavior made by certain psychologists and psychiatrists in terms of particular traits or characteristics, such as feeblemindedness or egocentrism."[65] In this respect Cooley's discussion of social process used with an impersonal referent looked promising. Applied in this manner, social process focused on social forms and not persons, "and no reference is made to wishes, emotions, attitudes, reasoning, habits, or other psychological processes of the person."[66] Cooley's conception of social process in such behavior problems as delinquency was an application of his general theory of social process. He believed delinquency, as everything else, had antecedent causes without which it could not occur. Delinquency could therefore only be understood "by tracing its history in the individual and in the group as a whole in relation to the rest of the social process."[67]
   Cooley explained behavior problems in terms of his two doctrines of human nature and social organization. As for human nature, Cooley stressed its lack of specific tendencies toward delinquency or law-abiding behavior. Human nature, he thought, was guided principally by, or took its form in, primary groups. In this sense, primary groups became the cause of delinquency if they were "degenerate." Absent "better influences," human nature slid into "depravity." Cooley wrote:

> There is, in fact, a certain practical truth in the idea of the "natural depravity" of human nature. That is to say, the higher life of the human mind is cooperative, is reached only through the higher sort of social organization; and, in the absence of this, human nature, thrown back upon crude impulse, falls into sensualism and disorder.[68]

   Sutherland expressed Cooley's thoughts on the cause of behavior problems this way:

> Conformity with social ideals can be acquired easily only if the co-operative efforts of other people are sufficient to build up and maintain an affirmative, constructive, and many-sided community life. Delinquency breaks out whenever these better influences are relaxed. In that sense human beings are naturally depraved. . . . The essence of his theory is that delinquency has increased in modern society, and that this increase is due to the weakening of the influence of the primary group due to mobility.[69]

Writing almost fifteen years after Cooley had expressed these thoughts,

Sutherland cited the more recent research of Shaw and McKay to support the idea that "high rates of delinquency are found in areas in which the so-called constructive influences are absent or underdeveloped."[70] Boys raised in neighborhoods in which the "spirit of the community" includes "hatred of the police and of the courts, belief in the general dishonesty of the police or courts against any member of their community, conflict with outside standards in many respects (e.g., compulsory school laws), and what may for want of a better term be called 'toughness,'" are likely to become delinquent.[71]

Cooley's idea of social process, especially as it referred to impersonal functional forms like the "spirit of the community," explained the findings of Shaw and McKay. This led Sutherland to suggest the following hypothesis as an explanation of the cause of delinquency:

> [i]t is not suggested as a total explanation of delinquency even in the delinquency area and it certainly does not explain the financial crimes of the white-collar classes. It is an attempt to add a general factor to the interpretation of the high delinquency rates in the areas of first immigrant settlement, where the delinquents are characteristically of the second generation of immigrants . . . The hypothesis is that the high delinquency rate is due to isolation from the private culture of America and contact with the public culture of America.[72]

This was the first statement of the theory of differential association (1932). Those second-generation immigrants exposed primarily to the public culture of America were more likely to become delinquent. Those exposed primarily to the private culture were more likely to become law-abiding. The public culture was that part of America that the immigrant's child would find readily accessible—urban politics, the practice and ethics of business, newspapers, sports, and other "public" activities. Sutherland wrote:

> The standards most frequently displayed in public activities are "easy money" and conspicuous consumption, or a luxury standard of life. These standards are in conflict with their native standards of hard work and thrift. The immigrants see in America exaggeration (as in advertisements), misrepresentation, sharp practices, graft, grasping competition, and disregard of human beings.[73]

Contrasted against this "depravity," against what Sutherland must have felt were the worst aspects of American culture, was the private culture of America—that part of the American ethic that the immigrant was unlikely to observe. The private culture was represented in the "homes and neighborhoods of the older American communities." The only chance for the immigrant to get a glimpse of the private culture was through cinema and newspapers, although in these media, as elsewhere, the view would be one distorted by commercial values. Sutherland was neither so naive nor so sentimental as to think that the private culture found in the homes of native-born, old-immigrant groups such as the English and Scottish was all good, "but it is the medium through which the older Americans secure their directions for behavior."[74]

Sutherland thought of private culture as "almost equivalent" to the primary group culture. For Sutherland's generation, the primary group represented not just a sociological concept with more or less explanatory value; it represented a moral good, a value preference that was used in an ideological as well as a scientific way.

> In general, the primary group is one in which a person is in contact with the other members in so many and such intimate ways that he is easily able to put himself in the place of these others and therefore has a sympathetic human relationship with them, while the public and secondary relationships involve contacts which are departmentalized and therefore institutional. . . . [Differential association with the public culture breeds] young bandits, reared in the slums, revel[ing] in dress suits, silk hats, automobiles, fine food, and similar luxuries.[75]

Beginning, then, in 1932, Sutherland moved away from multiple factor theory and toward the development of a positive generalized theory of criminal behavior. That theory, although not explicitly stated, was already formulated as "differential association." Snodgrass writes:

> The conditions of isolation and association were central to Sutherland's ideas about the causes of crime from the very beginning, and remained relatively unchanged through the course of his intellectual career. It was what one was isolated from, and associated with, that changed as the theory developed.[76]

By 1935 Sutherland was the author of the leading criminology textbook and on the verge of establishing himself as the major American criminologist of the twentieth century. However, when his contract at the University of Chicago was reviewed that year, Ellsworth Faris, the chair of the department of sociology, recommended that it not be renewed. Goff suggests the reason for Sutherland's dismissal was a personality clash between the two men.[77] In any event, Sutherland was "furious" at Faris and never forgave him for his decision. His bitterness toward Faris was accompanied by extreme embarrassment. Not even his closest friends and colleagues learned from Sutherland the truth surrounding his departure from the University of Chicago. "He hid this fact so well that two of his closest associates at Indiana University, A.R. Lindesmith and Karl Schuessler, never learned the real circumstances surrounding Sutherland's departure."[78] In March 1935 Sutherland wrote the following letter to Thorsten Sellin:

> Dear Sellin: Though there has been no public announcement, I am informing a few friends that I have just accepted the position as head of the department of sociology at Indiana, to begin next fall. My position here has been on short-term appointments, which is the policy of President Hutchins. But in view of the reported threats of the immanence [*sic*] of drastic reductions in expenditures soon, of the fact that the others on higher salaries are on permanent salaries since they were here before Hutchins, and of the fact that since I am doing research mostly I can be dropped with less disturbance of the class work than any other member of the staff of the department, I have felt very insecure here. When the Indiana offer was made, I told them I wanted assurance of permanence but I think they would not even give God a permanent appointment under the present conditions. . . . It won't be as good for research work in criminology, but I think I shall enjoy teaching some more. Cordially, EHS.[79]

To support Goff's claim, we can review Schuessler's discussion of Sutherland's departure from Chicago. In 1973, when Schuessler edited *Edwin H. Sutherland: On Analyzing Crime*, he described this event in Sutherland's life as follows:

> Although the reasons for his move from the University of Chicago to Indiana are obscure, we can imagine that he was more or less dissatisfied with his dispensation in the department at Chicago, which did not include permanent tenure. There was probably more push than pull.[80]

One suspects Schuessler's reticence reflects his sensitivity to Sutherland's deep feelings on this wrenching event in his life, and that words Schuessler used elsewhere in his Introduction apply here as well: "[T]his account, in my opinion, is colored more by the omission of facts rather than the slanting of them."[81]

Notes

1. *Scholarly Resources, Incorporated.* "Rockefeller Archive Center," 1980, quoted in Colin Goff, "Edwin H. Sutherland and White-Collar Crime" (unpublished Ph.D. dissertation, University of California, Irvine, 1982), p. 160.
2. Goff, p. 159.
3. Edwin H. Sutherland, "The Decreasing Prison Population of England," *Journal of Criminal Law and Criminology*, 24 (1934), p. 880.
4. Ibid., pp. 898-899.
5. Goff, pp. 160-161.

6. Karl Schuessler, "Introduction," in *Edwin H. Sutherland: On Analyzing Crime*, Karl Schuessler, ed. (Chicago: University of Chicago Press, 1973), pp. 229-230.
7. Schuessler, p. 230.
8. Ibid.
9. Edwin H. Sutherland, "The Michael-Adler Report," in *Edwin H. Sutherland: On Analyzing Crime*, Karl Schuessler, ed. (Chicago: University of Chicago Press, 1973), pp. 230-231.
10. Schuessler, pp. 227-228.
11. Ibid., p. 229.
12. Edwin H. Sutherland, Letter to Dean Johnson, 30 March 1930, quoted in Goff, p. 168.
13. Ibid.
14. Schuessler, pp. xi-xii.
15. Martin Bulmer, "Quantification and Chicago Social Science in the 1920s: A Neglected Tradition," *Journal of the History of the Behavioral Sciences*, 17 (July 1981), pp. 324-325.
16. Goff, pp. 175-176.
17. Schuessler, p. xi.
18. Goff, pp. 164-165.
19. Ibid., pp. 174-175.
20. Ibid., p. 169.
21. Ibid., p. 170.
22. Ibid., p. 171.
23. Edwin H. Sutherland and Harvey J. Locke, *Twenty Thousand Homeless Men: A Study of Unemployed Men in the Chicago Shelters* (Philadelphia: J.B. Lippincott, 1936), p. v.
24. Ibid., p. vi.
25. Ibid., pp. 113-143.
26. Edwin H. Sutherland, "Development of the Theory," in *Edwin H. Sutherland: On Analyzing Crime*, Karl Schuessler, ed. (Chicago: University of Chicago Press, 1973), p. 15.
27. Jon Snodgrass, "The Criminologist and His Criminal: The Case of Edwin H. Sutherland and Broadway Jones," *Issues in Criminology*, 8 (Spring 1973), p. 3.
28. Edwin H. Sutherland, *The Professional Thief* (Chicago: University of Chicago Press, 1937), p. vii.
29. Ibid., p. viii.
30. Snodgrass, "The Criminologist and His Criminal," p. 6.
31. Lyn H. Lofland, ed., "Reminiscences of Classic Chicago: The Blumer-Hughes Talk," *Urban Life*, 9 (October 1980), pp. 262-263.
32. Snodgrass, "The Criminologist and His Criminal," p. 6.
33. Ibid., p. 1.
34. Ned Polsky, *Hustlers, Beats, and Others* (Chicago: Aldine Publishing Company, 1967), p. 122, quoted in Snodgrass, "The Criminologist and His Criminal," p. 1.
35. Snodgrass, "The Criminologist and His Criminal," p. 5.
36. Ibid.
37. Sutherland, *The Professional Thief*, p. iv.
38. Edwin H. Sutherland, n.d., quoted in Snodgrass, "The Criminologist and His Criminal," p. 9.
39. Snodgrass, "The Criminologist and His Criminal," p. 10.

40. Sutherland, *The Professional Thief*, p. 205.
41. Snodgrass, "The Criminologist and His Criminal," pp. 4-5.
42. Sutherland, "Development of the Theory," p. 15.
43. Edwin H. Sutherland, *Principles of Criminology*, 2nd ed. (Philadelphia: J.B. Lippincott, 1934), pp. 51-52.
44. Sutherland, "Development of the Theory," p. 16.
45. Schuessler, p. xv.
46. Snodgrass, "The Criminologist and His Criminal," pp. 4-5.
47. Edwin H. Sutherland, *Principles of Criminology*, 3rd ed. (Philadelphia: J.B. Lippincott, 1939), p. 4.
48. Ibid., pp. 4-5.
49. Goff, p. 183.
50. Sutherland, *Principles of Criminology*, 2nd ed., pp. 48-49.
51. Ibid., pp. 64-67.
52. Ibid., p. 70.
53. Ibid.
54. Ibid. p. 71.
55. Edwin H. Sutherland, "Social Process in Behavior Problems," *Publications of the American Sociological Society*, 26 (1932), p. 56.
56. Ibid.
57. Charles Horton Cooley, *Social Process* (New York: Charles Scribner's Sons, 1918), p. 30.
58. Sutherland, "Social Process in Behavior Problems," pp. 56-57.
59. Ibid., p. 57.
60. Sutherland, "Development of the Theory," pp. 16-17.
61. Ibid. pp. 17-18.
62. Ibid. p. 16.
63. Ibid. p. 18.
64. Edwin H. Sutherland and Donald R. Cressey, *Criminology*, 10th ed. (Philadelphia: J.B. Lippincott, 1978), p. 66.
65. Sutherland, "Social Process in Behavior Problems," p. 56.
66. Ibid., p. 57.
67. Ibid., p. 58.
68. Cooley, p. 176, quoted in Sutherland, *Principles of Criminology* 2nd ed. p. 52.
69. Sutherland, "Social Process in Behavior Problems," p. 58.
70. Ibid., p. 59.
71. Ibid.
72. Ibid., pp. 59-60.
73. Ibid., p. 60.
74. Ibid.
75. Ibid., p. 60-61.
76. Jon Snodgrass, "The American Criminological Tradition: Portraits of Men and Ideology in a Discipline" (unpublished Ph.D. dissertation, University of Pennsylvania, 1972), p. 278.
77. Goff, pp. 184-185.
78. Ibid., p. 185.
79. Edwin H. Sutherland, Letter to Thorsten Sellin, 16 March 1935, quoted in Snodgrass, "The American Criminological Tradition," pp. 224-225.
80. Schuessler, p. xi.
81. Ibid., p. xxxiii.

6

The Development of the Theory

The first part of this chapter will recount the events leading to the first explicit statement of the theory of differential association in 1939. At the beginning we will see how Sutherland was influenced by Alfred R. Lindesmith's methodology of analytic induction. Once Sutherland had accepted this, he quickly abandoned multiple factor theory as unscientific and moved to develop a general theory of crime in keeping with the tenets of analytic induction. Second, we will learn how collaboration with Thorsten Sellin in writing *Culture Conflict and Crime* (1938) led Sutherland to use culture conflict as a general explanation of crime. Third, we will see how a question posed by a colleague at Indiana University, Frank Sweetser, prompted Sutherland to formulate the first explicit statement of the theory of differential association in *Principles of Criminology* (1939). The last part of this chapter will describe Sutherland's efforts during the 1940s to refine, improve, and apply his theory.

Development of the Theory, 1935-1939

When Sutherland arrived in Bloomington, Indiana, he became very active. Within four years he had published *Twenty Thousand Homeless Men* (1936), *The Professional Thief* (1937), the third edition of *Principles of Criminology* (1939), and seven articles and reports. In recognition of his scholarship and service to the profession he was elected president of the American Sociological Society in 1939. In 1940 he became the president of the Sociological Research Association. The SRA was founded in 1936 by Herbert Blumer, Roderick McKenzie, Edward Reuter, Stuart Rice, Kimball Young, Ellsworth Faris, George Lundberg, Robert Park, Ernest Burgess, Edwin Sutherland, and approximately forty other sociologists who wanted to establish a core group around which scientific sociology might develop. Even as the United States slid deeper into the morass of the Great

Depression, the Sociological Research Association dedicated itself loftily to research and avoided political activity. Its membership was limited to 100; new members were admitted only by majority vote of the entire association. In 1940 the SRA was a prestigious organization, and Sutherland's election to its presidency was a great honor granted him by his colleagues.[1] In 1941 he was made president of the Ohio Valley Sociological Society. As he entered his last decade of life, the profession bestowed its highest honors on him as a token of respect and appreciation.

Sutherland's coming to Indiana University in 1935 marked the beginning of an independent department of sociology there. Prior to this sociology had existed only as a joint department with economics, a pairing of disciplines that had begun in 1915. In 1935 the department of sociology at Indiana University consisted of only two sociologists, Sutherland and John H. Mueller, who also had arrived at Indiana in that year. In 1936 Sutherland lost no time in building a solid department, recruiting Harvey J. Locke, Alfred R. Lindesmith, and August B. Hollingshead. With the exception of Hollingshead, who received his Ph.D. from the University of Nebraska in 1935, all of the men in the deparmtent were graduates of the University of Chicago.

Harvey Locke and Sutherland had collaborated on *Twenty Thousand Homeless Men* while both were at Chicago. Locke arrived at Indiana in 1936 as an assistant professor. He stayed at Indiana until 1945 when he left for the University of Southern California. Locke's specialty was the sociology of marriage and the family. At Chicago he had worked closely in this area with Professor Ernest Burgess.[2] August Hollingshead was just twenty-nine years old when he joined Sutherland at Indiana. Over the next eleven years he rose in rank to full professor and, in 1947, left for Yale University to become professor of sociology and chair of the department. It was while he was at Indiana that he wrote his widely read book, *Elmtown's Youth*, which brought him prominence throughout the social sciences.[3]

Alfred R. Lindesmith and Analytic Induction

The third new sociologist attracted to Indiana by Sutherland in 1936 was Alfred R. Lindesmith. In 1932 he was a student in one of Sutherland's courses at the University of Chicago. After completing his course work there he came directly to Indiana University with the rank of instructor. Lindesmith spent his entire academic career at Indiana (1936-1975), where he was well liked and highly respected by his colleagues and students. Indiana University ultimately awarded him the title of university professor.[4]

Throughout his career Lindesmith was acknowledged as the leading sociological authority on drug addiction in the United States. His Ph.D. dissertation advanced a new theory on opiate addiction, which has stood up well to critical evaluation over the years. Unfortunately, due to the Depression and World War II, over a decade passed before it was published in 1947 under the title *Opiate Addiction*. Lindesmith explained his sociological theory of opiate addiction in these words:

> Addiction occurs when opiates are used to alleviate withdrawal distress, after this distress has been properly understood or interpreted, that is to say, after it has been represented to the individual in terms of the linguistic symbols and cultural patterns which have grown up around the opiate habit. If the individual fails to conceive of his distress as withdrawal distress brought about by the absence of opiates, he cannot become addicted, but if he does, addiction is quickly and permanently established through the further use of the drug.[5]

Lindesmith's work drew attention not only because of his theory, but also because of the methodological technique known as analytic induction that he used to develop it.

According to Lindesmith's methodology, a researcher's hypothesis should fit his facts for every case within its purview. Indeed, Lindesmith's conception of methodology encourages the researcher to seek cases with which to test his hypothesis. Theory development thus becomes a process involving numerous steps. Researchers first need to develop a rough definition of the behavior they wish to explain. Second, an initial hypothesis is developed to explain the behavior in question. Third, "one case is studied in the light of the hypothesis with the object of determining whether the hypothesis fits the facts in that case." Fourth, if the hypothesis does not fit the facts, the initial hypothesis must be modified to accommodate the negative case. "The negative case is viewed as a sign that something is wrong with the hypothesis. . . ." Fifth, the modified hypothesis is then tested against other cases, which may require its further modification. Sixth, this procedure of examining selected cases and modifying the hypothesis to accommodate negative cases is repeated until the researcher achieves what Donald Cressey calls "practical certainty" that a "universal relationship"[6] has been established.

Sutherland acknowledged his debt to Lindesmith for teaching him this conception of research methodology:

> [When] Lindesmith [came] to Indiana University . . . I became acquainted with his conception of methodology as developed in his study of drug addiction. According to this conception, a hypothesis should fit every case in the defined universe. . . . This methodology consists in searching for negative cases, one negative case disproving the hypothesis. Although this involves several cases, it is not concerned with averages, standard deviations, or coeffi-

cients of correlation. This conception of methodology assisted me greatly in formulating problems and in testing hypotheses.[7]

Sutherland's interpretation of Lindesmith's methodology is extreme: "This methodology consists in searching for negative cases, one negative case disproving the hypothesis." Sutherland's student Donald Cressey, the last to write a Ph.D. dissertation with him, also agrees with this position. "Should a person conduct research on a particular type of offender and find that the theory does not hold, then a revision of the theory is called for, provided the research actually tested the theory, or part of it."[8] The proof that Sutherland used Lindesmith's methodological technique is found not just in his acknowledgment of his indebtedness to him, but, more importantly, in the use he made of it as the theory of differential association was modified throughout the 1930s and 1940s.

Thorsten Sellin: *Culture Conflict and Crime*

In August 1936 Sutherland wrote in a letter to his friend Thorsten Sellin:

> I am opposed to an effort at this time to make criminology highly scientific (in the sense of universal propositions) because I think we will be trying to define things about which we do not have enough information. . . . My own position is much more eclectic and empirical: keep on getting information, searching for ideas and hypotheses by intimate contacts with criminals and with violators of nonlegal norms but do not subordinate this at present to a highly organized rational scheme.[9]

The year before (1935), the Social Science Research Council formed a two-person subcommittee on delinquency within the committee on personality and culture. Thorsten Sellin was named as chair and Sutherland as the second member. The Sellin-Sutherland correspondence suggests that both the SSRC and the two-person subcommittee had the Michael-Adler report very much in mind when the work began that eventuated in *Culture Conflict and Crime* in 1938. Sellin has written:

> The SSRC mandate was a headache for both of us. We were supposed to make criminology more "scientific"; how to do it was left up to us. In hunting for a focus we finally settled on "culture conflict," a not uncommon concept forty years ago. Ed felt that since I was chairman of the committee I should start the ball rolling even though neither of us had a clear idea of what the goal was. As it turned out, the onus of writing the monograph fell on me. The result was that instead of a dissertation on criminological theory with a new twist, it ended in an exercise in logic and scientific method. . . .[10]

Given Sutherland's position on the need for more information, ideas, and hypotheses before putting the stamp of "scientific" on criminology, he was not altogether pleased with Sellin's work. In fact, Sutherland wrote in a letter to Sellin: "Your paper is a statement of Mortimer Adler's position [i.e., the Michael-Adler report], though without his extreme demands and criticisms."[11] However, in a letter written to Karl Schuessler in 1972, Sellin expressed his belief that the subcommittee's effort to comply with the SSRC's mandate of the mid-1930s may have prodded Sutherland to do exactly what he was then reluctant to do and formulate his ideas on crime causation as formal propositions:

> One good thing may have come out of Ed's dissatisfaction with my production. I strongly suspect that this formulation of the differential association concept in the 1939 edition of the *Principles* crystallized out of his earnest efforts to set me straight.[12]

This statement is probably correct. Notwithstanding Sutherland's conviction about prematurely elevating criminology to the status of "science," he sensed as early as late 1936 that his more patient way may have been an epistemological dead end. "I am probably wasting my time in my method of research work, so that futility of the rationalistic approach does not constitute a very good basis of criticism."[13]

In regard to their conceptions of science, Sellin and Sutherland were not so far apart as Sutherland seemed to think, if his correspondence may be taken to represent his point of view. Sutherland appears to have set up two opposed conceptions of science, virtually unalterable. One formalistic, abstract, and based on armchair speculation; the other eclectic, empirical, and seemingly unguided by an explicit purpose. In contrast to Sutherland's position, Sellin saw the two men's views as not fundamentally in conflict. Sellin wrote:

> I am not sure of Adler's position, so I cannot judge the extent to which I have approached it or identified myself with it. If my assumption that the scientific method is applicable to the study of social phenomena commits me to it, I am afraid there is no recourse. The burden of Michael and Adler's book is, however, [their lack of] sympathy with the struggle to achieve [scientific knowledge]. I, however, regard science as the result of a stumbling and long pursuit, but I don't think you can get there solely by indiscriminate stumbling—you have to stumble with a purpose. Your opposition "to an effort at this time to make criminology highly scientific (in the sense of universal propositions) because we will be trying to define things about which we do not have enough information" is not quite clear to me. We cannot make anything scientific by verbalization, of course. . . .But the moment we get *some* information we are compelled to think in terms of comparisons and only when such comparisons rest on good theory—sound in the sense that it

works with concepts *assumed* to possess universality; stumbling in the sense that it is hypothetical until completely validated—can we make progress.

I have no criticism to make of your "eclectic and empirical" position; in fact, I see nothing in it which is out of harmony with my own. . . . It is important, however, to keep [the goal of a highly rationalized scheme] in mind and if we do, constant re-examination of our results in terms of integration becomes necessary. No rational scheme, at present, is therefore anything more than an effort at orientation. In other words, I don't believe that your own standpoint on close examination is any less "rational" than the one expressed in my analysis. . . . I don't for a moment believe that science can be made in the armchair (that, I am told, is an extreme characterization of Adler's position) but a little more armchair than many criminologists have used might have saved a lot of energy and have improved the formulation of the research projects and, therefore, the results.[14]

Sellin may have been overly modest when he wrote that Sutherland's formulation of differential association in the 1939 edition of *Principles of Criminology* may have resulted from Sutherland's efforts to set Sellin straight. Sutherland wrote:

Sellin and I were appointed members of a committee of the Social Science Research Council to organize a report on a nuclear problem in criminology. We selected culture conflict as the problem and spent considerable time organizing the data and problems of criminal behavior around that concept. Although Sellin is almost entirely responsible for the report, it had an additional influence on me.[15]

The "additional influence" may very well have been Sellin's persuasion of Sutherland to accept the methodological necessity of stating his ideas in propositional form if criminology was to make significant headway as a science. The Sellin-Sutherland collaboration had another influence on Sutherland aside from the hard thinking on theory building and research methodology that Sellin's argument prompted: an uncertainty that confronted him as he pondered the meaning of culture conflict and its significance for a theory of criminal behavior. In a letter to Sellin written on February 5, 1938, just a few months before *Culture Conflict and Crime* was published he wrote:

There has been some analysis and doubt as to the concept "culture conflict." When are cultures in conflict? . . . I am recording the question, so that we may say the point has been recognized. I think there is an answer to the question, but in general I have shifted to "social disorganization" as preferable to "culture conflict."

[I]t seems to me that the relatively low rate of the large [immigrant] colonies is due to "isolation" from conflicting patterns. They live their own life in the midst of an American city almost as in their home community. Consequently they have few conflicts. Conflicts must grow out of cultural contacts. Moreover, the family and the neighborhood in such situations work together consistently in the direction of control of the individual member, while in the smaller [immigrant] groups, there may be no such harmony between the patterns of these two primary groups, and consequently there may be a high delinquency rate. In other words, it seems to me that the cultural conflict should be regarded as taking the form of such divergences between the smaller groups as well as in the larger national groups. The probable conflict of cultures does not consist merely in the fact that the law of one group says thus-and-this, while the law of the other group says so-and-so. Rather more important I believe is the fact that the informal codes differ on hundreds of other things, thus undermining the legal codes of both groups.[16]

And, indeed, in the 1939 edition of *Principles of Criminology* Sutherland did write that although "cultural conflict is the underlying cause of differential association and therefore of systematic criminal behavior . . . social disorganization is the basic cause of systematic criminal behavior."[17]

Frank Loel Sweetser

The department of sociology at Indiana University—Sutherland, Mueller, Locke, Hollingshead, and Lindesmith its members—remained intact until the outbreak of World War II. Only one change occurred in the department's personnel during the late 1930s: the addition of Frank L. Sweetser in 1937. Added to Sutherland's association with Thorsten Sellin on the SSRC project and his enthusiastic reception of Lindesmith's concept of methodology, Sweetser acted as a third influence on Sutherland, moving him to formulate an explicit, positive hypothesis on crime causation. Sutherland wrote:

> Some of us organized a non-credit seminar which met monthly in Indianapolis for two years and was attended by members of the professional staff of the penal institutions and by Lindesmith, Sweetser, and me. We were concerned principally with neighborhood influences on delinquency. One evening as we drove home from Indianapolis Sweetser asked, "Why doesn't the explanation of juvenile delinquency in a slum area apply in principle to murders in the South?" That question was the specific occasion for the formulation of the statement of differential association. That statement was mimeographed, distributed to the Indianapolis seminar and to some of my classes, criticized, reformulated, and then included in the first chapter of the 1939 edition of my criminology.[18]

Sutherland's anecdote on the "birth" of differential association has been confirmed by Sweetser. In a letter written in June 1982 Sweetser states:

While I can't claim to remember the specific incident on the road between Bloomington and Indianapolis, I do recall very distinctly that Sutherland, Lindesmith and I discussed the issue of what came to be called differential association as it applied to delinquents and neighborhoods extensively and intensively on more than one ride back to Bloomington through the night. . . . Out of these discussions came the idea for my dissertation, on which I began in 1939, and . . . Sutherland's formulation of the theory of differential association. I suspect [Henry] McKay was right, and that the germ of the theory was already in the *Criminology:* the conversations in the car (and elsewhere) very likely served as a catalyst.[19]

Sweetser's dissertation, "Neighborhood Acquaintance and Association: A Study of Personal Neighborhoods," explored the general question, "What is the nature of person-to-person relations among neighbors in urbanized residential areas?"[20] This broad interest in the nature of personal relationships within cities was eventually narrowed to a study of what Sweetser labelled "personal neighborhoods." By this phrase he meant "*the circle* of neighbors, outside the immediate family, with whom an individual maintains a specific person-to-person *relationship*. This focus constitutes a special type of neighborhood concept (within the more general concept of neighborhood as an area), and the term *personal neighborhood* is applied to it."[21] In a letter, Sweetser explained that "[t]o me, the concepts of personal neighborhood and differential association have always seemed the structural and dynamic aspects of the same idea."[22]

In defining the individual's personal neighborhood as the circle of neighbors with whom he maintains primary relationships, Sweetser believed he was offering an explanation for the finding that a percentage of children, but not all, who grow up in high-delinquency areas become delinquent. The personal neighborhood of one individual is not identical to that of another—even though each may live in the same area, indeed in the same household.

"Personal neighborhood," later to be characterized as "neighborhood network," was the missing link in the chain of theoretical attempts to explain the occurrence of delinquency. While books such as *Delinquency Areas, The Jack Roller*, and *The Natural History of a Delinquent Career* presented a convincing description of delinquency areas and the development of delinquent careers, Shaw and McKay gave relatively less attention to the fact that many children grew up in these areas without ever becoming delinquent.

Sweetser wrote:

The theory that the delinquents are produced by the transmission to them of a neighborhood culture which is delinquent is satisfactory so far as it goes, but it leaves unanswered the question as to why some of the children in the area become delinquent while others do not. If, however it is recognized in addition that delinquency areas are law abiding areas as well, and that each inhabitant associates with some but not all others, then the answer to that question seems obvious: children whose. . . . personal neighborhoods include many delinquents and few law-abiders become delinquent; children whose . . . personal neighborhoods include many law-abiders and few delinquents become law-abiders.[23]

The discovery that neighborhoods are organized both for and against law-abiding behavior was not Sweetser's alone. Before he began research for his dissertation (1939), the third edition of *Principles of Criminology* already lay in the hands of Sutherland's publisher. In that edition he wrote that "society is composed of various groups with varied cultures. These differences in culture are found in respect to many values and . . . [t]hey exist, also, with reference to the values which the laws are designed to protect. . . . This criminal culture is as real as lawful culture and is much more prevalent than is usually believed."[24]

In 1939 Sutherland believed culture conflict was the "underlying" cause of systematic criminal behavior. This is not to say, however, that he thought culture conflict was bad per se. On the contrary, he wrote that "differences in culture . . . are generally regarded as desirable."[25] It is possible that writing in an impersonal, scholarly, third-person style prevented Sutherland from stating that he had come to recognize most forms of culture conflict as desirable. Earlier, he believed that any kind of culture conflict caused crime, but one of his graduate students, Mary Bess (Owen) Cameron, convinced him to restrict the concept to conflict over definitions of criminal behavior. He called this restricted conception the "principle of specificity in culture conflict," an idea that Sweetser described in his dissertation.[26]

Sweetser obviously saw his work as further evidence in support of Sutherland's theory of differential association. It is equally obvious that his perception of the personal neighborhood was guided by Sutherland's earlier work on the differential association within conflicting cultures that is the hallmark of modern, city-dwellers:

> The parallel between this conclusion [i.e., "children whose . . . personal neighborhoods include many delinquents and few law-abiders become delinquent; children whose . . . personal neighborhoods include many law-abiders and few delinquents become law-abiders], and E. H. Sutherland's theory that criminal (or delinquent) behavior is caused by differential association with criminals (or delinquents) is clear. Since one of these ideas emerged from a primary interest in delinquent and criminal behavior, and the other from a primary interest in neighborly relations, it would seem in addition that the close parallel affords corroborative evidence both for the above conclusion and for Sutherland's theory.[27]

Principles of Criminology (1939)

By the end of the 1930s Sutherland's ideas on crime causation had crystallized to the point where he allowed his friends Henry McKay, Hans
Riemer, and Harvey Locke to persuade him to place his theory in the first
chapter of *Principles of Criminology*.[28] Such prominent display of the theory made Sutherland uneasy because he "knew that every criminological
theory which had lifted its head had been cracked down by everyone except
its author."[29] In addition to this, the theory was changing "rapidly and
frequently," as his presidential address given at the annual dinner of the
Ohio Valley Sociological Society in April 1942 reveals. Only three years
after the theory had been unveiled, Sutherland took the opportunity to
relate in detail the changes in his thinking that made a major revision
already necessary.

The first explicit statement of the theory of differential association appears on pages 4-9 in the 1939 edition of *Principles of Criminology*.
Sutherland proclaimed his theory "tentative" and stated in it the form of
seven propositions.

> First, the processes which result in systematic criminal behavior are funda-
> mentally the same in form as the processes which result in systematic lawful
> behavior.
>
> Second, systematic criminal behavior is determined in a process of associa-
> tion with those who commit crimes, just as systematic lawful behavior is
> determined in a process of association with those who are law-abiding.
>
> Third, differential association is the specific causal process in the develop-
> ment of systematic criminal behavior.
>
> Fourth, the chance that a person will participate in systematic criminal be-
> havior is determined roughly by the frequency and consistency of his con-
> tacts with the patterns of criminal behavior.
>
> Fifth, individual differences among people in respect to personal charac-
> teristics or social situations cause crime only as they affect differential asso-
> ciation or frequency and consistency of contacts with criminal patterns.
>
> Sixth, cultural conflict is the underlying cause of differential association and
> therefore of systematic criminal behavior.
>
> Seventh, social disorganization is the basic cause of systematic criminal be-
> havior.[30]

Sutherland considered social disorganization to be the general condition
of modern society and cultural conflict its most apparent symptom. In this
sense, social disorganization is the "basic cause" of cultural conflict, which,
in its turn, is the "underlying cause" of systematic criminal behavior.

Each of these propositions was accompanied by a paragraph that amplified and clarified the idea contained in the proposition. Some of these were quite short, while others filled more than a page. For example, the first proposition is followed by the comment that "[i]f criminality were specifically determined by inheritance, the laws and principles of inheritance would be the same for criminal behavior and for lawful behavior. . . . Criminal behavior differs from lawful behavior in the standards by which it is judged but not in the principles of the genetic processes."[31] Sutherland believed that systematic criminal behavior was the result of social learning or sociological processes and not genetics or biological processes.[32]

The second proposition essentially reiterates the first. Sutherland's commentary includes these thoughts:

> Any person can learn any pattern of behavior he is able to execute. He inevitably assimilates such behavior from the surrounding culture. . . . This proposition, stated negatively, is that a person does not participate in systematic criminal behavior by inheritance. No individual inherits tendencies which inevitably make him criminal or inevitably make him law-abiding.[33]

The second proposition is therefore not only redundant, it is also tautological. Sutherland writes: "Since criminal behavior is thus developed in association with criminals it means that crime is the cause of crime."[34] This is no more (or less) insightful than the folk adage "Birds of a feather flock together." The only difference between "birds of a feather" and "those who participate in systematic criminal behavior" is that birds flock together on the basis of species, or genetic similarity, which is a biological process, whereas criminals associate together on the basis of social learning, which is a sociological process.

The third proposition—"differential association is the specific causal process in the development of systematic criminal behavior"—suggests, perhaps unintentionally, that criminality is the result of *two* kinds of association. In the first instance, Sutherland says: "The principles of the process of association by which criminal behavior develops are the same as the principles of the process by which lawful behavior develops, but the contents of the patterns presented in association differ."[35] This statement suggests that "patterns of criminal behavior" is the specific causal process. Indeed, he went on to write, "For that reason it is called differential association."[36] But the very next sentence appears to contradict this idea. "The association which is of primary importance in criminal behavior is association with *persons* who engage in systematic criminal behavior" (emphasis added).[37] Sutherland considered two distinct expressions as the "specific causal process in the development of systematic criminal behavior."

Whether he meant differential association with "patterns of criminal behavior" or "persons who engage in systematic criminal behavior" is not made clear. The problem may lie in the lack of precision in his choice of words. Or it may be that Sutherland lacked clarity of thought at this time, a more likely conclusion.

The fourth proposition stated that the "chance" or probability that a person will participate in systematic criminal behavior is determined by the "frequency" and the "consistency" of his contacts with the "patterns of criminal behavior." Sutherland asserted that it was impossible for an individual to come into contact *only* with lawful behavior, or *only* with criminal behavior and that the actual condition for all of us falls somewhere between these two extremes. Consequently, "[t]he ratio of criminal acts to lawful acts by a person is roughly the same as the ratio of the contacts with the criminal and with the lawful behavior of others."[38]

A criminal identity and career resulted, Sutherland believed, from a "long series of . . . experiences [with contacts with the criminal behavior of others]," but a single experience may be the "turning point" in a career:

> A boy who is arrested and convicted is thereby publicly defined as a criminal. Thereafter his associations with lawful people are restricted and he is thrown into association with other delinquents. On the other hand a person who is consistently criminal is not defined as law-abiding by a single lawful act. Every person is expected to be law-abiding, and lawful behavior is taken for granted because the lawful culture is dominant, more extensive and more pervasive than the criminal culture.[39]

Frank Tannenbaum's criminology textbook, *Crime and the Community*, was published the year before Sutherland wrote these words. In it he described the labelling process whereby some, but not all, who engage in unlawful behavior are singled out for special stigmatizing treatment. Having been "publicly defined as a criminal," a person's "ratio of contacts with the criminal and with the lawful behavior of others"[40] is likely to be altered to the extent that a criminal identity is formed and leads to the pursuit of a criminal career. Tannenbaum referred to this process as the "dramatization of evil." Tannenbaum described this process as follows:

> The first dramatization of "evil" which separates the child out of his group for specialized treatment plays a greater role in making the criminal than perhaps any other experience. It cannot be too often emphasized that for the child the whole situation has become different. He now lives in a different world. He has been tagged. A new and hitherto non-existent environment has been precipitated out for him.
>
> The process of making the criminal, therefore, is a process of tagging, defining, identifying, segregating, describing, emphasizing, making conscious

and self-conscious; it becomes a way of stimulating, suggesting, emphasizing, and evolving the very traits that are complained of.[41]

At the end of chapter two Sutherland recommended Tannenbaum's textbook to the readers of *Principles of Criminology.*

The fifth proposition—"individual differences among people in respect to personal characteristics or social situations cause crime only as they affect differential association or frequency and consistency of contacts with criminal patterns"—resulted from two bases. First, it was becoming increasingly clear that mental traits and social situations per se were uncorrelated with criminal behavior. Second, Sutherland had a strong antipathy for psychiatry. Schuessler believes this attitude was possibly acquired from W. I. Thomas,[42] whom Janowitz described as "fiercely anti-Freudian."[43] Thomas tried to develop through his "four wishes" an adequate alternative approach to the Freudian theory, which posited deep-seated and unconscious emotional complexes as the seat of human motivation. The four wishes were first presented in the paper "The Persistence of Primary-group Norms" (1917). At that time Thomas's conception of human behavior leaned somewhat toward a bio-psychological reductionism. However, in *The Polish Peasant* (1918-20) the four wishes were virtually synonymous with attitudes, were defined as partly biological and partly social, and thus changed character in this book. Here Thomas emphasized their role in social control and deemphasized their linkage to the "instincts" of hate and fear. "Society, through suitable appeals to the wishes as well as through punishments and rewards relating to their expression, can achieve effective social control since it is the essence of the wishes that they must be satisfied socially."[44] Thomas's final formulation of the four wishes in *The Unadjusted Girl* (1923) defined them as "forces which impel to action." Throughout the 1920s the four wishes were very popular in American sociology; they provided a theory of motivation that granted an independent disciplinary status to sociology vis-a-vis psychiatry and psychology.

As the four wishes gained in popularity within sociology, Thomas himself began to assume a detached attitude toward them. Apparently he hesitated to attach a great deal of importance to any of the various formulations he had given to the wishes, and by the middle of the period he was beginning to shift his emphasis to a "situational" approach, away from a theory of motivation with its suggestion that something *within* the individual, rather than without, incites a person to action.[45] The objective was to discover, rather than to merely assume, the behavioral determinants, some of which might be simple organic drives such as hunger or sex and some of which might spring from interpersonal relationships.

The situational approach represented an improvement over the four wishes, Thomas believed, in the sense that it was empirical and not merely based on "common sense" explanations of human behavior. By 1928 Thomas developed his famous concept of the definition of the situation: "If men define situations as real, they are real in their consequences."[46] That is:

> Behavior is determined by certain conditions, which comprise the "situation," including the state of the organism, the objective environment, and the subjective manner in which these are perceived, evaluated, and made conscious. Apart from sheer reflex, human action is preceded by this process of defining the situation, and even though the basis of action is subjective, the results are not.[47]

Sutherland's bias against psychiatry is perhaps most readily apparent in his later work on laws dealing with sexual psychopaths. While he was often described as a modest, gentle, soft-spoken scholar and gentleman, such topics as white-collar crime and psychiatry could raise Sutherland's ire. He enjoyed nothing quite so much as deflating pretention and the self-serving claims of rivals. Not long before his death, Sutherland wrote the following on psychiatry and psychiatrists; words all the more forceful when one considers that they were written for a professional journal in the late 1940s:

> Certain psychiatrists have stated that they are interested in the sexual psychopath laws principally as a precedent; they believe that all or practically all criminals are psychopathic, that all should be treated as patients, and that psychiatrists should have a monopoly on professional advice to the courts. These laws are dangerous precisely from this point of view; they could be passed over in silence otherwise, as a product of hysteria. The question is whether psychiatrists have a monopoly on knowledge of human personality and human behavior which warrants their nomination as "the experts" in the diagnosis and treatment of criminals.

> Other disciplines, such as psychology, social work, and sociology, require as much training as does psychiatry, and have points of view, hypotheses, and techniques which should be used, together with those of psychiatry, in the diagnosis and treatment of sex offenders and other offenders. At many points the theories of one of these disciplines are in conflict with the theories of the other disciplines, and one theory has as much scientific validity as the other. Moreover, the question of importance is not whether an offender has a low I.Q. or unstable emotions, but how this trait is related to the violation of the law and to a process of rehabilitation. There is no more reason for turning over to the psychiatrist the complete supervision of a criminal who is found to be psychopathic than for turning over to the dentist the complete supervision of a criminal who is found to have dental cavities. If the official agencies of the state are to use professional advice, the advisors should represent all the branches of knowledge and should be on an equal footing.[48]

Statements of this kind demonstrate Sutherland's loyalty to his discipline.

He was quick to jump to sociology's defense whenever he perceived a threat from outsiders. As a master of critical and searching analysis he fulfilled the role of vigilant guardian superbly. As a result he won the unflagging support of his colleagues.

Louis Wirth and Culture Conflict

We will recall that the sixth and seventh propositions in Sutherland's theory of criminal behavior in 1939 claimed culture conflict was the "underlying cause" of differential association and therefore of "systematic criminal behavior," and that social disorganization is the "basic cause" of "systematic criminal behavior." In "Development of the Theory" (1942) Sutherland credits Louis Wirth (1897-1952), his colleague at the University of Chicago between 1931 and 1935, for suggesting the value of culture conflict for a sociological theory of criminal behavior.

In 1914 Louis Wirth entered the University of Chicago, where he received the A.B., M.A., and Ph.D. degrees. Wirth was very much the product of the Chicago tradition of Small, Thomas, Mead, Park and Burgess. His European background and command of the German language made Max Weber's work accessible to him during his graduate school years. Park and Burgess, perhaps more than anyone else at Chicago, guided Wirth's graduate studies. His lifelong interests were primarily in urbanism, the ecology of human communities, race and international relations. Culture conflict seemed a particularly useful concept in understanding all of these phenomena.[49]

The preeminent concern of Chicago sociology in the 1920s was the city. Large industrial cities, populated by native-born Americans moving to the urban centers from the countryside, and waves of immigrants from the agricultural regions of Europe, were looked upon as "natural laboratories" by the Chicago sociologists. Chicago was and remains to this day a mosaic of highly segregated communities. "Little Italy," "Little Sicily", Germantown, Chinatown, the Polish district, and the Jewish and the black ghettos were not merely colorful images invented by journalists and other chroniclers of the time, but genuine ethnic settlements based on shared cultural identities. These urban groupings were the subject of intense interest in the 1920s and 1930s, "and a practice soon developed at Chicago, as elsewhere, of arranging class visits to such communities. Term papers and dissertations naturally followed, and in time, research volumes."[50]

Wirth's master's thesis, written in 1925, was titled "Culture Conflicts in the Immigrant Family." The next year he completed his doctoral dissertation on *The Ghetto*, which was published in 1928. Wirth's interest in the Jewish ghetto had several bases. First, he was a Jewish immigrant from

Germany as well as a sociologist deeply committed to social reform and individual freedom. He strongly believed that a "science of human behavior was not only possible but indispensable to social betterment."[51] On this subject he wrote:

> Our action has so far outrun our knowledge that we must concentrate our efforts for some time to come on fundamental research concerning the nature and functioning of prejudice and antipathy, on problems of discrimination, on segregation, and on intergroup tensions and conflicts that furnish a more reliable basis for social action.[52]

Second, Jewish communities were different in two important ways from most ethnic districts. Many of their members had come from European cities rather than agricultural regions. Unlike peasants, these urban immigrants were familiar with life in a city—with its commercial values, impersonality, and heterogeneity. Over centuries, as members of a despised religion, they had developed "customs and institutions to protect themselves and their cultural heritage from the destructive influences of the surrounding societies, and some of these protective devices were transplanted to their communities in the cities of the United States."[53]

Third, Wirth had an interest in the "natural history" of ethnic districts in general equal to his interest in the experience of Jews in European and American ghettos in particular. Given his definition of sociology as the "study of what is true of man by virtue of the fact that everywhere and always he lives a group life,"[54] Wirth wanted to contribute to the sociological knowledge of urban ethnic districts as a universal phenomenon. He discovered that Jewish ghettos in the United States differed from their European counterparts. In the first place, European ghettos had built up a much more stable social structure over the five hundred-year history of their existence than had those in the United States. Perhaps more important, the relatively greater religious and social tolerance within the United States made it possible for members of the Jewish ghetto to migrate to "second-settlement Jewish areas and afterward [scatter] into the general population and [undergo] assimilation."[55] In 1931 Wirth published an article in *Social Forces* titled "Culture Conflict and Misconduct." Culture conflict was not a new concept, but Wirth's use of it to analyze deviant behavior was an innovation.

In 1942 Sutherland wrote that he "undoubtedly owed much to Wirth's 1931 paper."[56] Indeed, culture conflict became an important concept for Sutherland's understanding of crime. Early in the 1930s he supervised the work on a dissertation on crime in China. The argument of the dissertation was that crime is due to cultural conflict. The dissertation was completed in 1934 under the title "Crime in Relation to Social Change in China." The 1934, 1939, and 1947 editions of *Principles of Criminology* contain citations from this work. In the 1939 edition Sutherland wrote:

> In preliterate and peasant societies the influences surrounding a person were steady, uniform, harmonious, and consistent. China until recently exemplified this situation perfectly except in a few of the coast cities. The individual was surrounded by all of his relatives and this larger family determined his career and his ambitions. His principal satisfactions were found in co-operation with that group, which was considered as extending beyond his own life into the distant future. Within this group he had perfect individual security, for the group cared for him in case of sickness, accident, old age, insanity, or other emergency and this care involved no stigma or disgrace whatsoever. This large family, moreover, was supported by the surrounding community which also was harmonious in its traditional culture. In that situation the behavior of the individual was almost completely predictable, for he had only one pattern to follow and only extraordinary emergencies could induce him to invent a new mode of behavior. The local group had little contact with outsiders, since the community was a self-supporting and self-contained society. Within this group almost no crimes were committed, and the occasional crimes were chiefly confined to crimes committed by non-residents upon the members of the group, or crimes committed by members of the group upon non-members. The standards of the outside political society meant little within this group and national loyalty was not significant.
>
> The industrial revolution in China is now producing the same consequences that it has in Western countries, though the change from familism to individualism is much more abrupt.
>
> The effects of mobility and culture conflict become more apparent when an isolated country is suddenly brought by mobility into contact with the rest of the world. This happened in China within the last fifty years, and has been accompanied by remarkable changes in criminality in that country. The old social relations and standards of behavior which had been quite adequate for control while the country was relatively isolated have proved very inadequate in the last generation when many foreigners have lived in China and when Chinese have gone to foreign countries, and when in addition the cultures of other communities have been introduced into China through impersonal means.[57]

The seventh—and last—proposition constituting the 1939 version of differential association suggested that social disorganization was the "basic cause" of "systematic criminal behavior." Sutherland believed "[c]ultural conflict is a specific aspect of social disorganization and in that sense the two concepts are names for smaller and larger aspects of the same thing."[58] The concept "social disorganization," of course, was part of Thomas and Znaniecki's theory of social change as presented in *The Polish Peasant*. But Sutherland wrote that social disorganization was an idea he had "borrowed from Shaw and McKay."[59] By social disorganization Sutherland meant a condition in which individual or small-group interests did not lead to collective reaction by the general society against a threat to values that they regarded as vital. For the most part, a "law-abiding person is more interested in his own immediate personal projects than in abstract social welfare or justice."[60] The consequence is that a disorganized society permits crime to persist in systematic form simply because it has not stirred itself to resist its presence. "Since the law-abiding culture is dominant and more extensive, it could overcome systematic crime if organized for that purpose."[61]

Sutherland described one such example:

> When a gang starts in a disorganized district of a city it keeps growing and other gangs develop. But when a delinquent gang started on a business street adjacent to Hyde Park, a good residential district in Chicago, the residents became concerned, formed an organization, and decided that the best way to protect themselves was by providing a club house and recreational facilities for the delinquents. This practically eliminated the gangs. Therefore, whether systematic delinquency does or does not develop is determined not only by associations that people make with the criminals, but also by the reactions of the rest of society toward systematic criminal behavior. If the society is organized with reference to the values expressed in the law, the crime is eliminated; if it is not organized, crime persists and develops. The opposition of the society may take the form of punishment, or reformation, or of prevention.[62]

In summary, differential association in 1939 was stated in the form of seven propositions that explained "systematic criminal behavior" in terms of social disorganization. That is, Sutherland thought of social disorganization as the underlying cause of cultural conflict with reference to values that laws were designed to protect. If it were not for social disorganization and cultural conflict with regard to the law, association with those who commit "systematic crime" would not exist. Some small, isolated societies may still exist where this is the case. In the past there were undoubtedly many more such societies—China, for example. But the forces of modernity lessen the likelihood that they will continue to exist. The result will be the development and spread of "systematic criminal behavior" until the point is reached "[w]hen a society or a smaller group develops a unified interest in crimes which touch its fundamental and common values,"[63] and then organizes to eliminate or at least greatly reduce such crimes.

Between these two empirical rarities—societies in which "systematic crime" is unknown and societies that have successfully organized to eliminate it—the vast majority of human societies will experience such crime to the extent that either the forces organized for or against "systematic crime" hold sway. Further, so long as individuals within societies marked by social disorganization and cultural conflict come into contact with those who commit "systematic crime," the process of differential association will insure and spawn its continuation.

Development of the Theory, 1940-1950

Almost immediately after the publication of the third edition of *Principles of Criminology*, Sutherland began to work at improving his theory of differential association. We know this from two articles he wrote in the 1940s that described his intellectual growth during the five years following the appearance of the 1939 edition. Neither article was published during Sutherland's lifetime; both were first printed in *The Sutherland Papers*, edited by Albert Cohen, Alfred Lindesmith, and Karl Schuessler in 1956. All three men were Sutherland's colleagues at Indiana University; Cohen and Schuessler were also among his most distinguished graduate students there. These articles are also found in *Edwin H. Sutherland: On Analyzing Crime* (1973), edited by Karl Schuessler.

The first article, "Development of the Theory," was an address given by Sutherland as retiring president of the Ohio Valley Sociological Society at its annual dinner (April 1942). It was a personal account (Sutherland called it a "biography") of the history of differential association. "It is a story of confusion, inconsistencies, delayed recognition of implicit meanings, and of much borrowing from and stimulation by colleagues and students."[64] Sutherland continued:

> The hypothesis has changed rapidly and frequently, for which I am doubly thankful, first because the hypothesis at any rate is not dead, and second because I have been able to retract many ideas about it before they were published. . . . And so, this is my account of how my theory of differential association has been produced by my own differential association.[65]

The second article, which Sutherland's editors titled "Critique of the Theory," apparently was intended for circulation only among Sutherland's closest associates. Within this critical yet sympathetic circle, he referred to his essay as "The Swan Song for Differential Association." This was merely an example of his puckish humor, for neither he nor they were disillusioned with the theory. Indeed, it may be seen as a sign of confidence that Sutherland would direct his formidable critical powers toward his own theoretical formulation. As his editor wrote, "the paper is Sutherland's own effort to make the strongest case for the critics of the theory."[66]

Sutherland's thinking changed rapidly in a number of ways during the years immediately following the publication of the third edition of his criminology textbook. One of the changes involved his conceptualization of social disorganization. By the end of the 1930s a number of sociologists were becoming dissatisfied with this concept. It was often used in a tautological manner, as both the explanation of certain social phenomena, such as mental illness, delinquency, broken homes and alcoholism, and as the social phenomenon to be explained. Additionally, social disorganization carried an ideological charge. Rather than merely denoting some aspect of the social environment, social disorganization came to represent that which was most abhorrent to those who feared and disliked the city. In 1941 Louis Wirth's article "Ideological Aspects of Social Disorganization" made this point. Just two years later the same theme appeared in C. Wright Mills's influential article "The Professional Ideology of Social Pathologists," which was published in the *American Journal of Sociology.*

Sutherland might have felt the sting of recognition in these two articles. Remember that he once wrote "I loathe Chicago as a place in which to live almost as much as I do New York City."[67] As a result he soon decided to abandon social disorganization for another term, differential social organization, "at the suggestion of Albert K. Cohen."[68] This new concept was chosen partly to avoid the evaluative notion that "their" social organization is disorganized, while "ours" is not. Sutherland also thought "differential social organization" better conveyed the idea that society is two-minded about crime—one part being organized for criminal activities, the other organized against them.

> This concept was designed to answer the question, Why does not criminal behavior, once initiated, increase indefinitely until everyone participates in it? The answer was: Several criminals perfect an organization and with organization their crimes increase in frequency and seriousness; in the course of time this arouses a narrower or broader group which organizes itself against crime, and this tends to reduce crimes. The crime rate at a particular time is a resultant of these opposed organizations.[69]

While Sutherland worked hard on developing his theory in the early 1940s, events outside the small world of American sociological criminology were making themselves felt even in Bloomington, Indiana. The Second World War raged on in the Pacific and in Europe. During the war most students and faculty members enlisted in the armed forces. Sutherland thought the quality of the work in the department of sociology had fallen off somewhat.[70] The department, which had been very stable in the late 1930s, began to change as the war ended and the students and younger faculty members returned. The new members of the department of sociology were Dinko Tomasic, Anselm L. Strauss, and Irwin Smigel. In 1947 two of Sutherland's most able graduate students, Karl Schuessler and Albert K. Cohen, joined the department. When Schuessler finished work for his doctorate at Indiana University he was appointed a member of the faculty. Cohen received his M.A. from Indiana University, but earned the Ph.D. from Harvard University in 1951. Although Schuessler and Cohen had earlier been Sutherland's students, he considered them, after they returned to Indiana University as faculty, to be valued colleagues whose critical judgments helped shape the development of his theory of differential association. Perhaps Sutherland's greatest strength as a teacher lay in his ability to take his students seriously as young scholars. He encouraged even beginning master's students to challenge his ideas. Sutherland brought them into the process of advancing criminology. He fired their imaginations and the most able among them responded in kind.

Sutherland's teaching style in his graduate seminars and tutorials combined an innate modesty about his own ideas, intellectual honesty, and a natural authority based on his reputation as a complete master of his field. The result was a no-holds-barred examination of "what other criminologists had done or were doing. . . . Surprisingly, he was most critical of his own theory of differential association. In his classes he absolutely tore the theory apart."[71] One of his former graduate students recalls:

> In his graduate seminars, Sutherland was noted for his ruthless criticism of all theories of criminal behavior, including his own. . . . A regular question on Sutherland's examinations required students to criticize his theory of differential association and to suggest how it could be improved. . . . If the student criticism had any merit, Sutherland attempted to integrate it into the theory that was under discussion.[72]

Sutherland's openness to criticism from fellow sociologists stands in sharp contrast to his vigilance against attacks from rivals outside the discipline. This is another instance of his eagerness to promote sociology and gain for it the respect and recognition he believed it deserved. Sutherland worked his influence on a generation of sociologists eager to develop a scientific sociology. His pedagogical values ("informal, collaborative, egalitarian and supportive")[73] were highly compatible with science building. Albert Cohen described the intellectual environment at Indiana University during the Sutherland years in a letter to Jon Snodgrass:

> It was not only that we felt that *Sutherland* was at the frontier; we felt that *we* were at the frontier. Although most of us were just beginning graduate students, we felt that we were participating in this work of pushing back the frontiers. I believe that any of Sutherland's students of those days will tell you that Sutherland, for all of his tenacity to his views, was never overbearing, never didactic, never arrogant. He invariably treated his students with respect, never humiliated them, always made them feel that we were partners in

a quest. This did wonders for our own sense of professional identity and competence. It made us think of ourselves as something more than students. It is one thing for a professor to engage his students in collective criticism of some other person's work or ideas. It is another thing for him to build his seminars around the work that he himself is doing, and to define for them their task as that of evaluating, criticizing, correcting, and extending his own ideas. His modesty was real, but his talents were large enough that our respect for him was never diminished.

It is also important, I am convinced, that we were not just a set of students surrounding a great man. We formed a real intellectual—*Gemeinschaft*. I suppose the smallness of the department, as well as Sutherland's distinctive role, had something to do with this. In any case, there were about eight of us who lived and breathed sociology. We ate together, drank beer together, some of us lived together, and we talked all the time, and mostly we talked about the burning issues of criminology. We taught one another; in a way we engaged in a perpetual seminar in which Sutherland was always present, if only in spirit. This is not altogether a metaphor, because Sutherland was, in fact, always accessible. I for one (possibly more privileged than some of the others but only in degree) felt free to drop in to his office or at his house at any time to continue our conversations. I submit that, for young budding sociologists, this was a very different kind of experience than is available to most graduate students today.[74]

Principles of Criminology (1947)

The influence of his students and colleagues and his own critical analysis of the 1939 statement of the theory, resulted in a number of changes in the version that appeared in Sutherland's fourth edition of *Principles of Criminology*. The number of propositions increased from seven to nine, but the explanatory paragraphs following each proposition were briefer than before. The revised theory of differential association now read:

1. Criminal behavior is learned.
2. Criminal behavior is learned in interaction with other persons in a process of communication.
3. The principal part of the learning of criminal behavior occurs within intimate personal groups.
4. When criminal behavior is learned, the learning includes (a) techniques of committing the crime, which are sometimes very complicated, sometimes very simple; (b) the specific direction of motives, drives, rationalizations, and attitudes.
5. The specific direction of the motives and drives is learned from definitions of the legal codes as favorable or unfavorable.
6. A person becomes delinquent because of an excess of definitions favorable to violation of law over definitions unfavorable to violation of law.

7. Differential association may vary in frequency, duration, priority, and intensity.
8. The process of learning criminal behavior by association with criminal and anti-criminal patterns involves all of the mechanisms that are involved in any other learning.
9. While criminal behavior is an expression of general needs and values, it is not explained by those general needs and values since non-criminal behavior is an expression of the same needs and values.[75]

While the language of the first proposition is changed, the idea is the same as in the 1939 version: criminal behavior is the product of social learning and is not inherited. The idea set forth in the second proposition could easily have been incorporated within the first. Perhaps Sutherland chose to separate them in order to give each the prominence he felt it deserved, given the importance he placed on social learning, interaction, and symbolic communication. This proposition shows the obvious effect that George Herbert Mead and Herbert Blumer had on the University of Chicago sociologists.

One of the students of the Chicago tradition in sociology has written:

I think one needs to develop a sense of the appreciation the Chicago sociologists had for *processes of communication*: among themselves, among residents of a neighborhood, between parents and children, and among peers. . . . They used life-histories because they communicated well to various audiences . . . the ways people communicate—or fail to communicate—with each other. One of the things people communicate is values: "traditions" of criminal values grow in an area, are passed on even to successive waves of immigrants. Old World parents are unable to communicate "conventional values" to their adventuresome New World children. But this is precisely what W. I. Thomas' "social disorganization" meant![76]

The third proposition expressed Sutherland's belief that the "principal part" of learning criminal behavior occurs within "intimate personal groups," i.e., within primary groups. This idea was widely accepted by the Chicago sociologists, and Sutherland's regard for Charles Cooley's work on social process is well documented here, as elsewhere. While acknowledging the relative importance of personal agencies of communication, Sutherland did not then go on to dismiss utterly the impersonal agencies of communication. Citing the work of Blumer and Hauser (1933), he wrote:

The motion pictures are unquestionably an extremely important agency in determining the ideas and behavior of people, and especially of children. . . . The pictures provide people with schemes of life, with ideas of rights and privileges, and standards of behavior. . . . In view of this significant effect produced by the pictures on conduct, the content of the pictures is highly important. . . . People are animated by goals of easy money and sex, and seldom by the goals of social achievement. The criminal and prostitute are often glorified and seldom receive official punishment in the pictures. Children play as gangsters after seeing the pictures and are influenced in other ways. . . . In fact the general tendency seems to be that the children who reside in areas where delinquency rates are high are influenced more significantly by the crime and sex pictures than are those who live in areas of low delinquency rates. . . . Upon people wo already have a fairly stable scheme of life, as adults and as children in good residential areas do, the influence of the motion pictures is less harmful than upon people whose habits are less definitely formed and whose environment is more distinctly limited.[77]

Sutherland's position is that learning which occurs in intimate personal groups is primary and that learning which occurs through impersonal agencies of communication, such as motion pictures, reinforces previously established behavior patterns. Learning which occurs in intimate personal groups is both temporally and causally antecedent to learning which occurs outside primary groups and through impersonal agencies of communication.

The fourth proposition is a more precise statement of the ideas contained in the 1939 version's second proposition. *What* is learned in interaction with other persons includes both techniques of committing crimes and the "motives, drives, rationalizations, and attitudes" to do so. By using terms that suggest the cause of behavior may be either inside the person in the form of "drives" or outside the person in the form of "rationalizations," Sutherland skirted the difficult issue of human motivation. Now, as then, social scientists cannot agree on whether human beings are like other parts of the biotic world whose behavior is thought to be a product of the interaction of genetic endowment and environment. Sutherland was loath to join this debate and simply left the question of the locus of human behavior to drift unanswered.

His fifth proposition contains the idea that was found in the sixth proposition in the 1939 version of the theory. It states that in most societies cultural conflict exists relative to the criminal law. "[C]ulture relating to criminal law is not uniform or homogeneous in any modern society."[78]

In some societies an individual is surrounded by persons who invariably define the legal code as rules to be observed, while in others he is surrounded by persons whose definitions are favorable to the violation of the legal codes. In our American society these definitions are almost always mixed and consequently we have culture conflict in relation to the legal codes.[79]

The sixth proposition—often referred to as *the* principle of differential association—refines the ideas contained in the second and fourth propositions of the 1939 version. The 1947 version reads: "A person becomes delinquent because of an excess of definitions favorable to violation of law over definitions unfavorable to violation of law." However, the meaning of the proposition is imbedded within the meaning of the five propositions which precede it. In that sense, then, the principle of differential association is contained not just in proposition six but in the nine propositions taken as a whole.

The seventh proposition both limited *and* extended the ideas contained in the fifth proposition of the 1939 version of the theory. It limited the discussion of personality traits. In the early 1940s Sutherland came to believe that the earlier version of the theory did not adequately address the effect of different personality traits on the development of criminal behavior.[80] He wrote in 1942:

> This proposition [fifth proposition in 1939] has been questioned more frequently and more vigorously than any other part of the theory. In view of the extent of the disagreement I must be wrong. In fact I am fairly convinced that the hypothesis must be radically changed at this point. My difficulty is that I do not know what to change it to. I am convinced that the basic principle is sound and that modification is preferable to abandonment.[81]

By the end of the 1940s Sutherland had changed his mind. When he wrote *White Collar Crime* in 1949 he concluded that personality traits per se did not constitute a special problem for the theory of differential association. He posed three questions for consideration by advocates of personality traits as supplements to differential association: What are the personality traits that should be regarded as significant? Are there personal traits to be used as supplements to differential association that are not already included in the concept of differential association? Can differential association, essentially a *process* of learning, be combined with personal traits, essentially the *product* of learning?[82]

His answer to these questions was implicit, rather than explicit. Essentially, Sutherland concluded that differential association and personality traits were incommensurable "because the two are not in the same frame of reference."[83] This applied most directly to the third question. He also concluded that "personality traits," "personality," and "psychogenic trait components" are synonyms for "unknown conditions" that must be explained, rather than explanations of such social phenomena as criminal behavior. Consequently, the seventh proposition of the 1947 version made no mention of "individual differences."

The seventh proposition, as previously indicated, also *extended* the ideas contained in the fifth proposition of the 1939 presentation of the theory. In the earlier version differential associations were said to vary in "frequency" and "consistency" of contacts with criminal patterns. The more frequent, the more constant, and the more stable the associations one had with criminals or their patterns of criminal behavior, the more likely it was one would become criminal. On the other hand, if one had more frequent and constant or stable associations with lawful persons or patterns of lawful behavior, lawful behavior was consequently more probable. In the 1947 version Sutherland dropped the term "consistency" and added the terms "duration," "priority," and "intensity." In explaining this change he merely asserted that "'[f]requency' and 'duration' as modalities of associations are obvious and need no explanation."[84] However, he later felt the need to offer a fuller explanation of his decision to drop "consistency." He wrote in 1942: "Consistency is the same as 'differential' association and therefore is not a variable, which leaves nothing except frequency."[85]

Despite Sutherland's "explanation," it is difficult to know exactly what he thought the proposition gained by replacing "consistency" with "duration." Since duration is defined as that which is persistent or consistent, it hardly seems more than a semantic quibble to prefer the one term to its replacement. In fact, in "Development of the Theory" (1942) he wrote of his displeasure with the term "consistency"—holding that it was redundant to use it to modify "differential"—yet he said nothing at the time about the need to use another modifier, such as "duration," to clarify differential association.

What he did write about in that article was his belief that associations not only varied in frequency, but also in "intimacy" and "prestige"; yet these terms do not appear in the 1947 version of the theory. Thus we know that Sutherland's thinking on this issue went through *at least* three stages. We cannot know, however, if there were other intermediary changes of mind, or if he had intended to change his mind in his proposed, but unfinished, revision to be published in the early 1950s.

Strictly speaking, neither intimacy nor prestige refer to the associations per se; they refer to the persons who are associating with each other, to the sources of the patterns of criminal behavior. Sutherland wrote:

> To some extent [prestige] duplicates [intimacy], and such duplication is the principal difficulty in adding to the number of variables. I have been asked, How do you explain the relatively low crime rate of prison guards and policemen who come into contact with criminals with great frequency? In the first place, I am not sure that they have a low crime rate, and second, they may not have frequent contacts with criminal patterns even though they have contact with criminals, for a prisoner seldom displays his criminal behavior to a prison guard. But waiving these points, we may say that policemen and prison guards seldom have intimate contact with criminals, and that criminals have little prestige with these agents of justice. A policeman or a prison guard has his most frequent, intimate, and prestigious associations with oth-

ers in the same occupation and with members of the police machine; and when he participates in criminal behavior, it is most frequently in graft, which he learns from these associates.[86]

By 1947 "intimacy" and "prestige," along with "consistency," were found wanting in Sutherland's opinion, and instead he used "priority" and "intensity." Priority referred to the age at which one is exposed to differential associations with lawful and criminal behavior patterns. Sutherland supposed that a child exposed to lawful behavior early in life might persist in following those early patterns. Associations to which one is exposed in childhood were thought to be more important than associations to which one is exposed at a later age. "Priority" refers not only to the temporal dimension of associations, but also to their strength of influence.

Intensity was the least clearly defined modality. Sutherland wrote: "'intensity' is not precisely defined but it has to do with such things as the prestige of the source of a criminal or anti-criminal pattern and with emotional reactions related to the associations."[87] It is unclear why he did not simply use the word "prestige," which he seemed to favor in 1942. The way in which he used the term "intensity" suggests he had two analytically distinct ideas in mind: the prestige of the source of the behavior pattern, and the intimacy that characterized the relation between the source of the behavior pattern and its recipient.[88] A lawful behavior pattern might be received as a cause of the opposite behavior if the source of the behavior pattern was judged to be low in prestige or if the affective feeling toward the source of the behavior pattern was negative. Sutherland was aware of the concept "differential response pattern," or the idea that a person's receptivity to a behavior pattern was influenced by the meaning the recipient attached to the source of the association.[89] His response to this question was his statement of the theory of differential association.

> One person who walks by an unguarded and open cash register, or who is informed of the presence of such a condition in a nearby store, may perceive the situation as a "crime-committing" one, while another person in the identical circumstances may perceive the situation as one in which the owner should be warned against carelessness. The difference in these two perceptions, the theory holds, is due to differences in the prior associations with the two types of definition of situation, so that the alternatives in behavior are accounted for in terms of differential association. The differential in "response pattern," or the difference in "receptivity" to the criminal behavior pattern presented, then, is accounted for by differential association itself.[90]

The eighth proposition was a refutation of his critics' claim that differential association was nothing more than a rewording of Gabriel Tarde's theory that crime is due to imitation. Sutherland's answer was to claim that "differential association takes into account not only imitation but all other processes of learning. For instance, seduction into illegal sexual behavior or other illegal behavior is not imitation."[91]

The ninth, and final, proposition was a statement about what were not causes of crime. He argued that neither "general needs" nor "general drives and values" can explain criminal behavior. Sutherland reasoned that this must be so, for "[t]hieves generally steal in order to secure money, but likewise honest laborers work in order to secure money."[92] If a cause does not differentiate between criminal and noncriminal behavior then it is no cause at all.

Apart from the differences between the 1939 and 1947 versions of the theory of differential association that are revealed through a proposition-by-proposition comparison, there are other significant differences that must be discussed in order to appreciate the extent to which these statements are different.

The 1939 statement of the theory is very casual in its specification of the *content* of differential association. In the second and third propositions Sutherland asserts it is the relative isolation from "those who are law-abiding" and the differential "association with those who commit crimes," "with criminals," and "with persons who engage in systematic criminal behavior" that is the explanation for "systematic criminal behavior." This version left Sutherland open to the double-barreled charge that his theory was not only tautological ("Since criminal behavior is thus developed in association with criminals, it means that crime is the cause of crime"[93]), but also "a contagion or imitation theory in which individuals caught crime from criminals."[94]

The 1947 version largely countered these criticisms. By 1942 Sutherland had defined precisely what the nature and content of the associations were that caused criminal behavior.

> With the general point of view which I had acquired as a sociologist and used particularly in relation to criminal behavior, it seemed to me that learning, interaction, and communication were the processes around which a theory of criminal behavior should be developed. The theory of differential association was an attempt to explain criminal behavior in that manner.[95]

Through "interaction with other persons in a process of communication," that which was learned was "definitions of the legal code as favorable or unfavorable." A major shift had occurred. Previously, the nature of the person was crucial—was she/he criminal or law-abiding? Now the nature and content of the communication in the association was identified as the causal agent. Snodgrass had described how significant this change was, not only in answering Sutherland's earlier critics but also in explaining how "bad associates" might not necessarily cause one to become criminal, and how "good associates" might not necessarily cause one to become law-abiding:

> The change in terms and emphasis focused on what was communicated, rather than who communicated. . . . Criminal behavior patterns and definitions thus could be communicated also by non-criminals. It meant also that the non-criminals could only communicate, but not commit, criminal behavior patterns. . . . Theoretically, an indivdual could be surrounded by criminals and not receive the communication of criminal behavior patterns, and therefore not become criminal. Similarly, association with non-criminals, whose communications were predominantly criminal behavior patterns, would lead to criminality. This was an important amendation, in regard to the contagion criticism, for then individuals in contact with criminals would not become criminal unless the content was criminal in nature.[96]

Another change that occurred between 1939 and 1947 was Sutherland's decision to drop the term "systematic criminal behavior"; in 1947 he referred simply to "criminal behavior." In 1939 Sutherland used the term "systematic . . . for practical rather than logical reasons."[97] He did not then feel that his theory could account for "adventitious" crimes, criminal acts that were accidental, casual, or trivial in nature. It is unclear what these adjectives meant when applied to crimes. Is one to believe that Sutherland thought they were accidental in the sense that they did not have causes? Or that they were engaged in by nonprofessional criminals? Or by persons lacking a criminal identity? Sutherland explained his decision to drop the modifier "systematic" in this way:

> A psychiatrist in the Indiana State Prison accepted the theory as it related to systematic criminal behavior but asserted that not more than two of the two thousand prisoners there were systematic criminals. My idea had been that practically all of the prisoners were systematic criminals. However, when some of our graduate students were attempting to test the validity of the hypothesis by case studies of prisoners, they found that the most difficult part of the work was to determine objectively whether a prisoner was a criminal systematically or adventitiously. Since the distinction had been made for practical purposes and did not seem to have practical utility, I abandoned it and stated the hypothesis as applying to every crime, regardless of its systematic quality. Some of my friends, especially [Alfred R.] Lindesmith, have insisted that I shall need to re-adopt this distinction or something much like it.[98]

The changes evident in the theory of differential association between 1939 and 1947 indicate that Sutherland was not content to lean back on his oars while the boat drifted on. What changes were planned for the theory in the projected fifth edition of *Principles of Criminology*, however, will never be known. By the end of the 1940s he had relinquished his administrative duties to devote more time and energy to teaching and writing. Goff reports that Sutherland "believed he would live until he was at least 80 years of age"[99] and that he could therefore take his time in working on his theory and its relationship to other sections of *Principles of Criminology*.

During the summer of 1950 he taught two criminology courses at San Diego State College. He returned to Bloomington, Indiana, at the end of the summer with an enthusiasm that he had not known since the mid-1940s. He was troubled periodically by ulcers, and the responsibility of administration exacerbated his condition. But with Clifford Kirkpatrick as chair of the department, Sutherland at age sixty-seven was free to do what he enjoyed most, teach and conduct research.[100] On October 11, 1950, as he walked from his home to his office he collapsed from a stroke, striking his head on the concrete walkway. He died en route to the Bloomington hospital. Apart from the personal loss felt by Sutherland's family, friends, colleagues and students, the field of criminology was thus denied the fruits of the further probing research he had planned for the coming years.

White Collar Crime (1949)

Sutherland's last major accomplishment before his death was the publication in 1949 of his monograph *White Collar Crime*, which analyzed the crimes committed by American corporations and executives. So famous is this book that its title has become part of the English language.[101] Since such crime is always inspired by economic gain and made possible by particular features of the capitalist economy it would seem to lend itself naturally to an economic analysis. However, Sutherland did not pursue this line of thought. Instead, he used his newly developed theory in a tentative fashion to account for a new type of crime.

> [Although] certainly not a complete or universal explanation of white collar crime . . . [t]he data which are at hand suggest that white collar crime has its genesis in the same general process as other criminal behavior, namely, differential association . . . . Businessmen are not only in contact with definitions which are favorable to white collar crime but they are also isolated from and protected against definitions which are unfavorable to such crime. . . . As a part of the process of learning practical business, a young man with idealism and thoughtfulness for others is inducted into white collar crime. . . . He learns specific techniques for violating the law, together with definitions of situations in which these techniques may be used. Also, he develops a general

ideology, . . . "we are not in business for our health," "business is business," or "no business was ever built on the beatitudes."[102]

The behavior of white-collar criminals could not be explained easily by biological theories. It was not the product of an economic condition such as poverty; nor were these people misfits from broken homes. All that seemed to remain was differential association theory. What made white-collar crime such a convincing test of the theory as a *general* explanation is that it could be applied to a behavior far removed from that of the police-blotter criminals on which it was spawned. Sutherland observed: "White collar criminals, like professional thieves, are seldom recruited from juvenile delinquents."[103] If Sutherland rejected biological theories as both undemocratic and perhaps un-Christian, economic explanations of crime implying criticisms of capitalism were likely rejected as being contrary to Protestant ideology. The link between the Protestant ethic and the spirit of capitalism is surely not new, and just as surely the Protestant ethic and the spirit of capitalism seem to have provided intellectual guidance for Sutherland. Like many Protestants of his generation, his theological upbringing made criticism of the institution of American capitalism unlikely. In spite of his considerable graduate training in political economy, in spite of the development of his theory during the Great Depression of the 1930s, and in spite of his own book demonstrating the flagrant economic abuses of American capitalists, Sutherland firmly stood by his differential association theory.

Notes

1. Robert E. L. Faris, *Chicago Sociology, 1920-1932* (Chicago: University of Chicago Press, 1967), pp. 121-122.
2. Delbert C. Miller, "The Sutherland Era, 1935-49," unpublished manuscript (1983), Indiana University.
3. Ibid.
4. Ibid.
5. Alfred R. Lindesmith, *Opiate Addiction* (Bloomington, Indiana: Principia Press, 1947), p. 42.
6. Edwin H. Sutherland and Donald R. Cressey, *Criminology*, 10th ed., (Philadelphia: J.B. Lippincott, 1978), p. 71.
7. Edwin H. Sutherland, "Development of the Theory," in *Edwin H. Sutherland: On Analyzing Crime*, Karl Schuessler, ed. (Chicago: University of Chicago Press, 1973), pp. 17-18.
8. Sutherland and Cressey, p. 88.
9. Edwin H. Sutherland, Letter to Thorsten Sellin, 29 August 1936. Indiana University.
10. Thorsten Sellin, Letter to Karl Schuessler, 13 May 1972, quoted in Karl

Schuessler, "Introduction," in *Edwin H. Sutherland: On Analyzing Crime*, Karl Schuessler, ed. (Chicago: University of Chicago Press, 1973), p. xxx.

11. Edwin H. Sutherland, Letter to Thorsten Sellin, 29 August 1936.
12. Thorsten Sellin, Letter to Karl Schuessler, 13 May 1972, quoted in Schuessler, p. xxx.
13. Edwin H. Sutherland, Letter to Thorsten Sellin, 29 August 1936.
14. Thorsten Sellin, Letter to Edwin H. Sutherland, 17 September 1936.
15. Sutherland, "Development of the Theory," p. 17.
16. Edwin H. Sutherland, Letter to Thorsten Sellin, 5 February 1938.
17. Edwin H. Sutherland, *Principles of Criminology*, 3rd ed. (Philadelphia: J.B. Lippincott, 1939), pp. 7-8.
18. Sutherland. "Development of the Theory," p. 18.
19. Frank Sweetser, Letter to Mark Gaylord, 15 June 1982.
20. Frank Loel Sweetser, Jr. "Neighborhood Acquaintance and Association: A Study of Personal Neighborhoods" (unpublished Ph.D. dissertation, Columbia University, 1941), p. 2.
21. Ibid. p. 3.
22. Frank Sweetser, Letter to Mark Gaylord, 15 June 1982.
23. Sweetser, "Neighborhood Acquaintance and Association," pp. 92-93.
24. Sutherland, *Principles of Criminology*, 3rd ed., p. 7.
25. Ibid.
26. Sutherland. "Development of the Theory," p. 20.
27. Sweetser, "Neighborhood Acquaintance and Association," p. 93.
28. Schuessler, "Introduction," p. xv.
29. Sutherland, "Development of the Theory," p. 17.
30. Sutherland, *Principles of Criminology*, 3rd ed. pp. 4-9.
31. Ibid., p. 4.
32. See Edwin H. Sutherland, "The Biological and Sociological Processes," *Papers and Proceedings of the Twentieth Annual Meeting of the American Sociological Society*, 20 (1926), pp. 58-65.
33. Sutherland, *Principles of Criminology*, 3rd ed., pp. 4-5.
34. Ibid., p. 5.
35. Ibid.
36. Ibid.
37. Ibid.
38. Ibid., p. 6.
39. Ibid.
40. Ibid.
41. Frank Tannenbaum, *Crime and the Community* (New York: Ginn, 1938), pp. 19-20.
42. Schuessler, "Introduction," p. xvii.
43. Morris Janowitz, "Introduction to W. I. Thomas," in *On Social Organization and Social Personality*, Morris Janowitz, ed. (Chicago: University of Chicago Press, 1966), p. xxii.
44. E. H. Volkart, "Thomas, W. I.," *International Encyclopedia of the Social Sciences*, 1968, Vol. 16 (New York: Macmillan), pp. 1-6.
45. Ibid.
46. W. I. Thomas and Dorothy Swaine Thomas, *The Child in America: Behavior Problems and Programs* (New York: Alfred A. Knopf, 1928), p. 572.
47. Volkart, "Thomas, W. I."

48. Edwin H. Sutherland, "The Sexual Psychopath Laws," *Journal of Criminal Law and Criminology*, 40 (January-February 1950), p. 554.

49. Eleanor Bernert Sheldon, "Wirth, Louis," *International Encyclopedia of the Social Sciences*, 1968, Vol. 16 (New York: Macmillan), pp. 558-559.

50. Faris, p. 70.

51. Sheldon, "Wirth, Louis".

52. Howard W. Odum, *American Sociology: The Story of Sociology in the United States through 1950* (New York: Longmans, Green and Company, 1951), p. 232, quoted in Sheldon, "Wirth, Louis".

53. Faris, p. 70.

54. Sheldon, "Wirth, Louis".

55. Faris, p. 71.

56. Sutherland, "Development of the Theory," p. 16.

57. Sutherland, *Principles of Criminology*, 3rd ed., pp. 69-70; p. 80.

58. Ibid., p. 8.

59. Sutherland, "Development of the Theory," p. 21.

60. Sutherland, *Principles of Criminology*, 3rd ed., p. 8.

61. Sutherland, "Development of the Theory," p. 21.

62. Sutherland, "Principles of Criminology, 3rd ed., pp. 8-9.

63. Ibid, p. 8.

64. Sutherland, "Development of the Theory," p. 13.

65. Ibid.

66. Karl Schuessler, in *Edwin H. Sutherland: On Analyzing Crime*, Karl Schuessler, ed., p. 30.

67. Edwin H. Sutherland, Letter to Dean Johnson, 30 March 1930, quoted in Colin Goff, "Edwin H. Sutherland and White-Collar Crime" (unpublished Ph.D. dissertation, University of California, Irvine, 1982), p. 168.

68. Sutherland, "Development of the Theory," p. 21.

69. Ibid.

70. Goff, p. 197.

71. C. Ray Jeffery, interview with Colin Goff, 12 November 1981, quoted in Goff, p. 194.

72. Goff, pp. 193-194.

73. Jon Snodgrass, "The American Criminological Tradition: Portraits of Men and Ideology in a Discipline" (unpublished Ph.D. dissertation, University of Pennsylvania, 1972), p. 231.

74. Albert K. Cohen, Letter to Jon Snodgrass, 7 September 1971, quoted in Snodgrass, pp. 232-233.

75. Edwin H. Sutherland, *Principles of Criminology*, 4th ed. (Philadelphia: J.B. Lippincott, 1947), pp. 6-7.

76. James Bennett, Letter to Mark Gaylord, 1 September 1983.

77. Sutherland, *Principles of Criminology*, 4th ed., pp. 191-193.

78. Sutherland, "Development of the Theory," p. 20.

79. Sutherland, *Principles of Criminology*, 4th ed., p. 6.

80. Sutherland, "Development of the Theory," pp. 25-27.

81. Ibid., p. 25.

82. Edwin H. Sutherland, *White Collar Crime* (New York: Holt, Rinehart and Winston, Inc., 1949), p. 265.

83. Sutherland, "Development of the Theory," p. 25.

84. Sutherland, *Principles of Criminology*, 4th ed., p. 7.

85. Sutherland, "Development of the Theory," p. 24.
86. Ibid., pp. 24-25.
87. Sutherland, *Principles of Criminology*, 4th ed., p. 7.
88. Snodgrass, pp. 282-283.
89. Edwin H. Sutherland, "Susceptibility and Differential Association," in *Edwin H. Sutherland: On Analyzing Crime*, Karl Schuessler, ed. (Chicago: University of Chicago Press, 1973), pp. 42-43.
90. Sutherland and Cressey, p. 90.
91. Sutherland, "Development of the Theory," p. 22.
92. Sutherland, *Principles of Criminology*, 4th ed., p. 7.
93. Sutherland, *Principles of Criminology*, 3rd ed., p. 5.
94. Snodgrass, p. 280.
95. Sutherland, "Development of the Theory," p. 19.
96. Snodgrass, pp. 280-281.
97. Sutherland, "Development of the Theory," p. 21.
98. Ibid., pp. 21-22.
99. Goff, p. 201.
100. Ibid., p. 204.
101. *Oxford English Dictionary*. Supplement (Oxford: Clarendon Press) Vol. 4, 1986, p. 128.
102. Sutherland, *White Collar Crime*, pp. 234, 240, 247.
103. Ibid., pp. 239-240.

7

Conclusion

The theory of differential association, which Edwin Sutherland was reluctant to make explicit as late as 1939, survives. Indeed, it remains vital nearly fifty years after its origin. This is remarkable when one considers that the theory has remained unchanged since 1947. As indicated earlier, Cressey has written: ". . . the most significant criminological works of the past half-century are those which have, in one way or another, tried to *extend* Sutherland's principle [of differential association], to say something he did not say, rather than trying to improve the form of his statements."[1]

The development of criminology has not been dissimilar to other social sciences. Kuhn[2] reports that "In the absence of a paradigm . . . all of the facts that could possibly pertain to the development of a given science are likely to seem equally relevant. As a result, early fact-gathering is far more nearly random activity . . . [with facts pulled] from established crafts like medicine." In the case of criminology there were a myriad of disciplines that were in an equally good position to capture criminology prior to differential association theory—including psychiatry, biology, and law. This diverse influence was reflected in a multiple factor theory, which was ideally suited to accommodate a variety of disciplines. Kuhn has found that it is not unusual for textbooks to play a pivotal role in the early development of a science.[3] Textbooks present and justify paradigms that can be used by other scientists as points of departure in their research. Then and only then will a textbook be likely to advance the reputation of the scholar who writes it. This clearly happened in the case of Sutherland.

Raised in a sober and pious midwestern Baptist home, Sutherland acquired his father's sense of duty, honesty, and fairness. One of his biographers has written of him as a man whose personality exemplified "decency, integrity, and compassion."[4] By all accounts he was revered by those who knew him. Sutherland also inherited his father's intellectual ambitions, and both men could be sharply critical of work that failed to meet their exacting standards. In the younger Sutherland's case these characteristics were combined with a first-rate mind. To fulfill his father's expectations and his own, he became a conscientious student and an obedient son. One Sutherland family member recalled Edwin as a boy who, "naturally wishing to please,"[5] conformed to his father's demands. The desire to please others and to win approval from authority figures was a characteristic that did not disappear when he left his father's house to begin his own life.

When he entered the University of Chicago in 1906 to begin graduate work, Sutherland's plans changed quickly. A course in sociology was required as a prerequisite for graduate work in history, his intended major. At the suggestion of a correspondence course instructor, he enrolled in Professor Charles Henderson's sociology course during the summer quarter of 1906. When Henderson showed a personal interest in him, Sutherland changed his major to sociology and began to pursue the kind of sociology that his professor represented.

For the first year that he was at the University of Chicago, Sutherland remained primarily influenced by Henderson. In many respects Henderson and Edwin's father were cut from the same cloth: both were self-confident, outgoing, and domineering. Just as Sutherland rarely returned to his parents' home once he was grown, after his first year at Chicago he turned away from the strong personality of Henderson to find another kind of sociology.

The city of Chicago both excited and repelled Sutherland. Before 1906 he had only *read* about the city; his experiences had been those of small-town midwestern life. While it is true that he "loathed" Chicago, it is also true that it influenced his ideas on social reform, the causes of crime, and the likelihood of the social control of crime. During his first year of graduate work he was a field worker for the city's Juvenile Protection Association. For the first time in his life he saw the conditions that the poor and the immigrants faced in large American cities at the beginning of the twentieth century. On this point, Goff has written:

> Almost 30 years later, in his study of homeless men in Chicago, Sutherland discussed how migration from the protective, rural countryside into the city had been disconcerting for so many shelter residents. And so it must have been for the young graduate student as well. It was through his involvement with the JPA that Sutherland saw "for the first time the conditions of life in the immigrant sections of a large city. These impressed me very much."[6]

Between 1906 and 1913 Sutherland drifted away from sociology. He grew increasingly disillusioned with the quality of his sociology instructors. In particular, he grew impatient with Henderson's social reform approach to sociology and with Albion Small's empty talk about methodology. Of all his sociology instructors, W. I. Thomas had the most positive influence on Sutherland. Mead, Dewey, and Thomas's evolving conception of social psychology was passed on to Sutherland in Thomas's courses. He turned to political science, history, and especially, political economy, for a method by which to put social science on a scientific footing. During Sutherland's last two years at the University of Chicago he became a disciple of political economist Robert Hoxie. By the time he graduated in 1913 he had earned a Ph.D. in sociology *and* political economy. At this point in his academic career Sutherland thought of himself more as a political economist than as a sociologist. This is indicated in his early research interests: labor unions, farmers' organizations, employment agencies, and socialism.

After graduation he accepted a position as professor of sociology at William Jewell College in Liberty, Missouri. Compared to those of his graduate school friends who were also just beginning their careers, Sutherland's immediate prospects were not bright. William Jewell was a small, underfinanced, and isolated Baptist institution for men in western Missouri. Although he determined to make the best of his situation, he soon realized the futility of trying to do "constructive work" in such a setting. It is no exaggeration to say that by 1918 he was desperate to leave and join a more prestigious sociology department. That year he wrote to Luther L. Bernard, "I am getting quite anxious to get away from here, for I am afraid of dying here."[7]

Fortunately, a major break came his way. Stuart Queen, a good friend during his student years at Chicago, recommended Sutherland for a vacancy at the University of Illinois. He was hired and thereby lifted to a level of academe where he at least had an opportunity to make a reputation for himself by working diligently in research activities. In 1921 Sutherland's department chair, Edward Hayes, asked him to write a criminology textbook. This request was the major turning point in Sutherland's career.

It is somewhat surprising to learn that the best-known criminologist of this century acquired his professional identity as a result of departmental fiat. While it is true, as Schuessler writes, that Hayes would not have asked Sutherland to write the book if he had doubted his competence and dependability, it is equally true that up to that point there is no evidence that Sutherland had ever considered writing such a book. Although he was nearly forty years old, his professional identity was still in a state of flux and he was as committed to political economy as he was to sociology. Hayes's request pushed Sutherland off dead center. From that point on he committed himself to criminology and never looked back to his former research interests. Sutherland's book won immediate acceptance from sociologists in large part because its treatment of criminology was so generously accommodative to the concepts and perspectives of sociology.

After the publication of *Criminology* in 1924, Sutherland's reputation soared. In 1926 he was offered a position at the University of Minnesota, then the fourth-ranked department of sociology in the country. Sutherland's three years at the University of Minnesota reveal three characteristics: by increasing his scholarly activity he moved to solidify his reputation as one of the country's leading criminologists; he became an effective spokesman for sociology as a scientific enterprise; and he worked conscientiously to promote sociology as a profession. Almost all of his articles during this period concerned criminological issues or stressed the value of sociology in shedding light on human behavior and in solving social problems. All the while he worked quietly behind the scenes to further the interests of sociology as a profession, serving on committees of the American Sociological Society, organizing conferences, and assisting his colleagues. He served as department chair during his last year at the University of Minnesota while F. Stuart Chapin was on leave. In the course of ten years (1919-1929) Sutherland had earned the trust and respect of his peers as a loyal and dedicated member of the profession.

After working for the Bureau of Social Hygiene in New York for one year, Sutherland was invited to join the department of sociology at the University of Chicago as a research professor. He jumped at the chance. Aside from the excellent research facilities and financial support that Chicago could offer him, he valued the opportunity to work with the people who constituted his professional reference group: Robert Park, Ernest Burgess, Louis Wirth, Clifford Shaw, and Henry McKay. While in Chicago between 1930 and 1935 he revised his criminology textbook, conducted the research later to be published as *Twenty Thousand Homeless Men* and *The Professional Thief*, edited (with Thorsten Sellin) a volume of *The Annals of the American Academy of Political and Social Science*, and wrote over a dozen articles and book chapters.

The 1934 edition of *Principles of Criminology* advanced three hypotheses that contained the germ of the theory of differential association. Depending on which version of the story one chooses to believe, either Sutherland did not recognize that he had developed a general theory of crime causation (his own version) or he was simply reluctant to draw attention to it for fear that such a move was premature (Schuessler's position). Schuessler reports:

> Sutherland had some misgivings about assembling his scattered ideas and calling them a theory, although there was ample warrant for that step. He was concerned that not enough was known to justify a general theory and that the mere presence of a theory might foster an unhealthy perseveration of thought, possibly in the wrong direction. He understood that a theory might gain adherents not because of its truth but because of its mere existence as a

rallying point in a jumbled field. Accordingly, he preferred to think of his propositions as an approach rather than a theory, as working hypotheses rather than universal laws.[8]

Four specific events occurred in the early 1930s that account for Sutherland's decision to try to develop a general theory of crime causation. First, Dean Beardsley Ruml of the University of Chicago called together several persons interested in criminology, including Sutherland, and asked them what they knew about the causes of crime. The best Sutherland could say was that they had certain facts about the incidence of high crime rates and that they had proved that certain propositions about the causes of crime were false. "I could state no verified positive generalizations. This turned me somewhat more toward a search for such propositions."[9] Second, the Michael-Adler report, which was highly critical of criminological research, stirred "emotional antagonism" within Sutherland upon its publication in 1932. After some time had passed, however, Sutherland found merit in much of its criticisms. In 1942 he wrote: ". . . I wish now to admit that it had a very important influence on me and turned my attention toward abstract generalizations."[10] Third, Sutherland's 1932 article "Social Process in Behavior Problems" suggests that he was beginning to appreciate the difference between integrated theory and multiple factors. He used Cooley's social process concept to move toward an abstract understanding of the process by which behavior can become delinquent behavior. Cooley's work gave Sutherland hope that a way might be found to organize all of the allegedly criminogenic factors that criminologists had accumulated over the years. Fourth, Sutherland was urged to develop a theory by his friends Henry McKay, Hans Riemer, and Harvey Locke. "With modesty, Sutherland would say that he was hardly aware of his theory until it had been brought to his attention by his perceptive friends."[11]

These four specific events assume greater importance when placed in the context of sociology in the 1930s and 1940s. Beginning sometime in the early 1930s and continuing through the mid-1960s, sociologists turned their energies toward building general theories of society and behavior. This activity reached its apex in the postwar years as structural-functionalism spread its influence throughout the discipline. While influential social theorists such as Talcott Parsons and Robert Merton made their mark on sociology *after* Sutherland developed his criminological theory, the professional rewards bestowed upon originators of general theories were already recognized by sociologists working in the mid-1930s. Sutherland was a keen student of sociology and a careful observer of the theoretical arguments within the discipline that appeared in the *American Journal of Sociology*. One imagines that he felt excited as he came to realize that he had created a general theory of criminal behavior. The only consideration that held him back from bringing forth his work was the possibility that he had not sufficiently thought out the implications of his theory. Although he was probably just as eager as anyone to receive recognition for his accomplishments, he feared that critics would demolish his theory just as he and others had done to other would-be general theories of criminal behavior. In 1934 the theory was included in *Principles of Criminology* almost as an aside. It was not highlighted in ways that would cause a reader to appreciate its importance, nor was it integrated with other materials on crime causation that constituted the first part of the book.

In 1935 Sutherland's contract was not renewed by the University of Chicago. America was in the depths of the Great Depression and he had been hired on an annual basis without promise of secure and continuing employment. The reasons for his dismissal are not totally clear. While a number of explanations have been offered, the most plausible is that Sutherland and department chair Ellsworth Faris had a falling out owing to their dissimilar personalities. Sutherland was stunned, embarrassed, and, perhaps most of all, furious with Faris. It is hard to imagine anyone not feeling these emotions in the face of such an event, which was undoubtedly an enormous blow to Sutherland's ego.

In 1935 he became the first chair of the newly established independent department of sociology at Indiana University. He quickly set about building a strong department by hiring able scholars such as Alfred Lindesmith and Harvey Locke, whom he had come to know at the University of Chicago. But administrative duties failed to prevent him from continuing his scholarly work. Within a few years he had published *Twenty Thousand Homeless Men, The Professional Thief*, and the third edition of *Principles of Criminology*. This 1939 edition of his criminology textbook contained the first explicit statement of the theory of differential association. Even at that late date he was reluctant to "rush" his theory into print.

> He was aware that a general theory would be premature in the absence of more factual information about crime and criminals. His ideal was a general theory of crime consistent with the widest possible range of data, and he realized that the factual materials on crime were fragmentary and unreliable and generally insufficient to bear the weight of broad generalizations.[12]

Two events in the late 1930s helped Sutherland clarify his ideas on crime causation and put them in explicit propositional form. First, in 1935 the Social Science Research Council asked Thorsten Sellin and Sutherland to form a two-person committee on crime and delinquency. Their mandate was to make criminology more scientific; how they were to accomplish this was left to their own collaboration. Three years later they produced a monograph called *Culture Conflict and Crime*. Sellin, as chair of the committee, actually wrote most of the manuscript; Sutherland's role was principally that of critic. They settled on culture conflict as an approach to a general explanation of crime. Neither man was entirely satisfied with their work, and Sellin believed that Sutherland's dissatisfaction may have prompted him to "crystallize" his ideas on crime causation and "go public" with his theory in 1939. Second, prior to publication of the 1939 edition of *Principles of Criminology*, Sutherland, Lindesmith, and Frank Sweetser were driving late one evening. Sweetser asked his colleagues, "Why doesn't the explanation of juvenile delinquency in a slum area apply in principle to murders in the South?" Sutherland concluded that his explanation of juvenile delinquency *did* apply to murders in the South. And so he set about putting his theory in propositional form for inclusion in the upcoming edition.

The next decade saw Sutherland working constantly to improve his theory. Unlike many scholars, who after completing one piece of work move on to other problems that interest them, Sutherland continued to polish his ideas. He frequently used the theory of differential association as the basis of graduate seminars at Indiana University. His students were encouraged to tear into the theory, to criticize it mercilessly. This they did, and without any fear that their distinguished teacher would punish them for their boldness. Indeed, the most able and telling critics among Sutherland's students became his favorites. In this and other instances Sutherland acted on his belief in democratic relations among fellow scholars, be they distinguished veterans like himself or beginning graduate students.

On the basis of materials that are in the hands of his former students it is clear that the changes in the theory which appeared in the 1947 edition of *Principles of Criminology* were the end result of numerous intermediary versions that were tried and rejected between 1939 and 1947. It is a safe assumption that if Sutherland had lived long enough to produce a fifth edition of his criminology textbook he would have introduced yet other modifications.

Sutherland's theory was first published in the bleak years of the Great Depression. The social and economic upheavals of the time undoubtedly made a theory claiming totally social origins for criminal behavior easier to accept. This is not offered as a complete explanation for the acceptance of Sutherland's work, but as a factor that should not be overlooked. A complete explanation of the positive reception that greeted Sutherland's theory must include the power of the ideas themselves, the temper of the times in which they were introduced, and, equally important, the esteem in which Sutherland was held by his colleagues.

This review of the major steps leading to the origination and development of the theory of differential association suggests three broad generalizations concerning Sutherland's career. First, he was a builder and defender of the discipline and profession of sociology, devoting his energy and intelligence to both ideas and organizational activity. He lent encouragement to his colleagues' efforts to build a scientific sociology just as he nurtured his students' developing professional identities. Sutherland was fiercely loyal and protective toward fellow sociologists. He had a keen sense of the importance of maintaining disciplinary boundaries and he used his sharp critical ability to attack outsiders, such as psychiatrists and psychologists, when they encroached on what he considered to be sociology's territory. The debate between Sutherland and sociologist-lawyer Paul Tappan on the question "Is 'White-Collar Crime' Crime?" is a good example of Sutherland acting as a disciplinary watchdog.[13] In this instance he defended the propriety of including actions he termed white-collar crimes within the subject matter of sociological criminology if these behaviors violated written laws, even if the actors were not convicted of a crime. That is, he insisted on a behavioral rather than a legalistic definition of crime. As noted earlier, he also discounted economic and biological explanations of behavior.

Second, Sutherland was ambitious to make his mark within academe. From the time of his first postdoctoral position, which he had looked upon as a "source of income and promotion," to the end of his life he was ever eager to advance. At the University of Illinois, he accepted Edward C. Hayes's offer to write a criminology textbook. Sutherland realized that a widely circulated textbook was an ideal way to gain visibility in the discipline. *Criminology* was generously accommodative to the concepts and perspectives then in general use within the discipline and its publication was greeted warmly. In 1926 he joined the fourth-ranked department of sociology when he was hired at the rank of full professor by the University of Minnesota. This was clearly a step up from the University of Illinois. During the 1928-1929 academic year he served as department chair in F. Stuart Chapin's absence. In 1930 he joined the department of sociology at the University of Chicago as a research professor. This, too, was clearly a career enhancement for Sutherland because Chicago was then the top-ranked department of sociology in the country. When he was forced out of the University of Chicago, Sutherland moved to Indiana University as the first chair of that school's department of sociology. He worked hard to make it a respectable department and by the end of the 1930s he had succeeded. By then Sutherland could be considered the dean of American criminology, respected and trusted for his ideas and service to the profession. In electing him to the presidency of the American Sociological Society in 1939 his colleagues bestowed upon him their highest honor. Other honors followed in rapid succession. In Westie's study of "professional immortality" within sociology, in which he measured the degree to which one's name and work are remembered by sociologists, Sutherland ranked tenth among past American Sociological Society presidents.[14]

Third, Sutherland's theory of differential association has not only survived the test of time; it has been the preeminent sociological theory of criminology for nearly fifty years. The reason is not difficult to understand—the theory of differential association is centered in the very heart of sociology. Sutherland's theory was determinedly sociological from its inception and continued to be so as it evolved throughout the 1940s. Since it embraced the concepts and perspectives of sociology, it represented the kind of criminological theory that sociologists found easy to accept and endorse.

Notes

1. Donald R. Cressey, "Fifty Years of Criminology: From Sociological Theory to Political Control," *Pacific Sociological Review*, 22 (October 1979), p. 462.
2. Thomas S. Kuhn, "The Structure of Scientific Revolutions." (Chicago: University of Chicago Press, 1967), p. 15.
3. Ibid., pp. 19-20.
4. Colin Goff, "Edwin H. Sutherland and White-Collar Crime" (unpublished Ph.D. dissertation, University of California, Irvine, 1982), p. 263.
5. Jon Snodgrass, "The American Criminological Tradition: Portraits of Men and Ideology in a Discipline" (unpublished Ph.D. dissertation, University of Pennsylvania, 1972), p. 221.
6. Goff, pp. 81-82.
7. Edwin H. Sutherland, Letter to Luther Bernard, 28 December 1918, quoted in Goff, p. 138.
8. Karl Schuessler, "Introduction," in *Edwin H. Sutherland: On Analyzing Crime*, Karl Schuessler, ed. (Chicago: University of Chicago Press, 1973), pp. xiv-xv.
9. Edwin H. Sutherland, "Development of the Theory," in *Edwin H. Sutherland: On Analyzing Crime*, Karl Schuessler, ed. (Chicago: University of Chicago Press, 1973), p. 16.
10. Ibid.
11. Schuessler, "Introduction," p. xv.
12. Ibid., pp. xv-xvi.
13. Edwin H. Sutherland, "Is 'White-Collar Crime' Crime?" *American Sociological Review*, 10 (April 1945), pp. 132-139; Paul W. Tappan, "Who Is the Criminal?" *American Sociological Review*, 12 (February 1947), pp. 96-102.
14. Frank R. Westie, "Academic Expectations for Professional Immortality: A Study of Legitimation," *American Sociologist*, 8 (February 1973), pp. 19-32.

Methodological Note

Data Sources

This study was based on interviews, personal files, and library archives. Sutherland's published works were reviewed, and interviews were conducted with Alfred Lindesmith, Karl Schuessler, Donald Cressey, and Frank Sweetser. Several other persons were contacted as especially knowledgeable informants about Sutherland's work. This second group includes Jon Snodgrass, Colin Goff, Gilbert Geis, Evan Thomas, James Bennett, and Delbert Miller. Both Snodgrass and Schuessler provided a number of useful materials from their Sutherland files. Schuessler's files contained several letters and unpublished manuscripts bearing on the origin and development of differential association theory. The Sutherland materials held by the Lilly Library at Indiana University were also reviewed. The special collections at the University of Chicago's Joseph Regenstein Library also contained many helpful documents. The complete Sutherland-Luther Bernard correspondence contained in the Luther L. Bernard Papers in the Pennsylvania Historical Collections and Labor Archives at the Pattee Library of the Pennsylvania State University was also obtained. A number of early twentieth century criminology textbooks were reviewed to gain greater insight into the intellectual context in which Sutherland wrote his textbook.

Diverse methods and data sources, such as interviews, manuscripts, and letters, were used to explore each aspect of this research problem. For example, it became clear that Alfred Lindesmith's research methodology influenced Sutherland's effort to develop a theory of crime causation. This conclusion was based on interviews with Lindesmith and others, on Sutherland's unpublished manuscript "Development of The Theory," and on his published work from the 1930s and 1940s.

Bibliography

Baker, Paul J.
   1974   "The Life Histories of W. I. Thomas and Robert E. Park."
           American Journal of Sociology, 79 (September): 243-260.
Bennett, James
   1981   *Oral History and Delinquency: The Rhetoric of Criminology.*
           Chicago: University of Chicago. Press.

——.
   1983   Letter to Mark Gaylord. 1 September.
Blumer, Herbert, and Hauser, Philip M.
   1933   *Movies, Delinquency, and Crime.* New York: Macmillan.
Blumer, Herbert
   1939   *An Appraisal of Thomas and Znaniecki's "The Polish Peasant
           in Europe and America."* New York: Social Science Research
           Council.
Bulmer, Martin
   1981   "Quantification and Chicago Social Science in the 1920s: A
           Neglected Tradition." *Journal of the History of the Behavioral
           Sciences*, 17 (July): 312-331.
Burgess, Ernest W.
   1925   "Book Review." *American Journal of Sociology*, 30 (January):
           491-492.

——.
   1948   "W. I. Thomas as a Teacher." *Sociology and Social Research*, 32
           (March-April): 760-764.
Carey, James T.
   1975   *Sociology and Public Affairs: The Chicago School.* Beverly
           Hills, California: Sage Publications.
Chambliss, William J.
   1984   "White Collar Crime and Criminology." *Contemporary So-
           ciology*, 13 (March): 160-162.
Chicago Daily Tribune
   1916   "Prof. R. F. Hoxie Takes His Life." 23 June: Sec. 2, p. 15, Col. 2.
Cohen, Albert, Lindesmith, Alfred, and Schuessler, Karl (eds.)
   1956   *The Sutherland Papers.* Bloomington: Indiana University
           Press.
Cohen, Albert
   1971   Letter to Jon Snodgrass. 7 September.

Cooley, Charles Horton
    1918   *Social Process*. New York: Charles Scribner's Sons.
Cressey, Donald R.
    1960   "Epidemiology and Individual Conduct: A Case from Crimi-
            nology." *Pacific Sociological Review*, 3 (Fall): 47-58.

_____.
    1979   "Fifty Years of Criminology: From Sociological Theory to Po-
            litical Control." *Pacific Sociological Review*, 22 (October):
            457-480.
Deegan, Mary Jo, and Burger, John S.
    1981   "W. I. Thomas and Social Reform: His Work and Writings."
            Journal of the History of the Behavioral Sciences, 17 (January):
            114-125.
Diner, Steven J.
    1975   "Department and Discipline: The Department of Sociology at
            the University of Chicago, 1892-1920." *Minerva*, 13 (Winter):
            514-553.

_____.
    1980   *A City and Its Universities: Public Policy in Chicago 1892-1919*.
            Chapel Hill: University of North Carolina Press.
Elliott, Mabel
    1952   *Crime in Modern Society*. New York: Harper and Brothers.
Faris, Robert E. L.
    1967   *Chicago Sociology, 1920-1932*. Chicago: University of Chicago
            Press.
Finestone, Harold
    1976   "The Delinquent and Society: The Shaw and McKay Tradi-
            tion." Pp. 23-49 in *Delinquency, Crime and Society*. James F.
            Short, Jr. (ed.). Chicago: University of Chicago Press.
Fisher, Berenice, and Strauss, Anselm
    1978   "The Chicago Tradition and Social Change: Thomas, Park and
            Their Successors." *Symbolic Interaction*, 1 (Spring): 5-23.
Geis, Gilbert
    1976   "Editorial." *Criminology*, 14 (November): 303-306.
Geis, Gilbert, and Goff, Colin (eds.)
    1983   "Introduction." Pp. ix-xxxiii, in *White Collar Crime: The Un-
            cut Version*. Edwin H. Sutherland. New Haven: Yale University
            Press.
Gibbons, Don C.
    1974   "Say, Whatever Became of Maurice Parmelee, Anyway?" *So-
            ciological Quarterly*, 15 (Summer): 405-416.
Gillin, John L.
    1926   *Criminology and Penology*. New York: Appleton.
Glaser, Daniel
    1976   "Marginal Workers: Some Antecedents and Implications of an
            Idea from Shaw and McKay." Pp. 254-266, in *Delinquency,*

Crime, and Society. James F. Short, Jr. (ed.). Chicago: University of Chicago Press.

Goff, Colin
1982   "Edwin H. Sutherland and White-Collar Crime." Unpublished Ph.D. dissertation, University of California, Irvine.

Hall, Jerome
1945   "Criminology." Pp. 342-365, In *Twentieth Century Sociology.* Georges Gurvitch and Wilbert E. Moore (eds.). New York: Philosophical Library.

Hayes, Edward C.
1915   *Introduction to the Study of Sociology.* New York: D. Appleton and Company.

Henderson, Charles R.
1899   "The Ministry of Today—Its New Equipment." *University of Chicago Record,* 3: 279-281.

———.
1901   *Introduction to the Study of the Dependent, Defective, and Delinquent Classes.* 2nd ed. Boston: D.C. Heath.

———.
1914   *The Cause and Cure of Crime.* Chicago: A.C. McClurg and Company.

Hinkle, Roscoe C., and Hinkle, Gisela J.
1954   *The Development of Modern Sociology: Its Nature and Growth in the United States.* New York: Random House.

House, Floyd Nelson
1936   *Development of Sociology.* New York: McGraw-Hill Book Company.

Howard, Lois
1981   Interview with Colin Goff. 15 November.

Hull House Maps and Papers
1895   New York: Thomas Y. Crowell.

Hunter, Albert
1980   "Why Chicago? The Rise of the Chicago School of Urban Social Science." *American Behavioral Scientist,* 24 (December): 215-227.

Janowitz, Morris
1966   "Introduction to W. I. Thomas." Pp. vii-lviii, in *On Social Organization and Social Personality.* Morris Janowitz (ed.). Chicago: University of Chicago Press.

Jeffery, Clarence Ray
1981   Interview with Colin Goff. 12 November.

Kobrin, Solomon
1971   "The Formal Logical Properties of the Shaw-McKay Delinquency Theory." Pp. 101-131, in *Ecology, Crime and Delinquents.* Harwin L. Voss and David M. Peterson (eds.). New York: Appleton-Century-Crofts.

Kuhn, Thomas S.
  1967   *The Structure of Scientific Revolutions.* Chicago: University of Chicago Press.
Lindesmith, Alfred R., and Levin, Yale
  1937   "The Lombrosian Myth in Criminology." *American Journal of Sociology,* 42 (March): 653-671.
Lindesmith, Alfred R.
  1947   *Opiate Addiction.* Bloomington, Indiana: Principia Press.
———.
  1982   Interview with Mark Gaylord. 23 June.
Lofland, Lyn H. ed.
  1980   "Reminiscences of Classic Chicago: The Blumer-Hughes Talk." *Urban Life,* 9 (October): 251-281.
Lombroso, Cesare
  1897   *L'Anthropologie criminelle.* 5th ed. Turin, Italy: Bocca.
Martindale, Don
  1976   *The Romance of a Profession: A Case History in the Sociology of Sociology.* St. Paul, Minnesota: Windflower Publishing Company.
Matthews, Fred H.
  1977   *Quest for an American Sociology: Robert E. Park and the Chicago School.* Montreal, Canada: McGill-Queen's University Press.
McCaul, Robert
  1959   "Dewey's Chicago." *School Review,* 67 (Summer): 258-280.
McKay, Henry D.
  1971   Letter to Jon Snodgrass. 3 March.
Mead, George Herbert
  1901   Letter to Helen Mead. 26 May. University of Chicago. Papers of the Presidents. Department of Special Collections.
———.
  1903   "The Definition of the Psychical." *Investigations Representing the Departments: The Decennial Publications of the University of Chicago.* First Series. Vol. 3, Part 2, 77-112.
———.
  1918   "The Psychology of Punitive Justice." *American Journal of Sociology,* 23 (March): 577-602.
———.
  1925   "The Genesis of the Self and Social Control." *International Journal of Ethics,* 35 (April): 251-277.
———.
  1934   *Mind, Self and Society.* Chicago: University of Chicago Press.
Miller, Delbert C.
  1983   Letter to Mark Gaylord. 18 August.

　　　　　.
1983　　"The Sutherland Era, 1935-49." Unpublished manuscript, Indiana University.

Odum, Howard W.
1951　　*American Sociology: The Story of Sociology in the United States through 1950.* New York: Longmans, Green and Company.

Oxford English Dictionary
1986　　Supplement. Oxford: Clarendon Press. Vol. 4, p. 128.

Park, Robert E. and Burgess, Ernest W.
1921　　*Introduction to the Science of Sociology.* Chicago: University of Chicago Press.

Park, Robert E.
1915　　"The City: Suggestions for the Investigation of Human Behavior in the City Environment." *American Journal of Sociology,* 20 (March): 577-612.

Parmelee, Maurice F.
1918　　*Criminology.* New York: Macmillan.

Parsons, Philip A.
1909　　*Responsibility for Crime.* New York: Columbia University Press.

　　　　　.
1926　　*Crime and the Criminal.* New York: Alfred A. Knopf.

Polsky, Ned
1967　　*Hustlers, Beats, and Others.* Chicago: Aldine Publishing Company.

Queen, Stuart A.
1932　　"Henderson, Charles Richmond." *Encyclopedia of the Social Sciences.* Vol. 7, (New York: Macmillan): 320.

　　　　　.
1980　　Interview with Colin Goff. 8 November.

Rucker, Darnell
1969　　*The Chicago Pragmatists.* Minneapolis: University of Minnesota Press.

Scholarly Resources, Incorporated
1980　　"Rockefeller Archive Center."

Schuessler, Karl
1973　　"Introduction." Pp. ix-xxxvi. in *Edwin H. Sutherland: On Analyzing Crime.* Karl Schuessler (ed.). Chicago: University of Chicago Press.

　　　　　.
1982　　Interview with Mark Gaylord. 23 June.

Sellin, Thorsten
1936　　Letter to Edwin H. Sutherland. 17 September. Indiana University.

———.
   1938   *Culture Conflict and Crime.* New York: Social Science Research Council.

———.
   1972   Letter to Karl Schuessler. 13 May. Indiana University.
Shaw, Clifford R.
   1930   *The Jack-Roller: A Delinquent Boy's Own Story.* Chicago: University of Chicago Press.

———.
   1931   *The Natural History of a Delinquent Career.* Chicago: University of Chicago Press.
Shaw, Clifford R., with the collaboration of Frederick M. Zorbaugh, Henry D. McKay, and Leonard S. Cottrell
   1929   *Delinquency Areas: A Study of the Geographic Distribution of School Truants, Juvenile Delinquents, and Adult Offenders in Chicago.* Chicago: University of Chicago Press.
Sheldon, Eleanor Bernert
   1968   "Wirth, Louis," *International Encyclopedia of the Social Sciences.* Vol. 16 (New York: Macmillan): 558-559.
Shils, Edward
   1970   "Tradition, Ecology, and Institution in the History of Sociology." *Daedalus*, 99 (Fall): 760-825.
Snodgrass, Jon
   1972   "The American Criminological Tradition: Portraits of Men and Ideology in a Discipline." Unpublished Ph.D. dissertation, University of Pennsylvania.

———.
   1973   "The Criminologist and His Criminal: The Case of Edwin H. Sutherland and Broadway Jones." *Issues in Criminology,* 8 (Spring): 1-17.

———.
   1976   "Clifford R. Shaw and Henry D. McKay: Chicago Criminologists." *British Journal of Criminology,* 16 (January): 1-19.
Sutherland, Edwin H.
   1912   Letter to Luther Bernard. 23 October. Luther L. Bernard Papers. Pennsylvania Historical Collections, Pattee Library, Pennsylvania State University, University Park, Pennsylvania.

———.
   1912   Letter to Luther Bernard. 24 November. Luther L. Bernard Papers.

———.
   1913   Letter to Luther Bernard. 31 January. Luther L. Bernard Papers.

———.
   1913   Letter to Luther Bernard. 17 April. Luther L. Bernard Papers.

_____.
1913   Letter to Luther Bernard. 16 October. Luther L. Bernard Papers.

_____.
1913   Letter to Luther Bernard. 13 November. Luther L. Bernard Papers.

_____.
1914   Letter to Luther Bernard. 7 January. Luther L. Bernard Papers.

_____.
1914   Letter to Luther Bernard. 4 February. Luther L. Bernard Papers.

_____.
1914   Letter to Luther Bernard. 11 March. Luther L. Bernard Papers.

_____.
1914   "What Rural Health Surveys Have Revealed." Proceedings of Missouri Conference for Social Welfare, published in Monthly Bulletin: State Board of Charities and Correction, IX (June 1916), 31-37.

_____.
1915   Letter to Luther Bernard. 26 April. Luther L. Bernard Papers.

_____.
1915   Letter to Luther Bernard. 13 August. Luther L. Bernard Papers.

_____.
1915   Letter to Luther Bernard. 1 November. Luther L. Bernard Papers.

_____.
1916   Letter to Luther Bernard. 6 February. Luther L. Bernard Papers.

_____.
1916   Letter to Luther Bernard. 6 July. Luther L. Bernard Papers.

_____.
1916   Letter to Luther Bernard. 11 July. Luther L. Bernard Papers.

_____.
1916   Letter to Luther Bernard. 10 November. Luther L. Bernard Papers.

_____.
1918   Letter to Luther Bernard. 28 December, quoted in Colin Goff, "Edwin H. Sutherland and White-Collar Crime" (unpublished Ph.D. dissertation, University of California, Irvine, 1982), p. 138.

_____.
1921   Letter to Luther Bernard. 16 March. Luther L. Bernard Papers.

_____.
1922   "The Isolated Family." *Institution Quarterly,* 13 (September-December): 189-192.

———.
1924   "Public Opinion as a Cause of Crime." *Journal of Applied Sociology,* 9 (September-October): 50-56.

———.
1924   *Criminology.* Philadelphia: J.B. Lippincott.

———.
1926   "The Biological and Sociological Processes." *Papers and Proceedings of the Twentieth Annual Meeting of the American Sociological Society.* 20: 58-65.

———.
1927   "Review of *Delinquents and Criminals: Their Making and Unmaking.*" *Harvard Law Review,* 40 (March): 798-800.

———.
1927   "Social Aspects of Crime." *Proceedings of the Conference of the National Crime Commission.* Washington, D.C.: 156-157.

———.
1927   "Is There Undue Crime Among Immigrants?" *National Conference of Social Work:* 572-579.

———.
1927   Letter to Luther Bernard. 13 July. Luther L. Bernard Papers.

———.
1928   "Is Experimentation in Case Work Processes Desirable?" *Social Forces,* 6 (June): 567-569.

———.
1929   "The Person versus the Act in Criminology." *Cornell Law Quarterly,* 14 (February): 159-167.

———.
1929   "Edward Carey Hayes: 1868-1928." *American Journal of Sociology,* 35 (July): 93-99.

———.
1930   Letter to Dean Johnson, 30 March, *Bureau of Social Hygiene.*

———.
1930   "Observations of European Prisons." Unpublished manuscript, Indiana University.

———.
1931   "Mental Deficiency and Crime." Pp. 357-375, In *Social Attitudes.* Kimball Young (ed.). New York: Henry Holt and Company.

———.
1932   "Social Process in Behavior Problems." *Publications of the American Sociological Society.* 26: 55-61.

———.
1934   *Principles of Criminology.* 2nd. ed. Philadelphia: J.B. Lippincott.

———.
1934   "The Decreasing Prison Population of England." *Journal of Criminal Law and Criminology.* 24:880-900.

————.
1935   Letter to Thorsten Sellin. 16 March. Indiana University.

————.
1936   Letter to Thorsten Sellin. 29 August. Indiana University.

————.
1937   *The Professional Thief.* Chicago: University of Chicago Press.

————.
1938   Letter to Thorsten Sellin. 5 February. Indiana University.

————.
1939   *Principles of Criminology.* 3rd ed. Philadelphia: J.B. Lippincott.

————.
1945   "Is 'White-Collar Crime' Crime?" *American Sociological Review,* 10 (April): 132-139.

————.
1947   *Principles of Criminology.* 4th ed. Philadelphia: J.B. Lippincott.

————.
1949   *White Collar Crime.* New York: Dryden Press.

————.
1950   "The Sexual Psychopath Laws." *Journal of Criminal Law and Criminology,* 40 (January-February): 543-554.

————.
1973   "The Michael-Adler Report." Pp. 229-246, In *Edwin H. Sutherland: On Analyzing Crime.* Karl Schuessler (ed.). Chicago: University of Chicago Press.

————.
1973   "Development of the Theory." Pp. 13-29, in *Edwin H. Sutherland: On Analyzing Crime.* Karl Schuessler (ed.). Chicago: University of Chicago Press.

————.
1973   "Susceptibility and Differential Association." Pp. 42-43, in *Edwin H. Sutherland: On Analyzing Crime.* Karl Schuessler (ed.). Chicago: University of Chicago Press.

Sutherland, Edwin, and Cresey, Donald R.
1978   *Criminology.* 10th ed. Philadelphia: J.B. Lippincott.

Sutherland, Edwin and Locke, Harvey J.
1936   *Twenty Thousand Homeless Men: A Study of Unemployed Men in the Chicago Shelters.* Philadelphia: J.B. Lippincott.

Sutherland, Edwin H., and Sellin, Thorsten (eds.)
1931   "Prisons of Tomorrow," *The Annals of the American Academy of Political and Social Science,* 157 (September).

Sutherland, Edwin; Shaw, Clifford R.; Gehlke, Charles Elmer; Glueck, Sheldon; and Stearns, Warren A.
1932   "Housing and Delinquency." Pp. 13-49, in *Housing and the Community: Home Repair and Remodeling.* J.M. Gries and James Ford (eds.), Washington, DC.: U.S. Government Printing Office.

Sutherland, Edwin H. . and Van Vechten, C.C. . Jr.
   1934   "The Reliability of Criminal Statistics." *Journal of Criminal Law and Criminology,* 25 (May-June):10-20.
Sutherland, George
   1935   "Reminiscences." Manuscript. Rochester, New York: American Baptist Historical Society.
Sweetser, Frank Loel, Jr.
   1941   "Neighborhood Acquaintance and Association: A Study of Personal Neighborhoods." Unpublished Ph.D. dissertation, Columbia University.

_____.
   1982   Interview with Mark Gaylord. 2 June.

_____.
   1982   Letter to Mark Gaylord. 15 June.
Tannenbaum, Frank
   1938   *Crime and Community.* New York: Ginn.
Tappan, Paul W.
   1947   "Who Is the Criminal?" *American Sociological Review,* 12 (February):96-102.
Thomas, W. I.
   1909   *Source Book for Social Origins.* Chicago: University of Chicago Press.

_____.
   1913   Letter to Luther Bernard. 16 October. Luther L. Bernard Papers.

_____.
   1923   *The Unadjusted Girl: With Cases and Standpoint for Behavior Analysis.* Boston: Little, Brown.

_____.
   1927   Letter to Luther Bernard. 13 July. Luther L. Bernard Papers.
Thomas, W. I. . and Thomas, Dorothy Swaine
   1928   *The Child in America: Behavior Problems and Programs.* New York: Alfred A. Knopf.
Thomas, W. I., and Znaniecki, Florian
   1958   *The Polish Peasant in Europe and America.* Reprinted. New York: Dover Publications.
Thrasher, Frederic Milton
   1927   *The Gang: A Study of 1,313 Gangs in Chicago.* Chicago: University of Chicago Press.
University of Chicago
   1911   "Circular of the Departments of Political Economy, Political Science, History, Sociology and Anthropology."
Volkhart, E. H.
   1968   "W. I. Thomas." *International Encyclopedia of the Social Sciences.* Vol. 16 (New York: Macmillan): 1-6.

Westie, Frank R.
    1973   "Academic Expectations for Professional Immortality: A Study of Legitimation." *The American Sociologist,* 8 (February): 19-32.

William Jewell College Bulletin 1920-1921. Liberty, Missouri.

Wirth, Louis
    1928   *The Ghetto.* Chicago: University of Chicago Press.

    ————.
    1931   "Culture Conflict and Misconduct." *Social Forces*, 9 (June): 484-492.

Index

181